CANADIAN MOUNTAIN PLACE NAMES

Mt. Moby Dick, north face. ROGER LAURILLA PHOTO

CANADIAN
MOUNTAIN
PLACE NAMES

The Rockies and Columbia Mountains

Glen W. Boles

Roger W. Laurilla

William L. Putnam

Rocky
Mountain Books
Calgary–Victoria–Vancouver

Rocky Mountain Books
#108 – 17665 66A Avenue
Surrey, BC V3S 2A7
www.rmbooks.com

Rocky Mountain Books
PO Box 468
Custer, WA
98240-0468

Library and Archives Canada Cataloguing in Publication
Putnam, William L. (William Lowell)
    Canadian mountain place names: the Rockies and Columbia Mountains / Glen W. Boles [artwork and photographs]; Roger W. Laurilla [photographs]; William L. Putnam [text]. —2nd ed., rev. and updated
Originally publ. under title: Place names of the Canadian Alps.
Includes index.

ISBN 13: 978-1-894765-79-4; ISBN 10: 1-894765-79-6

1. Names, Geographical—Rocky Mountains, Canadian (B.C. and Alta.).
2. Names, Geographical—British Columbia—Columbia Mountains.
3. Rocky Mountains, Canadian (B.C. and Alta.)—History, Local.
4. Columbia Mountains
(B.C.)—History, Local. I. Boles, Glen W. II. Laurilla, Roger W., 1959-
III. Title.

FC219.P88 2006   917.11001'4   C2006-906190-4

Library of Congress Control Number: 2006932788

Edited by Helen Godolphin
Proofread by Corina Skavberg
Book design by Frances Hunter
Cover design by Verge Design Works
Front cover photo by Glen Boles
Interior photos as credited

Printed in Canada

Rocky Mountain Books acknowledges the financial support for its publishing program from the Government of Canada through the Book Publishing Industry Development Program (BPIDP), Canada Council for the Arts, and the province of British Columbia through the British Columbia Arts Council and the Book Publishing Tax Credit.

This book has been produced on 100% post-consumer recycled paper, processed chlorine free and printed with vegetable-based dyes.

Gratefully dedicated to that tolerant gentleman,
toponymist of the world's oceans,
Gordon Frederick Delaney

CONTENTS

Mt. Louis. GLEN BOLES PHOTO

INTRODUCTION

In this edition, prepared in time for the centennial of the Alpine Club of Canada, we have been aided most usefully by the ubiquitous and scholarly alpinist of the Selkirks David Peter Jones, of the University of British Columbia, and his diligent wife, Jocelyn (Joie) Seagram. It's not that we didn't get input from others, but much of it was unprintable, and we still stand behind the bulk of what we wrote in 1990. Some picky persons may note that a few of those features we still call glaciers may be on the way out, due to climatic warming. But, being disciples of the late Milutin Milankovitch, we are of the opinion that the warming cycle noted by alpinists for the past century may be approaching its peak—unless the activities of humans have influenced the process unduly. Thus we believe there is hope that some of the world's ailing snowfields will survive other than in history books and old journals.

THIS BOOK IS A REVISED AND UPDATED VERSION of our earlier effort, on the derivation of some 1,800 current and historic mountain names in the Canadian "Alps." This mountain area is rather ill-defined, but for the purposes of this volume is the classic area of North American alpinism that was opened to the greater public by the Canadian Pacific Railway in the latter part of the 19th century and pioneered by historic figures of North American and European mountaineering. More precisely, this text covers the numerous ranges of the Rocky Mountains in Alberta and British Columbia, and the Selkirks, Purcells, Monashees and Cariboos of the Columbia Mountains—in the area between the 49th and 54th parallels of latitude. We are mindful that many interesting names have been applied beyond these lines, but every endeavour has to have some practical limits.

This is not a guidebook, but may well be a useful supplement to those people in possession of one. The compilers have contributed to a number of climbers' guides in years past. This is also **not a**

gazetteer; nor is it guaranteed to be exhaustive—though the authors have done their best to make it so—for every named peak over 2,740 metres (9,000 feet) in elevation and every other place name of significance to alpinists or students of alpinism.

Many names herein were given first to the peak and later to adjacent rivers, lakes, glaciers or other terrain features. However, this has not always been the case; the listing order in the text follows primogeniture as best we can determine it.

THE EARLIEST TOPONYMISTS were the various First Nations frequenting these mountains—mostly Shuswap, Stoney, Cree, Blackfoot and Kootenay. The Native people were reticent regarding names, as noted by such diverse authorities as Anglican bishop William Bompas and anthropologist Sir James Frazer, so their designations were not easily learned by the first white explorers. Thus the names they used were not retained in situ; they were either disregarded or subject to repeated interpretation, misinterpretation and relocation by subsequent generations of white travellers and "scholars." It is now impossible to reconstruct with certainty what names might have been applied, or where, by the first people who traversed the bulk of the Canadian Alps. Yet their names linger, appropriately applied or otherwise, as in such Yamnee features as Mount Assiniboine, Kananaskis River and Lake Minnewanka.

Less reticent name-givers, at least insofar as leaving written records, were the traders, trappers and explorers who moved through these mountains in the wake of Anthony Henday, Alexander Mackenzie and their associates. The names they left on the landscape reflect their special concerns and a few of their own personnel—Mount Robson, Whirlpool Pass and the Committee's Punch Bowl.

A subsequent tide of nomenclature came with the more formal explorations of the Palliser Expedition in the mid-19th century. Its members took inspiration from their patrons, their problems and what they saw—Mount Murchison, Kicking Horse River and Castle Mountain.

Many names owe their origin to the influx of miners, many from the United States, into this area from 1858 on. Miners' names, dreams and tribulations are especially prominent in the Purcells and southern Selkirks—Budweiser and Parridice, Bugaboo and Delphine.

The great national enterprise that became the Canadian Pacific Railway entered the naming game with vigour, starting with the first explorations for its tentative northern route in the 1870s, but finally concentrating along the CPR's present main line. Its names recorded those who helped make it happen (Mount Sir Donald and Revelstoke) or who might have (Exshaw and Field).

Then came the climbers, and they were prolific in this game. They went up out of the valleys and into the high country, seeing much of it for the first time. They found peaks that most likely had never been seen and country that had never been dreamed of. Their names honoured both their own friends and what they encountered—Freshfield and Julian, Tomatin and Austerity, Butters and Belvedere.

In due course there were survey teams moving through the backcountry, many of them led by the indomitable Arthur Oliver Wheeler, whose son and grandson were to continue the scientific process with equal distinction. In these mountains, Percy Carson, Ley Harris and Noel McConnell were the most prominent among those employed by the Dominion of Canada. They named what they saw for their own set of friends, patrons and landmarks—Mounts Kilpatrick, Deville and Intersection.

Finally the politicians entered the game, as is invariably the case with any good thing. Naming a piece of the nation for a person was a good way to honour someone, or pay off a political debt. But, as with all people, they were sometimes fickle—the Premier Group and Mount Willingdon or Kinbasket Lake and Mount Eisenhower.

During and shortly after the close of the First World War, the landmarks within a large part of the southern Rockies were named for major military figures of that conflict—Mounts Pétain and Cadorna, French and Haig.

Some of the major, early backcountry gentleman explorers like James Carnegie, Arthur Coleman, Howard Palmer and Roy Thorington were especially effective in naming things. This text tries to identify everyone's output, not in chronological order, for all their various "terms of office" overlapped and interlocked. Rather, we have set everything in strict alphabetical order. Many of the names were applied simply because they were descriptive, or at least imagined to be—Cobalt Lake, Mount Torii and the Mermaid.

Some name-givers, though, failed to stimulate our enthusiasm, for their contributions to toponymy have been commonplace, taking such forms as Roaring Creek, Blue Lake, Sheep Mountain, etc. There is little romance in researching the commonplace, and we have not spent much effort in those directions. Far more rewarding has been delving into the minds of those scores of persons who have left us a glimpse of their heroes, their dreams and their tribulations.

OVER A CENTURY AGO George Monro Grant, in chronicling the transcontinental journey of his friend Sir Sandford Fleming, noted, "The name of almost every river, creek, mountain or district is either French or Scotch." This statement had some validity then, in that all of his sources of information on names were of such ancestry. However, names have changed over the years, which has sometimes confused things. Indeed, the great mountaineer Dr. Tom Longstaff complained in the 1910 *Geographical Journal* about "the changing of geographical nomenclature being unfortunately only too common in Western Canada."

In this text we have attempted to acknowledge these changes but have given the primary listing of any point under the name by which we feel it is now best known. Some will take issue with our choice and they may be justified, but we have tried not to bruise too many feelings (for we, too, have been a part of this onomastic melange). A few of the names herein have not been approved by the Canadian Permanent Committee on Geographical Names (a group whose own name has been subject to change) or the provincial naming authorities in Alberta and British Columbia. Hence, some names are unofficial, even though well used in the mountaineering press and elsewhere. In every case, officially approved names are **boldfaced**.

Source documents are always worth consulting—we certainly have, beyond the great mass of mountaineering literature on these ranges that we have long had at our fingertips. Most informative is the three-volume series issued by the "Commission Appointed to Delimit the Boundary between the Provinces of Alberta and British Columbia." A good source is Holmgrens' *Place Names of Alberta*, now in its third edition (Saskatoon, 1976). Arthur Wheeler's *The Selkirk Range* (Ottawa, 1905) is authoritative and makes good reading, too. A reliable reference is the Akriggs' *British Columbia Place Names* (Victoria, 3rd ed. 1986). Jack Holterman's *Place Names of Glacier-Waterton National Parks* (1985), while primarily oriented to Montana, is very informative. The official *Gazetteer of Canada* series, produced by the federal government and covering each province, while exhaustive in its recitation, is unfortunately barren of rationales. James White's rare little work, *Place Names in the Rocky Mountains Between the 49th Parallel and the Athabaska River* (1916), is definitive for its time. We admire Thorington's 1928 opus *The Glittering Mountains of Canada*. Our own books, *The Great Glacier and Its House* (New York, 1982) and *The Guiding Spirit* (Revelstoke, 1986), are replete with historic photographs and contain much data on early alpinists. But, beyond all, the Champlain Society's 1968 edition of *The Palliser Papers*, by Irene Spry, is the most scholarly.

There is, of course, a large number of more localized and specific references we have consulted in this endeavour, and they are referred to, where useful, in the text. We have not even attempted to list the mountaineering journals we have consulted in this research. Those, however, are not arcane and can be readily found under the appropriate guidebook references for each peak. A large amount of biographical data on some of our sources can be found in Appendix A of *The Guiding Spirit*.

MANY OF THE NAME-GIVERS are identified biographically in the text, where their own names have found a place on the landscape, but some are missing, more through lack of chutzpah than lack of work. For these, an identification is given below, and they are referred to in the text by their last names only:

Douglas George **Anger**, psychologist, is one of the Harvard graduates who have been such an active group of alpinists. Illinois-bred, he is professor of experimental psychology at the University of Missouri.

Glendon Webber **Boles**, a native of New Brunswick, moved to Calgary in 1953 and was introduced to alpinism by Heinz Kahl. Now the honourary pesident of the ACC, he is a leading authority on the Canadian Rockies and has also climbed in Alaska, the Alps and the Selkirks.

Norman Henry **Brewster** was a long-time employee of the CPR, starting as a telegrapher. He worked in Glacier, Windermere and South Slocan and travelled frequently in these mountains prior to his retirement.

Alexander Cyril **Fabergé** (1912–1988), professor of genetics at the University of Texas and grandson of Peter Carl, jeweller to the czars, was an inventive contributor to alpine literature and nomenclature for many years.

Dr. Benjamin Greely **Ferris** Jr. (1919–1999), a 1940 graduate of Harvard, was for many years a professor at its school of public health. An exploratory alpinist, he was for 25 years the compiler of the AAC's world-famous safety report.

Edwin Rex **Gibson** (1892–1957) was a distinguished Canadian alpinist and official of the ACC. He died in the mountains, despite heroic rescue efforts by his friends Hendricks and Donald Hubbard.

Herbert Wendell **Gleason** (1855–1944), a clergyman and lecturer from Malden, Massachusetts, was a participant and chronologer of many trips into the mountains of western Canada, often in company with Harnden.

Edward Warren **Harnden** (1865–1949) of Boston was a lawyer and law reporter who climbed extensively in the Purcells during the years 1910–14, thereafter turning his attention to the Colorado Rockies.

Sterling Brown **Hendricks** (1902–1981), an American chemist, agronomist and scientist of distinction, was also the leader of a contingent of alpinists who made numerous exploratory ascents in Canada over dozens of years.

David Peter **Jones**, a native of Revelstoke, persists in making ascents, and has coupled his climbing with a scholarly series of guidebooks to the Selkirk Range, which has far and away set a new standard for this genre of literature.

Andrew John **Kauffman** II (1920–2000), Harvard '43, was one of the two North Americans to have made the first ascent of an 8,000-metre peak. He made explorations, particularly in the Battle Range and elsewhere in the Selkirks, from 1941 until his death.

Robert **Kruszyna**, an untiring alpinist of distinction, is a sometime writer and researcher who is largely responsible for the quality of climbers' guidebooks to the Northern Rockies and the Purcell Range.

Roger William **Laurilla**, mountain guide, skier and photographer, travelled the Selkirks extensively from his early youth and has been party to the compilation of the guidebook series for the Canadian Alps.

Alfred James **Ostheimer** III (1908–1983), a Philadelphian and graduate of Harvard, partook of three extended visits to the Columbia and Clemenceau icefields in the 1920s. Thereafter, he worked in the insurance business.

William Lowell **Putnam**, an honourary member of several alpine clubs, spent three years of the Second World War with the U.S. Army Mountain troops and has climbed in and written about these mountains ever since.

Peter **Robinson**, professor emeritus of geology at the University of Massachusetts, and authority on the geology of Norway, was a Dartmouth undergraduate during those years when he was most active in exploring the peaks of the Purcell Range.

Henry Baldwin deVilliers **Schwab** (1887–1935) was a descendent of a prime promoter of the Northern Pacific Railroad but worked in the family wool-importing business. He spent three seasons in the Canadian Rockies in the 1920s.

Samuel Charles **Silverstein**, a Dartmouth graduate and distinguished medical researcher at Rockefeller University, has a meritorious record of service to alpinism as a functionary of the AAC.

Curtis Arthur **Wagner**, a theoretical physicist and professor at Southwestern Minnesota State University, received his Ph.D. from Illinois, but prefers to mix music with his latter-day mountaineering.

George **Wallerstein**, a graduate of Brown University, has been an active research and teaching astronomer since 1956 and is presently emeritus with the University of Washington in Seattle.

Cyril Geoffrey **Wates** (1884–1946), a graduate of Worcester Polytechnic Institute, immigrated to western Canada and became a leading member of the ACC, making many ascents in company with Gibson.

Robert Culbertson **West** Jr., a native of New Jersey and professor of chemistry at the University of Wisconsin for 30 years, has made countless exploratory alpine trips into these mountains.

15

WE HOPE THE ARRANGEMENT of the text is simple and consistent. Each name is followed by the features, in the order in which we believe them to have been named. These are often followed by a number in square brackets giving the altitude in metres and then by a date—the first year in which we are sure the name was used. Then we give the general mountain grouping in which the feature is located. In the first edition we offered an abbreviated guidebook reference, but because some of the texts are now out of date (and print), we refer readers only to the operas of Jones on the Selkirks and of Atkinson and Piche on the Bugaboo and Vowell groups. We then give the rationale and a narrative statement pertinent to the name.

We have tried not to adorn the text with a multitude of parenthetical notations. If another name is used in the narrative part of any entry, additional data will often be found under that name. The entire book is arranged alphabetically, and all residual names not actually itemized in the text can be found in a separate index at the end.

The reader will recognize that there seem to be some landmark years in the bestowal of names. In 1916 James White's short but pithy monograph appeared; in it he records the derivation of many names, but unfortunately fails to stipulate the precise year when they were first applied. A similar event occurred in 1924, when the Geographic Board of Canada decided to eliminate a huge backlog of unfinished toponymic business. Its 18th Report was issued in that year and did much to wipe the official plate clean. Another surge of names reached these mountains in the early 1960s when Gordon Delaney, executive secretary (1968–73) of the Canadian Permanent Committee on Geographical Names (successor organization to the Geographic Board of Canada and the Canadian Board on Geographical Names), encouraged the provinces to apply names of deceased war heroes to unnamed topographic features within their boundaries.

For most of the names herein we supply one derivation, that which our research indicates is the logical and correct origin. But for certain names in this text, when we are in doubt, we offer alternative explanations. In these few instances, we have chosen to let readers decide.

OUR THANKS ARE MANY, for this second edition has profited greatly from friendly criticism. First, we must thank our predecessors, many of whom we have never met but whose names adorn this text. Next come our sources, mostly named above. Then come the unsung. Years ago the senior compiler hereof began an exchange of letters with J. Keith Fraser, then the de facto coordinator of toponymy in Canada. He helped straighten us out on several matters long before this book was thought of. His collaborator, the late Brigadier E. Douglas Baldock, continued the process with gentle suasion and much tolerance. In time this burden was inherited by Gordon Delaney, who continued our education with stimulating reminders and great personal cordiality. More recently, Alan Rayburn, Gordon's successor, and now retired in turn, was so good as to pass his critical and informed eye over some of the manuscript, thereby improving it immensely. And we take renewed pleasure in acknowledging the gracious help afforded us by Helen Kerfoot, successor Secretary of the Canadian Permanent Committee on Geographic Names and her small but friendly staff who have graciously answered inquiries and provided full access to official files.

For the first edition we owed thanks to: Lindsay Moir, Assistant Librarian at the Glenbow Institute of Calgary; various staff members at the Reference Room of the Springfield Public Library; the B.C. Archives; the Whyte Museum of the Canadian Rockies in Banff; the Sterling Library at Yale; the Robert Frost Library at Amherst; the Hayden Library of Arizona State College; the University of Massachusetts Library; the library of the Lowell Observatory in Flagstaff and the Houghton Library of Harvard. A.J. Francis of Her Majesty's Naval Historical Library in London, Ruby Nobbs of Revelstoke, Winnifred Weir of Windermere and Wilfrid Habart of Golden have been most helpful. A very informative morning was spent in Nelson, thanks to the Chamber of Mines of Eastern B.C. The RCMP has supplied answers with the same diligence they normally ask questions. Helen Butling, the grande dame of Kootenay mountaineering, was her usual cordial and helpful self; and we are indebted to Felix Poucette, councillor of the Stoney tribe at Morley, for his several helpful insights.

For this second edition, we have spent much time bothering other people to whom we owe further thanks. These mostly include the peripatetic scholar/alpinist of the Selkirks David Peter Jones of the University of British Columbia; the now retired geologist Peter Robinson, who corrected some mistakes of the first edition; our sometime climbing protege Anna Williams, who hounded the offices of Ottawa on our behalf; and the late Gordon Adams of Edinburgh.

The artwork with this text was again done by Boles; the photographs are the work of Boles and Laurilla, while Putnam again handled most of the text.

THE IDEA FOR THIS BOOK CAME ABOUT when, seated around a smouldering campfire in the Frontal Ranges of the Rockies, the junior compiler insisted to the senior, "You've got most of the material right in your head." It was a flattering comment, which survived long enough to get us started, but was soon found to be dreadfully untrue, as the next years of research made painfully apparent. But it has been fun—a labour of love for the mountains we love.

The first edition also contained the following final warning: "WE MAY BE WRONG, here and there, but if there are complaints and corrections to be made, the senior compiler hereof avers that he is too old to get involved and defers such honours to his more youthful associates, who will doubtless survive long enough to improve upon this effort." Even that caveat needed revision, for improvements in medical science have kept him tottering in the saddle sufficiently long to present this updated volume.

G.W. Boles, R.W. Laurilla, W.L. Putnam

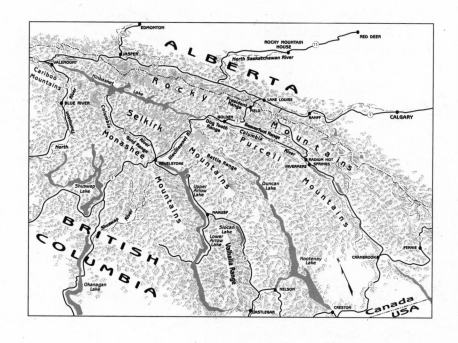

LIST OF ABBREVIATIONS

AAC   American Alpine Club (New York, after 1901)

ABC   Alberta/British Columbia Boundary Commission (1913–25)

AC   Alpine Club (London, after 1858)

ACC   Alpine Club of Canada (Banff, after 1906)

AMC   Appalachian Mountain Club (Boston, after 1876)

BCLS   British Columbia Land Surveyor

CMH   Canadian Mountain Holidays (an organization started by guide Hans Gmoser)

CNR   Canadian National Railways (after 1920)

CPR   Canadian Pacific Railway (after 1883)

DLS   Dominion Land Surveyor

GSC   Geological Survey of Canada

HBC   Hudson's Bay Company

IBSC   International Boundary Survey Commission (1858–1962)

NWC   North West Company

ABBOT: Pass [2925 m]; 1896; Lake Louise. Philip Stanley Abbot (1867–1896) was a young Boston lawyer and prominent member of the AMC, then in the process of forming an Alpine Section. He was killed in a fall from the upper ledges of Mount Lefroy. The pass between Mount Lefroy and Mount Victoria was then named in his honour. His death prompted the CPR to bring trained Swiss guides to these mountains, starting in the summer of 1899. A mountain hut was built on the pass in 1922 at the instigation of these guides and many members of the AMC were present for its subsequent dedication. **Peak** [2938m], **Creek**; 1894; Badshots; SS. Named after a miner who prospected on the lower slopes of this lesser peak.

ABBOTT: Mount [2465 m]; 1886; Sir Donald. This minor summit was named by the CPR for Harry Braithwaite Abbott (1829–1903), general superintendent of its western division when the famous Glacier House was built. Early on, a graded trail was laid out from the hotel up to a lookout near this point. Over the next 30 years the hotel evolved into the leading centre of alpinism in North America. *See also* Glacier. There is another **Mount Abbott** [2961 m] in the Badshot Group, named for an itinerant prospector.

ABEL: Mount [2746m], **Creek**; 1915; S Purcells. Willis Benson "Ben" Abel (1846–1915), a native of Vermont, prospected and worked the Carbonate Creek area and at one time owned the neaby Mineral King Mine.

ABERDEEN: Mountain [3151 m], **Glacier**; 1897; Lake Louise. Though Wilcox had called it "Hazel" in 1896, this summit was very soon renamed for Sir John Campbell Hamilton Gordon, seventh earl of Aberdeen (1847–1934), Governor General of Canada, 1893–98. His grandfather George (1784–1860), the fourth earl, was the British foreign secretary who negotiated the Oregon Treaty with the United States and was later rusticated for his part in the mismanagement of the Crimean War.

ABEY: Mount [2850m]; 1969; SW Purcells. Curt Wagner named this summit for Frank Abey, a farmer, horsepacker and "troublemaker" in the valleys below.

Adamant Group, left to right: West Blackfriars, East Blackfriars, Mt. Austerity, Turret (it blends into Austerity), Mt. Adamant and the Stickle. Farther to the right are Pioneer Peak and East Peak of the Gothics in the Gothics Group. GLEN BOLES PHOTO

ABRAHAM: Mountain [2820 m], **Lake** [1320 m]; 1973; Cline. The lake was not officially named until 1973, when the North Saskatchewan dam gates were closed; but the mountain goes back to Silas Abraham, a Stoney guide who worked for Mary Schäffer in 1906–07.

ABRUZZI: Mount [3267 m], **Glacier**; 1920; Italian. Luigi Amadeo di Savoia-Aosta (1873–1933) was Duke of the Abruzzi and one of the most famous alpinists and Arctic explorers of his age. He was also cousin to King Victor Emanuel and commander in chief of the Italian Navy during much of the First World War.

ABYSS: Glacier; 1962; W Selkirks. When Dr. Ferris first saw this glacier, as it descends into Downie Creek, he described it as being in such a deep slot as to be an abyss.

ADAMANT: Mount [3345 m], **Glacier, Range**; 1909. This mountain in the Northern Selkirks was named by Palmer for its forbidding south aspect. In later years the name was extended to other features—most notably the Adamant Pluton (batholith), one of the largest in western Canada, the quality of whose rock attracts many alpinists.

ADOLPHUS: Lake [1650 m]; 1907; Robson. Named by Coleman for Adolphus Moberly, a well-known Iroquois guide who helped on the professor's trip to Mount Robson that year.

AFTERNOON: Peak [3120 m]; 1927; Cline. Bridgland's party spent an afternoon taking observations (and building a cairn) on the north shoulder of this crumbling peak, 5 km north of Cline Pass.

AFTON: Mount [2553 m]; 1895; Sir Donald. This relatively unimpressive summit derives its name from an acronym of those in a party

Mt. Adamant, north glacier. ROGER LAURILLA PHOTO

making an early ascent along the ridge from Mount Abbott—Philip Abbot, Charles Fay and Charles Thompson.

AGNES: Lake [2118 m]; 1898; Lake Louise. Wilcox applied the name to honour Susan Agnes Bernard Macdonald (1836–1920), the second wife of Sir John A. Macdonald, who had visited this small lake on her one trip to the area in 1886.

AHA: Mount [3063 m]; 1949; Cariboo. Though Carpé, Chamberlin and Withers had made its first ascent in 1924, Hendricks's party named this peak, which lies only a short distance north of Penny Mountain, on the same day they had recovered Holway's 1914 penny.

AHAB: Mount [3075 m]; 1958; Battle. Anger named this subsidiary west peak of the Butters massif after Herman Melville's fictional skipper who had the vendetta with the great white whale, as part of the Melvilleana that marks this region. The mountain, however, might have been more properly named after Dr. Andrew J. Gilmour, who actually climbed on it. *See also* Moby Dick.

AIGUILLE: Peak [2999 m]; 1915; Waputik. This is the French word for needle and a generic term for any sharp alpine summit; it was applied in this instance by the ABC.

AKAMINA: Pass [1783 m]; 1861; Flathead. This Cree word for benchland was originally applied to an astronomical station occupied by the IBSC just north of the 49th parallel.

ALAN CAMPBELL: Mount [3030 m]; 1918; Freshfield. Wheeler named this lesser summit west of the Divide for Alan John Campbell (1883–1967), DLS 1909, one of his longer-lasting and lesser acknowledged assistants on the ABC. Campbell had trained under Louis Stewart and in 1910, prior to undertaking this years-long effort, had married Laura Alvina Pengelly (1884–1982), for whom Mount Pengelly, south of Crowsnest Pass, was named in 1914. On Collie's map of 1902, this summit is simply labelled "High Peak." Campbell's son became a notable field geologist for the GSC and his grandson, a licenced Canadian mountain guide.

ALBERT: Canyon, Peaks [3045 m], **Creek, Icefield**; 1883. Situated west of the Sir Donald/Glacier area, this name was first applied by Principal Grant for Albert Rogers, nephew and namesake of the pass-finding Major Rogers, who had assisted his famous uncle in the mountain surveys.

ALBERTA: Mount [3619 m]; **Glacier**; 1898; Churchill. Both the summit and the province are named for Princess Louise Caroline Alberta, Queen Victoria's fourth daughter, as was Lake Louise. Collie named the summit, while the princess's husband, as Governor General (1878–83), named the district (later part of the province). The summit is difficult to access and its first ascent was a mountaineering epic.

ALBREDA: River, Location [874 m], **Mount** [3075 m]; 1863; Monashee. Lady Albreda Elizabeth Wentworth-Fitzwilliam Lyveden was the Viscount Milton's aunt and the youngest daughter of the fifth earl of Fitzwilliam. Her brother, Robert Vernon Lyveden (1800–1873), was a British statesman who stood tall for the defence of Canada against the threat of Yankee imperialism.

ALCANTARA: Mount [2840 m], **Creek**; 1916; Blue. Origin unknown. Besides being the name of a city on the Tagus in western Spain, the seat of a military/religious order active in the late Middle Ages, this was the name of a British warship involved in the Battle of Jutland.

ALCOVE: Mountain [2810m]; 1920; Ramparts. This topographically descriptive name was given by the ABC.

ALDERSON: Mount [2692m], **Lake** [1875m]; 1918; Boundary. Lt. Gen. Sir Edwin Alfred Hervey Alderson (1859–1927) was the first commander of the Canadian Corps in the First World War, later appointed Inspector General of all Canadian Forces. The mountain had previously been called "Bertha."

ALDRIDGE: Mount [2637m]; 1916; Slocan. Walter Hull Aldridge (1867–1959) of Brooklyn joined the CPR in 1897 in charge of its mining operations. He served as managing director of the Consolidated Mining and Smelter Company of Trail from 1906 to 1911, and also had charge of coal supply development for the CPR in the vicinity of Crowsnest Pass. He later left Canada for an executive position with the Texas Gulf Sulfur Company.

ALEXANDRA: Mount [3388m], **River, Glaciers**; 1902; Alexandra. The summit was named by Collie for the consort of King Edward VII, the Danish princess Alexandra Caroline Maria Charlotte Louise Julia (1844–1925), eldest daughter of King Christian IX. After their marriage in 1862, the lady's beauty and charm helped enhance her popularity with her husband's subjects. The river was called "Nashan" by Schäffer in 1906 but that handle did not take.

ALICE: Lake [2380m]; 1898; Murchison. C.S. Thompson gave this name for the wife of his friend, the Reverend Harry Pierce Nichols (1850-1940), a very popular American clergyman and alpinist who was visiting the region at the time. Before this lake was named he had gone on a two-day excursion out from Glacier, which stretched into an unplanned three-day trip, but when he returned to civilization he immediately preached a sermon at Glacier House on "The Glory of Aspiration." In later years he became president of the AAC and a living legend in his native White Mountains of New Hampshire. *See also* Katherine.

ALLAN: Mount [2911m]; 1901; Ottertail. Whymper suggested this name for Sir Hugh Allan (1810–1892), late proprietor of the Allan Steamship Lines and a projector of the CPR. Allan had been involved in the election-financing scandal that brought down the first Macdonald Administration. Sir Hugh was a native of Glasgow and a long-time friend of Sir Donald Smith. **Peak** [2819m]; 1948; Kananaskis. Dr. John Andrew Allan (1884–1955) was for 37 years head of the department of geology at the University of Alberta, and did much to determine the extent of local coalfields. The Stoneys called this summit Chåse Tida Baha (Burnt Timber Hill). The eastern flank of this mountain was developed into the ski area "Nakiska" ("meeting place" in Stoney) on which were held the alpine ski events for the 15th Olympic Games in 1988.

ALLEN: Mount [3310 m]; 1898; Bow Ranges. Samuel Evans Stokes Allen (1874–1945) of Philadelphia was a graduate of Yale, an exploratory alpinist and the pioneer of present-day nomenclature in the Lake Louise area. In the years 1893, '94 and '95, with the help of Walter Wilcox, he prepared two maps of the area. This peak appears on his second map as "Shappee"—#6 of the Ten Peaks. Allen's parents' disapproval of his interest in alpinism precipitated severe depression, and he spent the final 40 years of his life in confinement for insanity.

ALLENBY: Mount [2995 m], **Creek, Pass** [2432 m]; 1919; Sundance. Edmund Henry Hynman (1865–1936) Field Marshal Viscount Allenby was commander in chief of the British Army in Egypt during the Great War and masterminded the defeat of the Turkish forces in the eastern Mediterranean area.

ALNUS: Peak [2976 m], **Glaciers, Creek**; 1920; Whirlpool. *Alnus* is the generic botanical name for alder. In the mountains of western Canada it is widespread and generally represented by the *rhombifolia* branch of the family, a notorious nuisance for backcountry travel. Not unexpectedly, the ABC crew found a lot of it in this valley.

ALPHABET: Group; 1965. For once Putnam ran out of meaningful names and labelled the lesser peaks east of Downie and north of Bachelor Pass with letters of the alphabet. His subsequent map submissions to Ottawa stuck. **Able** [2646 m]; **Baker** [2852 m]; **Charley** [2873 m]; **Easy** [2646 m]; **Folly** [2690 m]. Ley Harris occupied the northernmost of this group in 1929 as Goldstream South Station.

ALPHA CENTAURI: Mount [3094 m]; 1969; Starbird. This is opposite North Star Mountain and was named by West for one of the brightest stars in our galaxy. It is seen only in the southern hemisphere, in the constellation Centaurus, and, at a mere 4.3 light years away, is also the nearest stars to our solar system.

AMERY: Mount [3329 m]; 1927; Alexandra. Named by order-in-council for Leopold Charles Morris Stennet Amery (1873–1955), distinguished British statesman, alpinist, author and skier. He climbed the peak the year after it was named, in the company of Canada's celebrated Swiss-born guide Edward Feuz Jr.

AMETHYST: Lakes [1963 m]; 1920; Ramparts. One of the many descriptive names applied by the ABC survey teams that delineated the interprovincial boundary between the years 1913 and 1925. The variety of shadings of blue ascribed to mountain lakes seems to be endless. These large lakes, east of the most spectacular line of peaks in the Rockies, are among the most seen and photographed.

AMGADAMO: Point [2932 m]; 1906; Waputik. This is an acronym of the names of the party making the first ascent of this point on the south ridge of today's Mount Marpole—the reverends A.M. Gordon, A. Dunn and A.O. McCrae. These clergymen all shared the same first name, Alexander, and a belief in the Presbyterian church.

AMISKWI: River, Pass [1966 m], **Peak** [2822 m]; 1916; Van Horne. This is the Cree word for beaver, a creature that once abounded in this valley.

AMON RA: Mount [2911 m]; 1973; Commander. The highest in the line of peaks north of Jumbo Pass, known collectively as the Egyptian Peaks, Wagner very appropriately named it after the supreme god of ancient Egypt—generally depicted as a ram.

AMUNDSEN: Mount [3150 m]; 1923; Icefields. This peak, and several others nearby in the high country west of the Columbia Icefield, was named by members of the 1923 Mount Clemenceau expedition to honour prominent polar explorers or alpinists—in this case, Roald R.G. Amundsen (1872–1928) of Norway, the first navigator to finally clear the Northwest Passage.

ANCHORITE: Mountain [2880 m]; 1934; Ramparts. Gibson suggested this name because of the isolated position of this peak, which to him resembled a religious hermit.

ANCIENT WALL: Range; 1929; Starlight. So called by surveyors because of the linear, yet decrepit, aspect of this line of lesser peaks.

ANDERSON: Peak [2691 m]; 1882; Flathead. This relatively minor summit, northwest of Mount Blakiston, was named by Dawson for the British secretary of the IBSC, Capt. Samuel Anderson (1839–1881) RE, who later became chief British astronomer of the 1872–75 party marking the international boundary westwards from the Lake of the Woods to the crest of the Rockies. His final assignment was as inspector of submarine defences in England after 1876. There was another Anderson active in the region at this time. Alexander Caulfield Anderson (1814–1884) worked for the HBC after 1831, later taking a part in B.C. developmental activities and as Commissioner of Fisheries. He was a widely known authority on Native customs and beliefs.

ANDROMACHE: Mount [2996 m]; 1948; Murchison. This lesser point north of Mount Hector was named by members of the ACC for the Queen of Epirus, wife to the heroic Hector in Greek mythology.

After the sack of Troy and Hector's death, Andromache, along with Helenus, son of king Priam, was enslaved by Neoptolemus, the son of Achilles, and had a son by him. She later returned to Epirus with Helenus. Sir James Hector, for whom Mount Hector was named, had a wife of his own, Maria Georgiana (née Monro), whom he married in 1869 in New Zealand.

ANDROMEDA: Mount [3450 m]; 1938; Icefields. This prominent three-pronged peak near Mount Athabasca was named by Gibson for the mythological wife of Perseus. In ignorance of Gibson's prior designation, Thorington labelled this point "Janus" in 1939. Andromeda is also the name of the nearest galaxy to our Milky Way—a spiral nebula only two million light years away, but closing in on us at the rate of some 300 km per second.

ANDY GOOD: Creek, Peak [2637m]; 1916; Crowsnest. Andrew Good (d. 1916) ran the Summit Hotel in the town of Crowsnest, right at the height of land. He was a colourful character who kept a private zoo. His hotel straddled the provincial boundary, and he would move his bar from one end of the building to the other as necessary, depending on which side offered more liberality in liquor regulations. His freewheeling view of geography was brought to an end by the ABC, which found the hotel to be decidedly west of the line; his peak, however, still straddles the issue.

ANEMONE: Pass [1940 m]; 1950; Windy. Hendricks's party named the pass for the waving fields of this flower on and near the gentle crest at the north of the Windy Range.

ANGEL: Glacier; 1925; Jasper. Though Deville had called it the Glacier of the Ghost in 1916, because of its position relative to Mount Edith Cavell, it was soon renamed to honour the "Angel of Mercy."

ANGLE: Peak [2910m]; 1916; Ramparts. This name was applied by the ABC because there was a pronounced bend in the interprovincial boundary on this otherwise relatively minor summit.

ANNETTE: Lake [1975 m]; 1896; Bow Ranges. We don't know if he got a free meal or even more, but Wilcox chose this name in honour of the wife of the manager at the CPR's second Lake Louise Chalet. The original 1890 log structure had burned down in 1892; its replacement was considerably more stylish, but still not visible from the lake in Paradise Valley under Mount Temple. *See also* St. Piran.

ANNIVERSARY: Peak [2940m]; 1946; Bugaboo. This minor point on the east ridge of Howser Peak was named by members of the ACC on the 40th anniversary of the founding of Canada's national organization of mountaineering.

ANSTEY: Mount [2759 m]; 1929; Moloch. Francis Senior Anstey, a contemporary of Moberly and Lempriere, was a lumber baron of Shuswap Lake who profited handsomely from the patronage of the CPR. He became one of the promoters of the Waverly/Tangier Mines.

ANTEVS: Mount [3176 m]; 1969; Clearwater. A small glacial lake high on its west flank inspired Putnam to name this summit for Ernst Valdemar Antevs (1888–1981), the Swedish-born glaciologist notable for his study of varved clays in lake deposits and consequent dating of glacial advances and retreats.

ANTRIM: Peak [2938 m]; 1969; Starbird. This name comes from the county of Northern Ireland that contains the celebrated Giant's Causeway. It was applied here by Professor West.

AOSTA: Mount [2994 m]; 1918; Italian. Emanuele Filiberto (1869–1931), Duke of Aosta and cousin of King Victor Emanuel III, was the commanding general of the Third Italian Army in the First World War—until the disastrous Battle of Caporetto.

APEX: Peak [3240 m]; 1922; Premier. Carpé chose the name because this point was erroneously assumed to be the hydrographic apex of the Cariboos. The summit was not climbed until 1960. *See* Trigon. **Mountain** [3246 m] 1927; Icefields. There is no record of exactly who named this point in the middle of the Clemenceau Icefield, but it might well have been Ostheimer.

APPARITION: Mountain [2990 m]; 1963; Front. There are spectral references all through the nomenclature in this region northwest of Ghost Lake, this one applied by Dr. Thomas Wilson Swaddle.

APPRENTICE: Forepeak [2880 m]; 1948; Sorceror. Named by the 1948 Hendricks party because of its subsidiary relationship northwest of the prominent Sorceror Mountain.

AQUEDUCT: Mount [3180 m]; 1978; Icefields. Kruszyna was impressed by a waterfall spouting from the valley headwall below this peak and dropping into the Sullivan River; it was obviously fed by an underground source.

AQUILA: Mountain [2880 m]; 1916; Ottertail. This is the Latin word for eagle, one of which was seen circling the peak when Bridgland came by. This name also appears on 83D/9.

ARCHDUKE: Trio [2667 m]; 1963; Bugaboo. This minor but stimulating set of pinnacles was named by Robinson, though climbed by Kruszyna, both of whom enjoyed some of the same symptoms that later afflicted Wagner and Beck in the same area. **Mountain** [3155 m]; 1967; SW Purcells. Bruce Beck had a temporary hangup on Beethoven and applied this name in recognition of the B flat composition. He didn't settle for the short, though inspiring, trio, but went on to several other Beethoven-type names nearby. *See also* Emperor.

ARCS: Lac des [1290m]; 1858; Fairholme. This was given the French word for bow by Eugene Bourgeau because the lake is essentially an expansion of the Bow River.

ARCTOMYS: Creek, Peak [2793 m]; 1920; Lyell. This is the Greek word for marmot. These inquisitive and panhandling mountaineering woodchucks are all over the place, as this ABC name and several others denote.

ARCTURUS: Peak [2466m]; 1923; Starlight. Named for one of the brightest stars in the northern hemisphere, whose name in turn derives from the Greek for "bear guard," from its position in the constellation Boötes, near Ursa Major. The peak, though below our cut, is nevertheless the central summit of the Starlight Range and relatively near. The star, however, is a longer hike—40 light years distant—and in good company in these mountains, its neighbours being Sirius and Vega.

ARÊTE: Peak [2760m]; 1915; Waputik. From the French word for ridge, this name generally refers to a sharp, steep and exposed rock ridge above the timberline. It was applied in this instance by the ABC surveying team. **Mountain** [3010m]; 1970; 83C/7; Maligne; RN. This summit is blessed with a spectacular south ridge.

ARETHUSA: Mount [2912 m], **Creek**; 1917; Highwood. This name originally referred to the nymph of Greek mythology who was pursued by Alpheus. However, in this application it refers to a Russian light cruiser that was involved in the ill-fated Dogger Bank action and was shelled by the German ship *Frauenlob* only two days after being commissioned.

ARGENTINE: Mount [3018m]; 1907; Sorceror. Palmer, who viewed the shimmering effect of adjacent snowfields as seen from the north, named this peak at the head of the Gold River for its silvery connotations, though no quantity of any precious metal has ever been found in, on or adjacent to either peak or river.

ARGONAUT: Mountain [2975m], **Creek**; 1913; Windy. Palmer had submitted the name "Dentiform" in 1912, but the Board on Geographic Names failed to approve. The following year he tried again with "Big Tooth" and fared no better. The "Argonauts of '62" was another name applied to the Overlanders—some 200 immigrants who, stimulated by reports of gold, trudged across the continent from eastern Canada to prospect and then settled in various portions of British Columbia.

ARIES: Peak [2996m]; 1924; Waputik. This is the generic Latin name for ram or goat. The mountain variety (*Oreamnos montanus*) is frequently observed throughout this region. Aries is also the first sign of the zodiac.

ARMAGH: Mountain [2910 m]; 1969; Starbird. This name is not only a troubled suburb of Belfast, but also a County of Ireland. West applied it as part of the Irish pattern of nomenclature in this sub-range.

ARMSTRONG: Mount [2823 m]; 1918; High Rock. J.D. Armstrong, of the surveyor general's staff, was killed in action in 1917. **Mountain** [2667 m]; 1969; Gold. Capt. Francis Patrick Armstrong (1861–1923) of Golden, was the proprietor of several shallow-draft vessels regularly navigating the upper Columbia between 1885 and 1914. Among them were *Duchess* (I and II), *Cline, Marion, Pert, Gwendoline, North Star, Isabel*, and *Nowitka*. The opening of the Kootenay Central (part of the CPR) coincided with the beginning of the Great War, and Armstrong saw service as a boat skipper on the Nile, along with W.J. Astley. The final riverboat trip on the Columbia was that of the *North Star* in 1920. *See also* Marion and St. Piran.

ARRAS: Mountain [3090 m]; 1918; Lyell. This name is derived from the French city near Calais, which was the centre of much combat during both world wars. The historic old city was largely destroyed as a result. The name has a further usage in English as a wall hanging or tapestry.

ARROW: Lakes; 1830. Duncan Finlayson (1796–1862) of the HBC noted that the local First Nations had the custom of shooting arrows at a cliff above the lake prior to undertaking a journey. According to his sources, if a man's arrow stuck in a crack, he would enjoy good luck; if it fell back into the lake, he was heading for trouble.

ARTHUR MEIGHEN: Mount [3150 m]; 1927; Premier. Arthur Meighen (1874–1960) served twice as Conservative prime minister of Canada in the early 1920s and, according to MacMillan's *Dictionary of Canadian Biography*, "... seldom has a statesman of such ability and integrity been treated so unkindly by the Canadian electorate." Zillmer called this summit "Carpé."

ASGARD: Peak [2789 m]; 1964; Valhalla. This is the home of the gods in Norse mythology, within which Valhalla is the most luxurious palace.

ASSINIBOINE: Mount [3618 m], **Group, Pass** [2180 m], **Park**; 1884. Dawson named the most prominent summit of the southern Canadian Rockies after the Assiniboine people, sometimes called Stoneys because of their custom of cooking food by placing hot stones in bison-skin containers of water.

Mt. Assiniboine. GLEN BOLES DRAWING

ASTORIA: River, Pass [2315 m]; Ramparts. This name originated at the fur-trading post near the mouth of the Columbia River, established in 1811 by the German-American fur magnate John Jacob Astor (1763–1848). After the post was ceded to the NWC late in 1813, traders carried their furs up the Columbia and went eastwards over the Athabasca Pass for their annual rendezvous at the company headquarters on Lake Superior.

ASULKAN: Ridge [2847 m], **Pass** [2340 m], **River**; 1888; Sir Donald. This name is the Shuswap word for mountain goat. It was chosen by Green when visiting at Glacier House because of the numbers of these creatures originally seen near this height-of-land.

ATHABASCA: River, Pass [1750 m], **Falls, Mount** [3491 m], **Glacier**; 1790; Icefields. The name, sometimes spelled with a "k," first appears on Peter Pond's map and then on that of Aaron Arrowsmith in 1801. It is alleged to be the Cree word for "place where there are reeds," referring to the lake. As time went on the name migrated up the river to the pass and then onto the mountain and glacier. The pass became a celebrated route of the NWC and HBC fur brigades and its supposed high altitude became the base from which the unduly exalted heights ascribed to Mounts Hooker and Brown were in turn derived. Despite Coleman's authoritative findings on the matter, as late as 1911 no less an authority than Lawrence Johnstone Burpee (1873–1946), historian, civil servant and traveller, listed its altitude as 7,300 feet [2250 m].

ATLUNG: Mountain [3234 m]; 1971; Farnham. Named by Dr. David Peter Jones of Revelstoke, a notable Canadian alpinist and mountain author, for his friend Jan Atlung (1944–1971), who had been killed earlier in the year by a rock falling from high on Mount Commander, west across the valley from this summit.

ATMU: Mountain [2820 m]; 1973; Commander. North of Amon Ra, Wagner recalled Atmu, the Egyptian sun god.

AUGUSTA: Mount [3287 m]; 1927; Clearwater. Named by Palmer, whose companion, Ralph Melcer, made its first ascent. This name is from the title given to the wife of a Roman emperor; it is also the name of a lady who was the object of several communications by Lord Byron in 1816. This was Melcer's only trip into the mountains and we haven't been able to determine his rationale.

AUGUSTINE: Mount [3268 m]; 1902; Dawson. Named by Arthur Wheeler in conformance with the new name for the entire massif, Bishops Group. Its prior name was East Mitre, given by Topham because of the peaked shape of the two major summits. There were two saints Augustine; the more famous was bishop of Hippo from A.D. 390 to 430 and a Doctor of the Christian Church, remembered in the liturgy of August 28. A lesser known bearer of the name was a Benedictine of Italian ancestry (d. *c.* 607), the first archbishop of Canterbury, who became known as the "Apostle of the English" and is remembered on May 27. *See also* Cyprian.

AURORA: Mountain [2790 m]; 1910; Blue. Origin unknown. Wheeler applied this same name to a prominent peak with "a hanging glacier" that lay directly south of the Four Squatters. That should place it among today's Macbeth Group. *See also* Eyebrow.

AUSTERITY: Mount [3337 m], **Glacier, Pass** [1815 m]; 1911; Adamant. Named by Palmer, whose party finally climbed it after a long, strenuous and circuitous approach via the west. Butters accompanied him, but it was Holway who led the critical moves of the ascent.

AVALANCHE: Mountain [2861 m], **Glacier, Crest**; 1881; Sir Donald. Applied here by Maj. Rogers, whose party of Shuswap companions was only the first to be caught in a snowslide on the west slope of this aptly named summit. Edward Wheeler's party suffered a more serious accident in 1908 and a subsequent ACC party came a cropper too, almost in the same spot. The CPR ultimately erected a mile of snowsheds to protect its original line, which ran below this side of the mountain.

AVENS: Mount [2970 m]; Sawback. This is a widespread flower of the Rocky Mountains, a white-flowering dwarf shrub forming flat cushions in calcareous, gravelly places, mainly above timberline. Locally known as "mountain avens."

AYE: Mount [3243 m]; 1913; Assiniboine. This name was applied by the ABC, but their records are devoid of explanation. We attribute it to the Scottish heritage of many Canadians and a remembrance of the Forest of Aye in the auld country.

AYESHA: Peak [3065 m]; 1901; Waputik. White states, "the crest of the mountain resembles a beautiful face turned upwards and, owing to the wild surroundings, suggested the name (of the sorceress heroine) in Rider Haggard's *She*." Sir Henry Rider Haggard (1856–1925) had published this African adventure story in 1887, the second book of his very successful career as a writer. Haggard's own name was applied to a minor point near Jasper after he visited that area as guest of the Grand Trunk Pacific Railway.

AYLMER: Mount [3163 m]; 1890; Palliser. Matthew, eighth Baron Aylmer (1842–1923), became inspector general of Canadian militia, then turned his attention elsewhere and served as president of the Kootenay Gold Mines in British Columbia. His younger brother, Frederick Whitworth (1850–1920), a location engineer for the CPR, platted the city of Golden and surveyed many mining claims in the upper Columbia valley. McArthur named the mountain in honour of his birthplace in the province of Quebec, which town was named for Matthew and Frederick's grandfather, Matthew, the fifth Baron Aylmer (1775–1850) who had been Governor-in-Chief of Canada, 1831–35. The family name had originally been Athelmer—traceable back through English history from Alfred the Great to its application in the upper Columbia valley.

AZIMUTH: Ridge [2624 m]; Notch [2515 m]; 1911; Sir Sandford. Named by Palmer, who used its highest point as one of the two central triangulation stations for his historic map of the Sir Sandford region.

AZTEC: Mount [3125 m]; 1928; Maligne. To early viewers, the twisted rock formations exposed on the northeast face of this summit suggested an ancient Aztec symbol.

AZURITE: Mountain [2682 m], **Pass** [2237m]; 1953; N Purcells. Named by Peter Robinson after a trace ore of copper which is found in nearby prospects. Azurite is a hydrous copper carbonate, distinguished by its blue colour from the chemically similar anhydrous malachite, which is green.

For my name and memory,
I leave it to men's charitable speeches,
To foreign nations, and the next ages.
—FRANCIS BACON, *LAST WILL*

BAAL: Mount [2997 m]; 1915; Moloch. Named by Sissons, whose party made its first ascent, from its association with Mount Moloch. Baal was the Canaanite god of agricultural fertility, worshipped by several pre-Biblical cultures in the Middle East.

BABEL: Mount [3101 m], **Tower** [2360 m]; 1899; Bow Ranges. Wilcox first applied this name to the striking tower north of the peak proper, highly visible as one approaches Moraine Lake by the modern highway. He fancied a resemblance to the biblical tower in the land of Shinar (Babylonia) that was meant to reach to Heaven (Gen. 11:4).

BACCHUS: Ridge [2826 m]; 1969; SW Purcells. Wagner named this crest not for the Roman god of pleasure but for Eric and Noel Bacchus, two bachelor brothers from England who homesteaded near Birchdale on Duncan Lake. Eric, a trained musician and erudite person, outlived his elder brother.

BACHELOR: Creek, Pass [2120 m]; 1907; Sorcerer. This creek, and nearby Spinster Creek, were both named by Carson, who offered no rationale for the names.

BACK: Mount [3009 m], **Lake** [2121 m]; 1861; Royal. Palliser set out to honour one of his predecessors in Canadian exploration, Admiral Sir George Back (1796–1878), a prominent British naval officer and explorer of the Canadian Arctic.

BADGER: Pass [2539 m]; Front; RS. Named for some member of the Meles family, of whom a number have been known to frequent the lower reaches of these mountains.

BADSHOT: Peak [2599 m], **Group**; 1894. Origin unknown. Perhaps a corruption of Bagshot, or a commemoration of some explorer's poor skills. In any case, it was certainly applied to a mining claim at 2179 m in altitude, prospected on the slopes above the then town of Ferguson.

BAGHEERA: Mountain [2765 m]; 1901; Hermit. Wheeler took this name from Kipling's *Jungle Book*, derived from the Bengali word *begh*, meaning tiger, with reference to the many cougars then found in this vicinity.

BAKER: Mount [3172 m]; 1898; Waputik. Collie named this summit after his occasional climbing companion, George Pierce Baker (1866–1935), a prominent member of the AMC and Harvard professor of dramatics and English literature.

BALCARRES: Mountain [2888 m]; 1870; Maligne. Here the earl of Southesk honoured his friend, Sir Coutts Lindsay (1824–1913), whose family's estate in Scotland bore that name. North across the Medicine Tent Valley he also labelled Mount Lindsay [2705m].

BALDYR: Mount [2980 m]; 1972; Valhalla. The Norse god of light was the most beautiful and gracious of all those residing in Asgard. He fell victim to a mistletoe dart prepared by the mischievous Loki, but was revived by the other gods.

BALFOUR: Mount [3272 m], **Group, Glacier, Pass** [2454 m]; 1859; Waputik. John Hutton Balfour, MD (1808–1884), was a Scots botanist who provided training to Dr. James Hector and much encouragement to the Palliser Expedition.

BALINHARD: Mount [3130 m], **Creek**; 1859; Maligne. This was one of the titles held by James Carnegie, earl of Southesk (1833–1908). He was lucky to have retained any of them, his great-grandfather having been under a bill of attainder for his part in assisting the abortive Highland rebellion of 1715. Balinhard is a locality in Forfarshire, which was renamed the County of Angus after the Jacobite wars.

BALL: Mount [3311 m], **Pass** [2210 m], **Range**; 1860; Ball. Hector gave this name to honour John Ball (1818–1889), a British public servant of Irish birth. At that time Ball was on his way to becoming one of the most illustrious of British alpinists. He authored the original guidebooks to the Swiss Alps and was the first president of the AC. However, it was in his capacity as undersecretary of State for Colonies that he lent great support to the Palliser Expedition.

BALU: Pass [2039 m], **Peak** [2670 m]; 1901; Hermit. Bridgland, then an assistant to Wheeler in the Topographical Survey, applied this name with reference to Bear Creek, using the Hindi word for bear.

BANDED: Peak [2934 m]; 1896; Opal. Applied by AMC members with reference to the bands of sedimentary rock making up the peak. *See also* Outlaw.

BANFF: Town [1383 m], **Park**; 1888. Sir William van Horne gave this name to honour and please the two largest stockholders of the CPR, Scotsborn Donald Smith and George Stephen, both of whom were born in Banffshire.

BANQUO: Mountain [3002 m]; 1960; SW Purcells. Though a chemist, West had his copy of *Macbeth* with him and obviously read from it freely while circling the icefield, around which rise a series of summits named for its principal characters. Banquo, a nobleman in Shakespeare's drama, was murdered by the ambitious and ruthless Macbeth. He reappeared in ghost form, his chains rattling, but seen and heard only by Macbeth. This portent of impending retribution brought on Macbeth's emotional downfall. *See also* Canmore.

BANSHEE: Mountain [2758 m], Tower; 1976; Starbird. Though it might have been a bad day, we doubt that West actually saw one of these. A banshee is a female spirit of Gaelic derivation who warns of approaching death by her mournful wailing.

BARBETTE: Mountain [3072 m], **Glacier**; 1924; Waputik. This name was derived from a gun turret used on armoured naval vessels of the late 19th century.

BARBICAN: Peak [3120 m]; 1921; Ramparts. The ABC continued its fortification motif on nomenclature all through the area of the Ramparts.

BARIL: Peak [2998 m]; 1918; High Rock. Named to honour M.C.L. Baril, a Dominion surveyor who was killed in action on November 9, 1915, during the Great War.

BARLOW: Mount [3120 m]; 1916; Freshfield. The Topographical Survey honoured the memory of Alfred Ernest Barlow (1861–1914), cartographer to the GSC and consulting geologist who contributed greatly to the knowledge of the nation. He and his wife were drowned when the steamship *Empress of Ireland* sank after a collision in the St. Lawrence River near the city of Quebec.

BARN: Mountain [2911 m]; 1931; S Purcells. Thorington named this mountain for its shape as he saw it when struggling with his pack train up Findlay Creek.

BARNARD: Mount [3339 m]; 1924; Freshfield. Named after Sir Frank Stillman Barnard (1856–1936), Lieutenant-Governor of British Columbia from 1914 to 1919. This is one of the better known peaks of the group.

BARONET: Group, Glacier; 1958; Adamant. This was a substitute for "Nobility," a name that did not honestly pertain, either. Both were the result of a toponymic hoax that got out of hand.

BARRICADE: Mountain [3180 m]; 1914; N Rockies. As one travels upstream along the Jackpine River this summit appears to block the head of the valley. Mary Jobe named it, just before easing south to cross Jackpine Pass.

BARRIER: Mountain [2957 m]; 1928; Front. The derivation of this name is similar to the preceding entry, though located a good many miles distant.

BASILICA: Mount [3390 m]; 1920; Jasper. Appropriately, this summit overlooks the Forum and lies 1 km north of the Curia and 2 km west of the much lower Rostrum.

BASTILLE: Mountain [3066 m]; 1972; Commander. This fortress-like summit, 6 km north of Jumbo Pass, was first climbed on July 14. There is a second summit of the same name on map sheet 93H/16, west of the interprovincial boundary, and a third near Anemone Pass. They were all climbed for the first time on Bastille Day.

BASTION: Peak [2970 m]; 1923; Ramparts. This term of military defence was also applied by the ABC to another of the Ramparts.

BATH: Creek, Glacier; 1881; Waputik. Maj. Rogers was thrown from his horse into the stream, receiving an involuntary bath. Hector's map shows it at as "Noore's Creek," which subsequent scholars have suggested may be a copyist's error for "Moose."

BATTISTI: Mount [3155 m]; 1918; Italian. Named to honour Cesare Battisti (1875–1916), an Italian alpinist, patriot and journalist who was captured by the Austrians and hanged as a spy.

BATTLE: Brook, Range, Mountain [2817 m], **Overlook** [2774 m]; 1901. The name first appears on Wheeler's map but is known to have predated that by some years and been applied because of a legendary battle between a grizzly bear and a prospector. There is no record (or even a strong rumour) of when, who won or where this battle actually took place, but everyone agrees it must have happened south of Glacier National Park, east of the Incomappleux and west of the Duncan River.

BATTLEMENT: Mountain [2910 m]; 1953; N Purcells. West named this mountain for its castellated, impregnable appearance.

BATTLESHIP: The [2606 m]; 1937; Kokanee. Twentieth-century versions of these naval vessels had up to a foot of armour plate and as many as nine 16-inch diameter guns, plus various smaller pieces. This summit, when viewed from the northwest, resembles the prow of such a warship.

BEACON: Peak [2986 m], **Lake** [2150 m]; 1922; Whirlpool. Lying east of the Divide, and thus the interprovincial boundary, this peak is substantially higher than any of the summits actually on the demarcation line. The ABC used it, therefore, as a primary point of reference.

BEAK: Peak [2813 m]; 1970; Badshot. A subsidiary point to the west of

Mount Pool, Wagner's party fancied a resemblance to a bird's beak among the summit rocks.

BEAMAN: Mount [2750m]; 1965; Cariboo. Wilfrid W. Beaman of Quesnel was killed in action during the Second World War (Septermber 1, 1944).

BEAR: Creek; 1888; Hermit. Perley was impressed with reports of the number of bear sighted in this valley; the name, however, was changed to Connaught Creek in 1916. **Glacier**; 1948; Sir Sandford. Applied by Putnam because a grizzly bear was shot while his party was traversing southward over Moberly Pass, toward which this glacier drains from the Sir Sandford Névé.

BEATRICE: Peak [3125 m]; 1912; Ball. Named by ACC members after Beatrice Schultz, a club member who made her graduating climb on this lesser summit on August 8, 1912, en route to neighbouring Mount Ball.

BEATTY: Mount [2999 m], **Creek**; 1924; British. Of Irish ancestry and with a distinguished early career in the Royal Navy, David Beatty, first earl of the North Sea (1871–1936), commanded the Battle Cruiser flotilla at Heligoland Bight, Dogger Bank and the Battle of Jutland. He was First Sea Lord from 1919 to 1927 and represented Great Britain at the 1921 Washington naval armament reduction agreements.

BEAUPRÉ: Mount [2778 m]; 1923; Maligne. Named by the ABC after Sandford Fleming's guide during his overland trip of 1872.

BEAVER: River, Glacier, Mountain [3212 m], **Overlook** [2990 m]; 1882; Battle. Named by Maj. Rogers for the great number of beaver frequenting this large valley up which he was the first white man to venture. The name was expanded beyond the river by Topham in 1890.

BEAVER-DUNCAN: Divide [1378 m]. This low pass, at the common head of the Beaver and Duncan rivers, has been noted and traversed from the earliest days of mountaineering exploration. It is a landmark of the Purcell geological trench, subsidiary to the more important Rocky Mountain Trench, and is occupied by those two streams.

BEAVERFOOT: River; 1884; Van Horne. Dawson stated this to be a translation of its original Stoney name.

BEAVERMOUTH: Station [741 m]; 1883; Dogtooth. This name was given by CPR crews for the place where the Beaver River empties into the Columbia. It was soon established as the base point for helper engines used to push trains over Rogers Pass from 1885 to 1914. In fact, though, the station was situated at the mouth of Quartz Creek, a short distance up the Columbia from the actual mouth of the Beaver River.

Mt. Begbie. GLEN BOLES DRAWING

BEEHIVE: The [2274 m]; 1894; Bow Ranges. This is a generically descriptive name found in many localities, applied here by Allen because of the shape of this minor peak as seen from the northeast, near Lake Louise. There is a Beehive **Mountain** [2895 m] in the High Rock area, which is also shaped appropriately.

BEGBIE: Mount [2732 m], **Creek**; 1907; Gold. Sir Matthew Baillie Begbie (1819–1894) was judge of the crown colony of Vancouver Island from 1858, and after 1870 Chief Justice of British Columbia. Begbie's role in vigorously asserting the supremacy of British law in this isolated colony was critical in holding this region to the Crown and hence in the formation of Canada. Begbie deserves a much higher summit than he has received.

BEGUIN: Mount [2850 m]; 1969; SW Purcells. Wagner gave this name in recognition of Charles and Ruth Beguin, natives of French Switzerland, who homesteaded in Argenta and provided a quietly intellectual environment for visiting alpinists.

BELANGER: Mount [3120 m]; 1921; Fryatt. Named by the ABC to honour André Belanger, a member of an 1814 party that had crossed the Athabasca Pass from Astoria and was drowned while descending the Athabasca River.

BELL: Mount [2910 m]; 1929; Bow Ranges. This mountain was initially "Bellevue" but the name was shortened by the ACC to honour Dr. Frederick Charles Bell (1883–1971), one of its founding members and its president from 1926 to 1928. Bell worked as a ship's surgeon for the CPR and Chief Medical Officer for Veterans Affairs in British Columbia. The doctor's sister, Nora, was a member of the first recorded ascent party.

Bennington Glacier. GLEN BOLES PHOTO

BELVEDERE: Peak [2978 m]; 1910; Sir Sandford. Given by Palmer, in appreciation of the fine and expansive views of the nearby major peaks obtained from this point at the head of the Silvertip Glacier.

BENITO CERENO: Mountain [3058 m]; 1970; Battle. This name was taken by Kruszyna from a character in Melville's *Piazza Tales*.

BENNINGTON: Peak [3265 m], **Glacier**; 1921; Ramparts. One of several names applied by the ABC in recognition of Simon Fraser, who was born in Bennington, Vermont.

BEOWULF: Peak [2830 m]; 1947; Battle. Given by Kauffman in keeping with the battle concept, recalling the hero of the greatest surviving epic of early Anglo-Saxon literature. *See also* Grendel.

BERG: Lake [1638 m], **Glacier**; 1908; Robson. Coleman chose this name because of the number of icebergs floating around in this lake, which lies just south of Robson Pass. The glacier tumbles steeply from the north face of the "King of the Rockies" and calves into the lake.

BERGNE: Mount [3175 m]; 1908; Freshfield. Named by the Topographical Survey for Sir John Henry Gibbs Bergne (1842–1909), an English alpinist and diplomat of distinction, whose son Frank had climbed in Canada and was killed in a fall in the Alps in 1907 while accompanied by Wheeler.

BERTRAM: Peak [3060 m]; 1967; Cline. Named for Bertram Perry, the young son of one member of an AMC party climbing in the area.

BESS: Mount [3216 m], **Pass** [1620 m]; 1910; Resthaven. This name is not from one of Curly Phillips's horses, contrary to some reports, but was given in honour of Miss Bessie Gunn, who was a member of the pack-train party led by John Yates in support of Collie and Mumm.

BEVERLY: Peak [2760 m]; 1953; N Purcells. Professor West borrowed the name from a mining claim down in McMurdo Creek. *See also* David.

B FLAT: Peak [3033 m]; 1963; SW Purcells. This name derives from a snow formation on the southwest face that was felt to have the shape of a musical note and follows the theme of principal summits nearby, named by Wagner for Beethoven compositions in this key.

BIDDLE: Mount [3319 m], **Pass** [2606 m]; 1894; Bow Ranges. Given by Allen in honour of his friend, Anthony Joseph Drexel Biddle (1874–1903) RGS, author and publisher "of Philadelphia, an extensive and enthusiastic traveller."

BIDENT: Mountain [3084 m], **Tower**; 1916; Bow Ranges. This summit has two peaks nearly equal in height. *See also* Quadra.

BIG GREEN: Peak [2841 m]; 1961; Battle. The name originally proposed by Anger and Silverstein was Dartmouth (where they were attending college), but since that name was already taken, the Committee on Geographical Names accepted the college's nickname as an alternative.

BILL'S: Pass [2560 m]; 1954; Bugaboo. Peter Robinson named this after a prospector who had earlier crossed the pass and left a note in a cairn that was discovered by Robinson and his party during their exit eastward from East Creek and the "Fountain of Youth" on August 2, 1954. The note read: "Bill H. Aug.14 45."

BILLY BUDD: Mount [2795 m]; 1970; Battle. This piece of Melvilleana was conferred by Kruszyna after he made its first ascent. *Billy Budd* was not published until 1924, 33 years after Melville's death.

BILLY WHISKERS: Glacier; 1947; Battle. Given by Brewster because a group of goats was crossing the ice as he and the Kauffmans first sighted the glacier on their final, and successful, attempt to reach Mount Proteus.

BINOCULAR: Peak [2740 m]; 1972; Lardeau. This is a granitic horn, named by the first ascent party, led by Spokane resident William Fix, for its proximity to Spyglass Mountain.

BIRDWOOD: Mount [3097 m], **Creek**; 1919; British. Field Marshal Sir William Riddall Birdwood (1865–1951) was commander during the First World War of the ANZAC forces in the mismanaged Gallipoli campaign and later in France.

BIRTHDAY: Peak [3185 m]; 1915; Starbird. Given by Capt. MacCarthy because the peak was first climbed on August 10, 1915, the 32nd birthday of Conrad Kain, the Austrian guide who led the way up.

BISHOP: Range; 1901; Dawson. Originally called "The Mitre" by Harold Topham, it was renamed by Wheeler to distinguish its various summits. **Mount** [2850 m]; 1918; High Rock. Named in memory of Air Marshall William Avery Bishop (1894–1956), who achieved fame initially by shooting down 72 enemy aircraft in the Great War and later became Canada's authority on civil aviation. **Peak** [3060 m]; 1978; 83C/4; W Rockies; RN. This is not the dominant point of the Chess group, but Kruszyna felt it to be one of the better peaks; furthermore, the summit has a pronounced notch.

BISON: Creek, Tower [3185 m]; 1973; Murchison. The creek drains from the several towers south of the main massif of Mount Murchison; its name is of long standing. In the 1972 Climbers' Guidebook, Putnam added specific names to each of the towers for future ease of identification.

BIVOUAC: Peak [3000 m]; 1924; Cariboo. This name commemorates an occurrence that punctuates many alpine accounts—sometimes planned, sometimes otherwise. In this instance Carpé and Chamberlin planned it. The peak is in the Premier Range southeast of Mount Sir Mackenzie Bowell but has not yet been renamed. **Tower** [3002m]; 1933; 82F/15; S Purcells; CS. McCoubrey, on the other hand, did not plan his party's night out while attempting this Leaning Tower.

BLACK: Glacier, Creek; 1901; Dawson. Originally called "Dirty Glacier" by Topham, from the quantity of rock debris covering its lower reaches in 1890; it was renamed more artistically by Wheeler.

BLACK DIAMOND: Mountain [2941 m]; 1916; Farnham. Stone named this mountain, noting the black, friable shale of which much of it is composed, but drawing his inspiration from a mining claim on its lower slopes, filed in 1898 by Ben Abel and Charles Watt. No one lost climbing equipment or ran a scary ski trail on this mountain.

BLACK FANG: Mountain [3002 m]; 1952; Starbird. Robinson meant this to be a descriptive name for this nunatak/pinnacle—rising, in those more glaciated days, some 30 metres sheer above the surrounding snowfield.

BLACKFRIARS: Peaks [E–3226 m, W–3190m]; 1909; Adamant. Applied by Palmer to a pair of prominent granitic summits south of the main Adamant massif. He fancied them as hooded monks. The lesser reaches only 100 m lower than the higher. **Mount** [3210m]; 1927; Chaba. Though there is only one summit here, Ostheimer felt it had the outline of a hooded monk.

BLACKHORN: Peak [3000m]; 1923; Jasper. This name was applied by the ABC. The first ascent came several years later, under the leadership of Bradley Baldwin Gilman (1904–1987), who became president of the AAC and gained fame for his high-angle climbing exploits.

BLACK PRINCE: Mount [2932 m]; 1917; Blue. A light cruiser bearing this name sank with all hands during the Battle of Jutland. It had been stationed on the starboard wing of the First Squadron and was badly damaged and set afire during the second phase of the battle. It blew up shortly after midnight on June 1. The original Black Prince, the eldest son of Edward III, wore distinctive black armour in combat and fought against the French in the Hundred Years War. He died in 1376 at age 46 before he could assume the English throne.

BLACKROCK: Mountain [2910m]; 1921; Whirlpool. Black Ordovician sediments, encountered here and there throughout the Rockies, outcrop prominently on this summit, appropriately named by the ABC.

BLACKWATER: Creek, Mountain [2732 m], **Range**; 1916; W Rockies. White asserts this name was applied simply because it was descriptive of the colour of the water. But this stream's water is actually quite colourless, one of the few non-glacial tributaries to the upper Columbia. There is, of course, a Black Water in Glenshee, Scotland, a name quite well known to many of the early travellers on the Columbia.

BLADE: The [2910m]; 1960; Opal. This spectacular gendarme on the south ridge of Mount Blane was so christened by members of the Calgary Mountain Club who had been repulsed on their initial attempts to ascend it.

BLAEBERRY: River; 1859; W Rockies. Named by Hector for the great number of huckleberry bushes he encountered while descending this valley.

BLAKISTON: Mount [2910m], **Creek**; 1861; Boundary. Lt. Thomas Wright Blakiston (1832–1891), an amateur ornithologist, was in charge of magnetic observations for the Palliser Expedition and was largely assigned to the southern area of exploration where he could coordinate with the International Boundary Survey Commission, whose work was to carry the 49th parallel line from the crest of the Rocky Mountains to the Pacific Ocean. Blakiston was difficult for Palliser to deal with and was sent home after two years. In later years he served in China and Australia, but married an American in 1885 and died in San Diego.

Mt. Blane. GLEN BOLES PHOTO

BLANE: Mount [2993 m]; 1922; Opal. Sir Charles Rodney Blane (1879–1916) commanded the battleship HMS *Queen Mary*, which was completely destroyed by German gunfire early in the Battle of Jutland, May 31, 1916.

BLANKET: Mountain [2817 m], **Creek**; 1930; Gold. L.E. Harris made this name official while refining the topographical survey of the Gold Range. The name appears to be derived from François Norbert Blanchet (1795–1883), an early Catholic missionary to British Columbia who became the first bishop of Oregon in 1845.

BLOCK: Mountain [2935 m], **Lake**; 1920; Sawback. Bridgland chose this name because of the mountain's shape. Tower [2941m]; 1973; S Purcells. This is the next, less imposing, summit south of Wall Tower.

BLOCKHEAD: Mountain [3063 m]; 1916; S Purcells. MacCarthy and Stone gave this name because of the blocky nature of the granite making up the mountain's summit, not in honour of any of their companions.

BLUEROCK: Mountain [2789 m]; 1913; Highwood. The ABC observed that the rocks on part of this mountain have a bluish cast to their colour.

BLUEWATER: Creek; 1916; W Rockies. The waters of this stream, a tributary from the east to the upper Columbia, really are bluish, being derived in part from glacial sources, but mellowed from the harsh grey tint of heavy rock-flour content by the infusion of clear water runoff.

BOAT ENCAMPMENT: Location [594 m]; 1811. David Thompson camped here, at the northerly apex of the Columbia, after his first traverse of Athabasca Pass and bushwhacking descent along the Wood River. Here, the men made canoes for the descent of the Columbia River. Their attempts to use local birch ended in failure, as the Pacific birch is a different subspecies from the Atlantic birch used for canoes. For the next generation this spot was used as a depot during overland trips by NWC and then HBC employees. This historic site is now flooded behind Mica Dam, under the waters of Kinbasket Lake.

BOBAC: Mountain [3087 m]; 1966; Murchison. This is the Polish word for marmot, of which many are found in the High Tatra of that nation. Several families of their Canadian relatives were encountered by the first ascent party near the base of this peak.

BOBBIE BURNS: Creek; 1890; N Purcells. This name derives from a mining claim in the headwaters of the creek, named for the famous Scots poet (1759–1796). The name first appears in gold commissioner A.P. Cummins report of 1890 and was shown on his map three years later. The Robert E. Burns claim (covering 51.6 acres) was filed in this basin on July 29, 1893, by John Bamford and surveyed by Fred Aylmer. Five years later, in September 1889, Alfred Beardmore filed a Bobbie Burns claim on Copper Stain Mountain, in the Dogtooth Range considerably north of the creek. At one time the name was applied to much of the Vowell Group of peaks near the head of the creek that is the major south fork of today's Bobbie Burns Creek. The third major facility of Canadian Mountain Holidays was later built in this valley.

BOGART: Mount [3144 m]; 1928; Kananaskis. Donaldson Bogart Dowling (1858–1925) was a Canadian geologist who pioneered the exploitation of Alberta's large fossil fuel resources.

BONNET: Peaks [3235 m], **Glacier**; 1890; Clearwater. This name was alleged to describe the appearance of the cap of snow on one of the peaks.

BONNEY: Mount [3100 m], **Glacier, Névé**; 1889; Sir Donald. Applied by Green to honour Thomas George Bonney (1833–1923), FRGS and professor of geology at both Cambridge and University College, London. He met Whymper at Zermatt in 1864, but was not a member of the fateful Matterhorn first ascent party. The process of global warming has caused the snow formations on its north side to dwindle in recent years.

BOOM: Lake [1893 m], **Mountain** [2760 m], **Pass** [2301 m]; 1908; Bow Ranges. When first seen by ACC members, driftwood near the outflow of the lake gave the appearance of a log boom.

BOR: Mount [2789 m]; 1937; Valhalla. The Norse motif of this area would naturally have to include the father of the gods Odin, Vili and Ve.

BOSTOCK: Creek, Summit [1850 m]; 1924; Sorceror. Hewitt Bostock (1864–1930) founded the Vancouver *Province* and took an active role in Liberal politics and, over time, held several federal posts, including Speaker of the Senate. In 1896 he represented most of this mountain area as a member of Parliament.

BOSWORTH: Mount [2771 m]; 1903; Waputik. This name was advanced by Whymper to honour his supporter, George Morris Bosworth (1858–1914), who was vice-president and freight traffic manager for the CPR, having been an employee of the railway since 1882.

BOULDER: Camp [2195 m]; 1938; Bugaboo. This spot, at timberline among the huge boulders above the Bugaboo Glacier, has been a favourite campsite for mountaineers since the area was first visited. Though used earlier, its name first appeared in print by the 1938 climbing party that included the distinguished Fritz Herman Ernst Wiessner (1900–1988). The BC Parks Department presently maintains a hut here. Its construction in 1972 was largely funded by donations made to the ACC in honour of Conrad Kain. **Peaks** [2764 m]; 1959; NW Selkirks. Originally named "bolder" by the first party to climb adjacent Downie Peak, in recognition of the sharp outline of these five peaks against the northern sky, the spelling was changed in the course of becoming officially accepted.

BOURGEAU: Mount [2930 m]; 1860; Ball. Eugene Bourgeau (1813–1877), a native of Brizon in the Department of Hautes-Alpes in France, was botanist with the Palliser Expedition. He had previously been a botanical collector in Spain, North Africa and the Canary Islands. Bourgeau was very popular with his associates on the three-year trip to western Canada.

BOW: River, Lake [1891 m], **Pass** [2069 m], **Glacier, Peak** [2868 m], **Range**; 1822; Waputik. This is a translation from the Cree. The members of that tribe found supplies of wood for bows along its banks. The lake was "Upper Arrow" on Collie's 1897 map. The river has sometimes been called the "South Saskatchewan."

BOWERS: Mount [3000 m]; 1913; Whirlpool. Named by Howard after Lt. Henry Robertson Bowers (1883–1912), an officer of the Royal Indian Marine and the "untiring meteorologist" who accompanied Scott in the Antarctic and died with him. *See* Oates.

BOWLEN: Mount [3072 m]; 1953; Bow Ranges. This was "Yamnee" on the Allen map of 1896; #3 in the row of the Ten Peaks. It was renamed in memory of John James Bowlen (1876–1959), a native of Prince Edward Island who moved west in 1902 and went into ranching. Bowlen took an active interest in public affairs, being elected an honorary chief of the Blackfeet and serving as lieutenant-governor of Alberta from 1950 until his death.

BOWRON: Lakes [956 m], **Park**; 1910; Cariboo. This name honours the memory of John Bowron (1837–1906), an Overlander of 1862 who became a mining recorder, government agent and finally gold commissioner of the Cariboo.

BRAS CROCHE: Mount [3286 m]; 1920; Icefield. The ABC recalled here the nickname of an early Metis trapper who was known by the peculiar set of his arm, which had been broken in his youth.

BRAZEAU: River, Lake [1808 m], **Mount** [3470 m], **Icefield**; 1860; Maligne. Hector gave this name to the river in honour of Joseph Etienne Brazeau, of a prominent St. Louis Creole family, who was the HBC factor at Rocky Mountain House and of great help to the Palliser Expedition. Brazeau was known for his command of the various Native languages spoken throughout the Rocky Mountains. The lake was named by Coleman in 1892, and the mountain in 1902 (formerly known as Mt. McGillivray on the 1862 map of D.G.F. MacDonald).

BREAKER: Mountain [3058 m]; 1917; Waputik. The ABC scribe who logged this one in felt that the snow cornice, curling over the crest of the peak, resembled a breaking wave.

BRENNAN: Mountain [2901 m]; 1928; S Purcells. James Brennan, prospector, worked the area near Ainsworth in 1889.

BRENTA: Spire [2941 m]; 1916; Bugaboo. Kain felt the shape of this peak to be similar to the Guglia di Brenta [3220 m] of the Italian Dolomites, with which he had been familiar in his youth.

BRETT: Mount [2984 m]; 1916; Ball. Dr. Robert George Brett (1851–1929) established a hospital at Banff in 1886. He later took an active part in Conservative politics and held several public offices, concluding with that of lieutenant-governor of Alberta, 1915–25.

BREWER: Mount [2789 m], **Creek**; 1911; S Purcells. Samuel Brewer was a prospector and businessman of the Windermere area. Six kilometres northeast of this summit is one [2688m] named for his contemporary, George Goldie, the mining recorder who logged in all the local claims for many years.

BREWSTER: Creek, Mountain [2859 m], **Rock**; 1934; Sawback. James Irvine Brewster (1882–1947) was probably the best known of the four sons of John Brewster, who settled in Banff in 1887 and opened a dairy. The sons branched out into guiding and outfitting and in time the name of Brewster came to be practically synonymous with all forms of transportation and much commerce within the Canadian Rockies.

BRIDGLAND: Mount [2930m]; 1957; Jasper. **Peak** [2984m], **Pass** [2060m]; 1956; NW Selkirks. All these features are named in honour of Morrison Parsons Bridgland (1878–1948), DLS 1905, a sturdy topographer and sometime chief mountaineer of the ACC, who travelled and surveyed much of the Canadian Alps in the course of his work. The name was first suggested for the peak by Sissons in 1912 but only officially adopted after Putnam's later resubmission.

BRISCO: Range, Locality [790m]; 1859; W Rockies. Capt. Arthur Brisco (1829–1860), a member of the 11th Hussars of the famous "Light Brigade," was a gentleman officer who attached himself to the Palliser Expedition during part of its existence. He had sold his commission in 1853 and was visiting North America in company with Capt. Mitchell.

BRITISH MILITARY: Group; 1918. These peaks lie south of Banff. The majority of the names in this area have been applied in remembrance of major British military figures of the Great War.

BROCK: Mount [2902m]; 1922; Opal. Rear Admiral Sir Frederick Edward Errington Brock (1854–1929) was one of the commanders during the Battle of Jutland. His detachment was based in the Shetland Islands and charged with defending them and the Orkneys. Reginald Walter Brock (1874–1935) was a distinguished Canadian geologist, director of the GSC after 1908, and sometime Dean of the School of Applied Science at the University of B.C.

BROUILLARD: Mountain [3210m]; 1919; Chaba. This was the "Misty Mountain" Coleman sighted during his trip to Fortress Lake in 1892. The name is frequently found in the mountains; it is derived from the French word for mist. The renaming was done by the ABC.

BROWN: Mount [2799m], **Glacier**; 1820; Whirlpool. Applied by David Douglas to honour one of his patrons, Robert Brown (1773–1858), the notable Scots botanist. Douglas estimated and publicized the height of its summit as being many thousands of feet greater than it was, much to the confusion of subsequent explorers. He assumed the height of the pass to be 11,000 feet (an error derived from his predecessors) and the mountain some 5,000 feet higher. Collie's map of 1898 shows it nearly correct at a bit over 9,000 feet. When the ABC performed the first precise triangulation of this area in 1920 they found it difficult to identify exactly what features Douglas was referring to. *See also* Hooker.

49

BRUCE: Mount [3090 m]; 1923; Icefields. The leader of the 1922 British attempt on Mount Everest was Gen. Charles Granville Bruce (1882–1965). His name, along with those of several other prominent explorers and alpinists, was placed on this summit by Schwab in the course of the 1923 expedition to Mount Clemenceau. **Mount** [2515 m]; 1921; S Purcells. The name on this lesser point recalls Robert Randolph Bruce (1863–1942), a native of Scotland who had been on the engineering staff of the CPR for ten years after 1887. Resigning to take up mining interests, he later became president of Columbia Valley Irrigated Fruit Lands, Ltd., served as lieutentant-governor of British Columbia (1926–31) and as minister plenipotentiary to Japan. The most notable of his mining interests was in Toby Creek, where he came to control the Parridice [Pair o' Dice] Mine, which was finally closed in 1906.

BRUINS: Pass [2485 m]; 1901; Hermit. Chosen by Bridgland for its relationship to Bear Creek.

BRUSSELS: Peak [3161 m]; 1920; Fryatt. Given by the ABC for *Brussels*, an unarmed merchant ship that had been commanded by the heroic Capt. Fryatt.

BRUSSILOF: Mount [3005 m]; 1916; Blue. Alexei Alexeivitch Brussilof (1853–1926) was one of the more successful Russian generals in the First World War. He later served as Supreme Military Commander during the brief Menshevik regime and then held important military commands under Lenin.

BRYANT: Mount [2629 m], **Creek**; 1901; Fisher. Henry Grier Bryant (1859–1932) was an Arctic explorer and American alpinist who visited the Canadian Rockies in 1899 and 1901 with mapmaker and writer Walter Wilcox. During the second of these trips he was the first person to attempt the ascent of Mount Assiniboine. Bryant later served as president of the AAC.

BRYCE: Mount [3507 m], **Creek**; 1898; Icefields. James, Lord Bryce (1838–1922) was a British jurist, historian, alpinist and diplomat. His 1888 volume *The American Commonwealth* established him as a friend of the United States, where he was ambassador from 1907 to 1912. He was elected president of the AC in 1899, the year after Collie named the mountain.

BUCEPHELUS: Peak [3130 m]; 1863; Ramparts. This was the name of Dr. Cheadle's mount, on whose back he travelled these mountains. He had derived the name from that of the favourite horse of Alexander the Great.

BUGABOO: Creek, Pass [2240 m], **Spire** [3185 m], **Glacier, Group**;

Bugaboo Spire and Howser Spire in the Bugaboo Group.
ROGER LAURILLA PHOTO

1893; Purcells. This name, used by miners elsewhere in the Kootenay district and now famous in North American skiing and climbing, appears on gold commissioner A.P. Cummins' map of 1893. The first mining claims were filed near the pass in 1895, precipitating a short-lived gold rush. Telesphore and Zepherine Mercier staked out the "Last Chance" and "Surprize" claims in 1896. They found the area a bit crowded the next year when the Golden and Fort Steele Development Company staked out five more. The mineralization at the pass, however, was largely galena and pyrite, and two years later everyone had left, though Telesphore continued to prospect the region for another quarter century.

BULLER: Mount [2805 m], **Creek**; 1927; Kananaskis. This name honours the memory of Major Herbert Cecil Buller (1882–1916), who had been aide-de-camp to the Governor General of Canada, 1911–14. He received the DSO in 1915 but was killed later in fighting near Zillebeke.

BULMER: Mountain [2789 m]; 1969; SW Purcells. Wagner applied this name in honour of an early settler in the Argenta area. George Bulmer was the owner of substantial orchards.

BULYEA: Mount [3304 m]; 1924; Freshfield. George Hedley Vicars

Bugaboo Spire and Vowell Glacier in the Bugaboo Group.
ROGER LAURILLA PHOTO

Bulyea (1859–1926) came west with the CPR and held several public offices. He was the first lieutenant-governor of the province of Alberta, serving from 1905 to 1915.

BURGESS: Mount [2599 m], **Pass** [2182 m], **Formation**; 1886; Waputik. Klotz gave this name after his superior officer, the honourable Alexander MacKinnon Burgess (1850–1908). A sometime journalist and deputy minister of the Interior, Burgess became Commissioner of Public Lands for Canada in 1897. The Burgess shale, prominent on the lower slopes of this mountain, is world renowned for its wealth of fossils (over 140 invertebrate species).

BURNEY: Mount [2934 m]; 1922; Opal. Admiral Sir Cecil Burney (1858–1929) led the First Battle Squadron in the Battle of Jutland from his flagship *Marlborough*. He became admiral of the fleet in 1920.

BURNHAM: Mountain [2910 m]; 1963; Gold. Brig. Gen. Frederick M.W.E. Burnham, M.D. (1870–1955), became a specialist in the treatment of rheumatic and arthritic diseases. He had served with distinction as a surgeon in company with Montenegran forces in the Great War and its aftermath. In 1924 he established a sanatorium and resort at Halcyon Hot Springs on the east side of Upper Arrow Lake. He died in a fire that consumed the premises. *See also* Grady.

BURNS: Mount [2936 m]; Highwood. Patrick Burns (1856–1937) of Calgary was locally known as the "Cattle King" because of his prominence in the meat-packing industry. He became a member of the Senate and also dabbled in the coal-mining business.

BURSTALL: Lakes [1966 m], **Mount** [2760 m], **Creek**; 1936; British. Lt. Gen. Henry Edward Burstall (1870–1945) served as aide-de-camp to the Duke of Connaught when the latter was Governor General. He later commanded Canadian forces during and after the Great War.

BUSH: River, Lakes [724 m], **Pass** [2395 m], **Mountain** [3300 m]; **Peak** [3090 m]; 1901; W Rockies. The name surely predates its first appearance in the literature, given for the difficulty of travel encountered by all who entered this valley's forests. The area became notorious—until finally conquered in the late 1960s by loggers armed with bulldozers and chainsaws. Collie was the first to reach Bush Pass, in 1902. After construction of the Mica Creek Dam, the shallow, mosquito-ridden lakes were subsumed into the much greater Kinbasket Lake. *See also* Icefall and Rostrum.

BUTTERS: Creek, Mount [3139 m], **Lake** [1957 m]; 1946; Battle. Frederick King Butters (1878–1945) was a botanist at the University of Minnesota and an authority on ferns. He climbed extensively in Canada, often with Palmer and Holway. In 1947, unaware of a request submitted a year earlier by colleagues at the University of Minnesota, Kauffman gave this name to the highest point of the Battle Range, now Proteus, which had been the unattained objective of Holway and Butters a generation earlier. They had failed to get far enough through the lower valleys and climbed, in 1914, only the peak that now bears this name. The peak was called "Ishmael" by Anger in 1958, following the Melville motif, and the creek was called "Holway's Creek." The Geographic Committee, however, had already established Holway's name in the area west of Tangier Summit and turned the prime nomenclature in this area over to the memory of his younger companion.

BUTTRESS: Peak [2752 m]; 1915; Ottertail. The Topographical Survey applied this name because the peak is essentially the large east buttress of the slightly higher Manganese Mountain.

BUTWELL: Peak [2942 m]; 1894; Ottertail. Allen had enjoyed the company of Frank Butwell, hunting guide of Golden and sometime game warden at Leanchoil.

BYNG: Mount [2940 m]; 1918; Blue. Julian Hedworth George Byng (1862–1935), Baron of Vimy Ridge, served as commander of the Canadian Corps in this famous and bloody battle of 1916 and was Governor General of Canada from 1921 to 1926.

It is not names which give confidence in things,
But things which give confidence in names.
—St. John Chrysostom (345–407),
Patriarch of Constantinople

CADORNA: Mount [3145 m], **Creek, Lake** [1935 m]; 1918; 82J/6; Italian. The aging commander in chief of the Italian armies during much of the Great War was Luigi Cadorna (1850–1928). After the disastrous battle and rout at Caporetto [Kubarid] in the Julian Alps in the autumn of 1917, he was replaced by Diaz.

CAIRN: Peak [2850 m]; 82K/11; N Purcells. This is the Scots word for a pile of rocks. Mountaineers have long been in the custom of building cairns as trail markers, summit adornments, landmarks and for no useful purpose at all. Some of the biggest and most striking fall into the latter category. The cairn, or a monolithic rock, was the symbol of the Celtic god Pen, whose name can be found in many mountain areas of Europe.

CAIRNES: Mount [3060 m], **Glacier**; 1917; 82N/10; Freshfield. This name was applied by Bridgland in honour of Delorme Donaldson Cairnes (1879–1917), a field geologist with the GSC, mostly specializing in the Yukon. His nephew, Clive Elmore Cairnes (1893–1954), wrote the definitive geological memoir on the Slocan Mining District.

CALEDONIA: Mount [2856 m]; 1926; 83D/15; Jasper. Origin unknown. This was the Roman name for northern Britain.

CALUMET: Ridge, Peak [2907 m]; 1922; 83E/6; Robson. Applied here by the ABC, this refers to the ceremonial pipe of North American First Nations, smoked on special occasions and passed from hand to hand as a symbol of friendship.

CAMBRAI: Mount [3134 m]; 1920; 82N/15; Lyell. This summit was named after one of the many towns in northeastern France that were liberated by Canadian troops in October 1918, as the German Imperial Army began to collapse after Gen. Paul von Hindenburg's final offensive.

CAMELS: Ridge [2720 m]; 1888; 82N/6; Hermit. This long easterly spur of Mount Tupper was named by unknown guests at Glacier House for the series of humps adorning it. The ridge remained unclimbed for a generation after its naming.

CAMERADE: Point [3016 m]; 1929; 82N/3; Dawson. Guide Christian Häsler Jr. named this point east of Mount Augustine and overlooking the expanse of the Deville Névé after leading its first ascent.

CAMP: Peak [3094 m]; 1928; 82K/7; Starbird. This summit stands above the site used by the ACC's 1928 annual camp in the valley of Horsethief Creek below Lake Maye, now Lake of the Hanging Glaciers. It was climbed frequently during their two-week stay.

CAMPUS: Peak [2810 m], **Creek, Pass** [2240 m]; 1926; 83D/9; Ramparts. The ACC followed the Roman motif in the area not far from the Forum.

CANAL: Flats [810 m]; 1883; S. Purcell. Lying at the high point of the Rocky Mountain geological trench, this was once called McGillivray's Portage, between the headwaters of the Columbia and the southbound Kootenay River. In 1883 it became the site of a canal project promoted by the British-Austrian alpinist and adventurer William Adolph

Baillie-Grohman (1847–1921). His plan was to divert floodwater from the Kootenay into the Columbia so as to successfully develop farmland around Kootenay Lake. Pressure from the CPR, which feared damage to its bridges downstream on the Columbia, caused the government to forbid full implementation of the project, though two riverboats did make the passage in 1886.

CANMORE: Town [1309 m]; 1883; this name comes from the Gaelic *ceann mor*, meaning "big head." It was initially applied to King Malcolm III of Scotland, who drove the usurper Macbeth from the throne in 1054 (and to his death three years later) after a troubled 17-year reign. When the somewhat irreverent Maj. Albert Rogers was working his way into the mountains in 1881, he referred to this spot as "Padmore."

CANOE: River, Pass [2050 m]; 1811; W Rockies. It was on the banks of this stream that David Thompson's party built their canoes for descending the Columbia River after crossing Athabasca Pass in the winter of 1811. An amateur botanist, he was the first to note the differences between the birch trees of the Pacific drainage and those of the East with which the voyageurs were more familiar. They had great difficulty in "raising the bark" to make their canoes, and ultimately realized they were dealing with a different subspecies of birch. The ABC applied the name to the pass in 1920.

CAPRICORN: Glacier, Lake [2175 m]; 1921; Waputik. This zodiacal name suggests the presence of *Oreamnos montanus*, the mountain goat. (After all, alpinists may sometimes appear to be uncouth and goatish, particularly when emerging bedraggled and unkempt after weeks in the woods.)

CARBONATE: Creek, Mountain [2780 m], **Group**; 1892; N Purcells. The Carbonate Mountain Mining Company, which staked out several claims in this area in 1892–93, operated here. Its proprietors had determined that the interesting ore bodies of the Northern Purcells were formed by the intrusion of magmatic fluids into a carbonate-rich country rock. This was also the name of a landing point on the Columbia, 20 miles upstream from Golden, where ores from the mines in the Spillimacheen River basin were transferred from wagons to boats. *See also* McMurdo.

CARCAJOU: Pass [1570 m]; 1928; Whitehorn. This is the French word for wolverine, an overgrown relative of the weasel and a rugged and resourceful denizen of these mountains. Wolverines have been known to raise hell with caches and untended campsites.

CARDINAL: River, Mountain [2688 m], **Pass** [1905 m]; 1918; Maligne.

There were several employees of the HBC bearing this name. One served as a guide to the earl of Southesk, another was manager of Rocky Mountain House. Jacques Cardinal, however, was buried on the banks of the north fork of the Brazeau River, which was renamed in his memory.

CARIBOO: Mountains; 1861. The name for the northernmost of to-day's Columbia Ranges first appears (with this spelling) in a dispatch from HBC governor Sir James Douglas (1803–1877) to the duke of Newcastle. He was referring to a wide but then undefined area of in-terior British Columbia.

CARMATHEN: Peak [2941 m], **Glacier;** 1969; Starbird. Professor West applied this name after the seaport of South Wales that had originally been settled as a Roman encampment.

CARNARVON: Mount [3040 m]; 1900; Waputik. Burgess put this name on its present location in honour of Henry Howard Molyneux Herbert (1831–1890), fourth earl of Carnarvon, who had been the parliamen-tary author of the British North America Act of 1867, which initiated the process of political self-determination for Canada. He served for many years as secretary of state for colonies. Drewry and McArthur had already used the name on the southerly high point of the Van Horne Range, now known as Mount King. They occupied it as a primary triangulation point and determined its altitude as 9488 feet above sea level. The present Carnarvon had been called "Emerald Mountain" previously.

CARNES: Creek, Peak [3051 m], **Towers** [2902 m]; 1865; NW Selkirks. The creek was named by Walter Moberly after Henry Carnes, a gold seeker who, with William Downie, Joseph LaForme, Louis Lee and Nelson deMars, prospected tributaries of the Columbia in the 1860s. The peak and towers were collectively called Serenity by Palmer in 1912 when he saw them from the east, but that name was not officially adopted. In 1956 Putnam suggested the present name.

CARPÉ: Mountain [2895 m]; 1949; Premier. Hendricks named this one after Allen Carpé (1894–1932), a brilliant American telephonic engi-neer and alpinist who had climbed in the Canadian Rockies, visiting the Athabasca Pass area in 1920, and been among the first to visit the Cariboo Mountains. Carpé lost his life after falling into a crevasse on Mount McKinley in Alaska.

CARSON: Mount [2742 m]; 1908; Sorceror. This relatively unimportant point was named after 31-year-old Percy Alexander Carson, Dominion Land Surveyor, who headed the topographical survey team that mapped much of the Railway Belt north of Glacier and Rogers passes, the field work being done in 1907–8. Carson later became an authority on the toponymy of Alberta.

CARTIER: Mount [2610 m]; 1885; W Selkirks. The CPR named this lesser point, prominent in the easterly view from Revelstoke, after Sir George Etienne Cartier (1814–1873), the leading French-Canadian statesman of Confederation and strong supporter of Sir John Macdonald and the Pacific Railway concept.

CASCADE: Mountain [2998 m], **River,** 1858; Sawback. Aptly named by Dr. Hector as a translation of the Stoney words for "mountain where the water falls." With the advent of overly enthusiastic alpinism, more than water has been known to fall off the south and easterly faces of the mountain. This is a common name and has also been applied to a **Rock** [2821 m] on map sheet 82J/13 and a **Mountain** [2941 m] on 82K/6. The best of the cascades in these mountains can be observed just east of Rogers Pass, where it bursts forth, full grown, from the side of Mount Tupper and is still spanned by one of the CPR's finer examples of 100-year-old masonry.

CASEMATE: Mountain [3090 m], **Glacier;** 1920; Ramparts. The ABC continued its fortification motif throughout this entire area.

CASKET: Pass [1640 m], **Lake, Creek;** 1924; N Rockies. This name was applied by the ABC for a funereally shaped rock formation near the crest of a nearby mountain.

CASTELNAU: Mount [3005 m], **Glacier;** 1918; French. Noel Marie Joseph Edouard de Castelnau (1851–1944) commanded the Second French Army in Lorraine during much of the Great War, later serving as Chief of Staff to the Allied Supreme Commander, Gen. Joffre.

CASTLE: Mountain [2766 m]; 1858; Sawback. This striking summit was aptly named by Dr. Hector because of its commanding shape and dominant position in the Bow Valley. It was renamed in early 1946, by direct order of Mackenzie King, to honour Gen. Dwight David Eisenhower, Allied commander in chief in Europe during the Second World War, who was then visiting Canada. There was much resentment on both sides of the 49th parallel about the renaming and it was officially changed back in 1979, leaving Eisenhower's name only on the separate tower east of the main massif. This name has intermittently been applied to quite a number of other impressive mountains.

CASTLEGUARD: Mountain [3090 m], **Glaciers, River, Meadows** [2130 m]; 1918; Icefields. The mountain was named by the ABC for its shape and startling aspect when seen from below. The meadows are wide and pleasant with isolated groves of timber, underground streams and abundant flora. They have become a popular camping area for alpinists.

CASTOR: Mount [2779 m]; 1896; Sir Donald. Named by Professor Fay for the mythological twin, in company with the adjacent peaks, Pollux and Lada, on the Jupiter massif which lies west of the Asulkan Valley. Fay may have been making a pun, as "castor" is also Latin for beaver, of which many have been found in the adjacent valleys.

CAT: Peak [2940 m]; 1937; Monashee. N.E. McConnell conferred a number of brief names to his triangulation points in the course of his travels in this region. *See also* Feline, Hat.

CATACOMBS: Mountain [3330 m], **Creek**; 1920; Fryatt. Chosen by the ABC because of the number of caves and grottoes in the approaches to the mountain.

CATAMOUNT: Peak [2733 m]; 1902; Hermit. The Topographic Survey applied this name, which refers to a variety of wildcats, in consonance with nearby "Cougar," "Bagheera," etc. **Glacier**; 1952; 82K/10; N Purcells; CS. Professor Robinson's party saw wildcat tracks in the early summer snow on this glacier.

CATARACT: Creek, Pass [2515 m]; 1892; Maligne. Given by Professor Coleman as a translation from the Stoney name for "rapid river." **Peak** [3333 m], **Brook**; 1908; Clearwater. This application was made from the numerous minor waterfalls in this area near the head of the Pipestone River.

CATHEDRAL: Mountain [3189 m], **Crags** [3073 m], **Pass** [2225 m], **Formation**; 1900; Waputik. The name was given first to the mountain by Outram because of its imposing walls, and then extended to adjacent features. Those walls are composed of a sturdy limestone/dolomite of mid-Cambrian age, found throughout much of the Canadian Rockies as a cliff band 100-200 metres in height and occasionally extending unbroken for several miles at a time. Its slightly younger companion formation (Eldon) shows similar characteristics. Collectively they make up some of the better rock in the otherwise "rotten Rockies." Near the mountain's crest is a small intermittent lake, which has periodically burst from under its glacial dam and raised havoc with the CPR tracks west of Kicking Horse Pass to the north. The railroad has, therefore, installed pumps and monitoring equipment on the diminutive Teacup Lake and makes periodic inspections by helicopter.

CATHERINE: Mount [3124 m]; 1911; S Purcells. Harnden named this summit after the wife of his occasional companion in the exploration of the Purcell Range, Catherine (Mrs. George) Emerson, who herself made several ascents in the area.

CAULDRON: Mountain [3216 m]; 1916; S Purcells. When Stone's party first approached the mountain it was wreathed in clouds boiling up from the south, resembling a gigantic cauldron.

CAUTLEY: Mount [2880 m]; 1928; Assiniboine. This summit was named for Richard William Cautley (1873–1953), DLS 1896 at Edmonton. He was born in Ipswich, England, but was raised in Vancouver and became the Alberta and Dominion representative on the ABC. His party was responsible for precise delineation of the boundary where it traversed the more usable passes. Wheeler, who represented British Columbia, managed the surveying party that covered the high points.

CAVE: Mountain [2656 m]; 1916; Assiniboine. The ABC applied this name south of Og Pass because there is a colossal cave entrance near the skyline.

CEGNFS: Mount [2807 m]; 1972; Kananaskis. This unpronounceable mouthful is an illogical acronym from the initials of the names of the members of the first ascent party, led by Bernie Schiesser.

CENTAURUS: Glacier; 1969; Starbird. Named for the man-horse of Greek mythology, as was a constellation of the southern hemisphere, of which Alpha Centauri is the foremost star. While Professor West's erudition extends beyond chemistry, in 1899 Manuel Dainard filed the Centaur claim not far distant.

CENTER: Peak [3002 m]; 1939; Bugaboo. This unimaginative name was applied by Georgia Engelhard, along with a number of other equally prosaic terms, during her first visit to what was then called the Bobbie Burns group.

CENTURION: Peak [2790 m]; 1920; Assiniboine. This point lies just southwest of Mount Sturdee and bears the name of Admiral Jerram's First Division flagship during the Battle of Jutland. **Peak** [2850 m]; 1907; Sorceror. Carson applied this name to the isolated summit near Argentine, but left no record as to why.

CHABA: River, Icefield, Peak [3210 m], **Group**; 1892; Chaba. Coleman knew this as the Stoney word for beaver and applied it to the river, a tributary of the Athabasca. Habel, following in 1901, carried that handle to a peak [3150 m] about 2 km northeast of the one presently designated by this name. The name was moved by the ABC in 1920.

CHAK: Peak [2798 m]; 1916; Jasper. The ABC named this peak from the Stoney word for eagle.

CHAMBERLIN: Peak [3110 m]; 1949; Premier. This lesser peak was chosen by Hendricks to honour Thomas Chrowder Chamberlin (1843–1928), American geologist and cosmologist notable for his part in formulating the spiral nebula theory for the origin of the solar system. Chamberlin's son, Rollin Thomas (1881–1948), had been a member of the 1924 and 1928 parties in this area. He was also a geologist and glaciologist of note, a professor at the University of Chicago and, for the final 20 years of his life, editor of the prestigious *Journal of Geology*.

CHANCELLOR: Peak [3280 m]; 1898; Ottertail. This name commemorates Sir John Alexander Boyd (1837–1916), the last chancellor of Ontario, who served as arbitrator in a dispute between the Dominion of Canada and the CPR over certain mineral rights. The matter was put to rest in 1886 and Sir John returned to his duties as president of the High Court of Justice.

CHAPERON: Mountain [2627 m]; 1896; Sorceror. This name appears on the First Report of the Board on Geographical Names, but none of the contemporary writers on the Selkirk Range explain its derivation, leaving a lot to speculate about.

CHAPMAN: Mount [3075 m]; 1917; N Selkirks. Palmer suggested this name after his occasional mountaineering companion, Robert Hollister Chapman (1868–1920), a geologist and surveyor who had briefly been superintendent of the (U.S.) Glacier National Park and served as secretary of the AAC from 1916 until his death.

CHARITY: Peak [3038 m]; 1966; Albert. This is not a very difficult peak to climb, but it took perseverance as well as some other of the cardinal virtues. Since this summit is the highest in the Albert Group, West felt it was the most deserving of his name taken from the words of St. Paul to the Corinthians (1 Cor. 13:13): "... and the greatest of these is charity." Some years earlier Putnam had suggested this be dubbed Bain Peak, since it lies near the head of the creek of that name. Thomas Bain (d. 1921) had opened the Lanark Mine in its lower reaches in 1891, operating it a few years before becoming Revelstoke's first police chief in 1901. *See* Fortitude.

CHARLES STEWART: Mount [2809 m]; 1928; Bow Ranges. This name commemorates the 1917–21 premier of Alberta (1868–1946), a native of Ontario, minister of interior under Mackenzie King and later the Canadian chairman of the International Joint Commission. The west shoulder of this summit is known as Princess Margaret Mountain.

CHARLTON: Mount [3217 m]; 1911; Maligne. Named by Mary Schäffer (Warren) after the general advertising agent of the Grand Trunk Pacific, Henry Ready Charlton (1866–1919). An employee of the CPR for five previous years, Charlton held his position with the GTP from 1898 until his death.

CHARYBDIS: Mountain [2850 m]; 1946; Battle. Named by Kauffman and Brewster for the mythological whirlpool in *The Odyssey*, encountered by Ulysses and his companions in conjunction with the sea monster of Scylla. The alpinists noted the defile between two hazards through which they felt it necessary to pass during an attempt to reach Mount Proteus. Kauffman, whose ashes now lie on that summit, had been after this objective for several years.

CHEADLE: Mount [2660 m]; 1863; Monashee. Viscount Milton suggested this name in honour of his companion, Walter Butler Cheadle (1835–1910), the English physician whose book *North-West Passage by Land* appeared in 1865, the same year he was elected to the Royal College of Surgeons. The book describes their journey through Canada in 1862 and 1863, and especially their tribulations due to the unwelcome company of an traveller named O'Beirne.

CHEOPS: Mountain [2583 m]; 1890; Hermit. Named after the pharaoh by Canadian astronomer Otto J. Klotz for its prominence in the western view from Rogers Pass and the strikingly pyramidal shape of its summit.

CHEPHREN: Mount [3266 m], **Lake** [1722 m]; 1918; Waputik. Originally called "Black Pyramid" by Collie, the name was changed by the ABC to avoid confusion. Chephren was the son and successor of Khufu (Cheops), builder of the great pyramid at Giza. His reign began in 2565 B.C. and his face is alleged to have been the model for that of the Sphinx.

CHERUB: Mountain [2968 m]; 1907; Sorceror. Carson chose this, along with a variety of other gentle-sounding names, because of the tranquil appearance of these summits in comparison with the nearby mass of Iconoclast.

CHESSBOARD: Glacier; 1978; 83C/4; Icefields. Kruszyna put this handle on the glacier that drained away from his major pieces at its head, which, however, he neglected to arrange in the traditional order. *See* King, Queen, etc.

CHESTER: Mount [3054 m]; 1917; Blue. HMS *Chester*, of the Fourth Light Cruiser Squadron, was involved in the Battle of Jutland in 1916, and although severely damaged, with 81 casualties, she was back on duty two months later. Incidentally, the CPR was not without influence in local nomenclature, and Thomas Edward Chester was manager of its mountain hotels during the same year.

CHETTAN: Mount [3040 m]; 1936; Icefields. Gibson, a well-read alpinist, applied this name after a famous and highly regarded Sherpa who lost his life in an avalanche (the probability of which he had predicted) during the course of the 1930 International Expedition to Kanchenjunga.

CHEVRON: Mountain [2880 m]; 1916; Jasper. This summit has twin crests and shows crisply synclinal structure in its bedrock. Thus the name aptly describes rock formations exposed on its northeast slopes.

CHIEF: Mountain; 1859; Boundary. The actual summit of this one is not in Canada, but the mountain stands clearly in front of the Rockies and has great geological significance. Fossils in the rocks of its upper 2,000 feet are considerably older than those in the sediments on which they rest, yet both formations appear to be essentially flat-lying and conformable. This was a considerable mystery to geologists until the nature of the famous Lewis overthrust fault of Montana and Alberta finally became apparent in 1902. The Earth's crust, in this area, had been shortened by three dozen kilometres of compressive movement.

CHIEF WARDEN: Mount [3126 m]; 1975; Maligne. This is the highest of a line of peaks climbed for the first time by rangers of Jasper National Park. Various names were applied by a party led by Willi Pfisterer in what they jocularly referred to as the Warden Range. Some of them stuck.

CHILKST: Peaks [2820 m]; 1960; Cariboo. This is the Shuswap word for "five," the number of peaks in this group. The name was applied, after personal inspection of the premises, by Rollin Chamberlin's daughter, Frances Carter, herself an alpinist of no mean distinction.

CHIMNEY: Peak [3000 m]; 1910; Bow Ranges. This is a generic mountaineering name and usually is applied because a wide crack, or chimney, is used in making the ascent, as in this instance by Longstaff and E.O. Wheeler.

CHINAMAN'S: Peak [2680 m]; 1886; Rundle Peaks. This name was given by local residents because a miner of Chinese origin, inspired by a wager, was the first person to ascend it. Rumour has it that he was disbelieved upon his return and so made a second ascent, this time constructing a cairn visible from Canmore. Research has uncovered the miner's name, and as of 2003 this peak is officially named Ha Ling.

CHINESE: Wall [2605 m]; 1946; Battle. The Kauffmans and Brewster were prevented from proceeding farther on their route toward the "Big Battle Mountain" [Proteus] by this wall, which forms the north shoulder of Scylla Mountain, effectively blocking the head of a valley above Kellie Creek. They had been warned about this difficulty by Cyril Grey Metzler, a trapper from Beaton, who worked this area from 1927 to 1952 and used the name to describe this feature's impact on his own wanderings.

CHISEL: Peak [3049 m], Creek; 1928; Chaba. ACC members felt this summit to be sharper than the Wedge.

CHOCOLATE: Mountain [3050 m]; 1935; Maligne. The mountain is composed largely of dark brown and very loose scree.

CHOWN: Mount [3381 m], **Creek, Glacier**; 1928; Resthaven. Samuel Dwight Chown (1853–1933) of Winnipeg was a prominent Methodist clergyman who helped to form the United Church of Canada in 1912. His cousin, Alice Amelia Chown (1866–1949), was a vigorous women's rights activist and author.

CHRISTIAN: Peak [3390 m]; 1972; Lyell. This southernmost peak of Mount Lyell and its associated high points were named after the Swiss-born guides who settled in Golden in 1912 and were employed by the CPR thereafter. Christian Häsler Jr. (1889–1942) was a native of Meiringen in the Bernese Oberland. *See also* Walter. **Mountain** [3134 m]; 1974; Cline. This point, east of Sunwapta Pass, was named by Putnam for the same gentleman, as it had been his last climb.

CHRISTIE: Mount [3103 m]; 1859; Fryatt. This name was applied by Hector to honour William Joseph Christie (1824–1886), chief factor at Fort Edmonton, who had provided winter quarters in 1858–59 and been of considerable other help to the Palliser Expedition. Christie's father, Alexander, had been Councillor of Ruperts Land until 1849.

CHRISTINE: Mount[2941 m];1929;S Purcells.J.M.Thorington climbed this peak and named it for his wife. *See also* Griswold and Katherine.

CHRYSLER: Peak [2548 m]; 1936; SW Rockies. This peak in the Top of the World area was named by Ben Rosicki, a local hunting guide of Jaffray, B.C., for the Chrysler Building in midtown Manhattan. Then famous for its height, the building is one of the peripheral accomplishments of American industrialist Walter Percy Chrysler (1875–1940), who first came to fame as president of the Buick Automobile Company. *See also* Empire State.

CIRQUE: Peak [2637 m]; 1972; S Purcells. Applied by Wagner, this is another of the common descriptive names that are found in all mountain areas of the world. A cirque is the open-ended, steep-walled bowl at the upper end of a glacially carved mountain valley.

CIRRUS: Mountain [3270 m]; 1935; Cline. In 1928 Bridgland suggested the name of Huntington for this summit but the Board on Geographical Names took a dim view (perhaps because of the cloudiness) and left Huntington to a nearby glacier.

CITADEL: Mountain [2926 m]; 1910; Sir Sandford. Palmer applied this name as a part of his concept of the fortifications surrounding and defending the main peak of the area—this one lying to its west. **Peak**

[2635 m], **Pass** [2350 m]; 1913; Sundance. The Topographical Survey gave this name for the summit's imposing appearance. The name was applied by the ABC but not made official until 43 years later.

CLACHNACUDAINN: Group, Creek; 1911; W Selkirks. Wheeler was party to the application of this name, taken from the "Stone of the Tubs," the historic centrepiece of the city of Inverness, north of Scotland's Great Glen.

CLAGGART: Peak [2786 m]; 1970; Battle. Kruszyna named this peak, 2 km west of Oasis Lake, after the petty officer and villain in Melville's *Billy Budd*.

CLARK: Range; 1910; Boundary. Daly suggested this name for the American explorer Capt. William Clark (1770–1838), who saw but never got near the place. A lesser summit in the Purcell Range was named by Wagner after William Clark, a prospector of Howser, on Duncan Lake.

CLARKE: Peak [3023 m], **Glacier**; 1901; Sir Donald. Given by Wheeler to honour Charles Clarke (1878–1935), who was British-born but resident in Interlaken. He came to Canada with the first contingents of Swiss guides, in part as a professional but also to help them as an interpreter. Clarke's father had been court physician to King Luis I of Portugal and had retired to Switzerland in 1890, building a fine home on Alpen Strasse (evolving later into a rooming house). Clarke went on to be an interpreter to the occupation forces in Germany after the First World War and was an unsuccessful applicant for the Mount Everest Reconnaissance of 1921.

CLEARWATER: River, Mountain [3275 m], **Pass** [2329 m], **Group**; 1792. The name is generic and was first applied, in this instance, by HBC surveyor Philip Turnor (1762–1800), who travelled the area between the major forks of the Saskatchewan River. See the Arrowsmith map of 1795.

CLEAVER: The [3255 m]; 1922; S Purcells. Mrs. Cora Best originally called this summit "Conforjohn," but by the time she made her submission she had apparently thought better of such a clumsy acronym for the first ascent party and offered the present name. *See also* Commander.

CLEMENCEAU: Mount [3658 m], **Icefield, Creek**; 1919; Icefields. Given by the ABC in honour of Georges Clemenceau (1841–1929), who was a great French political figure. A war correspondent with Ulysses Grant, he became a vigorous advocacy journalist and entered the political arena. Known as the "Tiger," he served twice as premier of France, from 1906 to 1909 and from 1917 to 1920, when he was in-

Mt. Clemenceau. ROGER LAURILLA PHOTO

strumental in writing the debasing terms of the Versailles Treaty. In 1892 this mountain was Coleman's "Pyramid."

CLIMAX: Col [2620 m]; 1953; N Purcells. Professor Robinson's party finally struggled to the crest of this high pass on their epic traverse of the Purcell Range.

CLIMBING: Ridge [2760 m]; 1954; Bugaboos. Robinson's party simply pulled this name out of the air when they came close to this ridge. The granite rock looked good, but in fact very little climbing has been done on this ridge, then or since.

CLINE: River, Mount [3361 m], **Pass** [2760 m], **Group**; 1898; Cline. Named by Collie for Michel Cline (sometimes also spelled Klyne or Klein), a fur trader and trapper in this vicinity in the early 19th century. Hector called the river Wapaktehk, meaning "white goat," a name that later migrated upstream to some peaks. Collie's first map of the area showed this simply as "Pointed Rock Peak." *See also* McDonald.

CLITHEROE: Mount [2747 m]; 1916; Jasper. Bridgland applied this, taking it from a local name in Lancashire, possibly derived from the Old Scandinavian words meaning "rock by the water."

CLOISTER: Mountains [3002 m]; 1892; Cline. Coleman travelled up the Cline River valley and was impressed with the imposing, cathedral-like walls on either side. *See also* Minster.

CLUTTERBUCK: Mount [3063 m]; 1930; S Purcells. Thorington, in his migrations up Findlay Creek, gave this name after Walter John Clutterbuck (1853–1937), a Cambridge-educated British author and traveller who visited the region and later wrote a volume entitled *BC 1887* as well as several other travel books. *See also* Lees.

COBALT: Lake [2323 m], **Spire** [2667 m]; 1946; Bugaboo. Alex Fabergé, alpinist and biochemist and descendant of the jewellers to the Czar, knew good colour when he saw it.

COCKSCOMB: Mountain [3180 m]; Lyell; RN. **Mount** [2770 m]; Sawback. This is another of the self-evident names frequently applied by alpinists.

COFFEE: Creek, Pass [2301 m]; 1906; Kokanee. George Thomas Coffee, a 35-year-old native of California and a hydraulic-mining expert, stopped off in this area en route to the Yukon. He finally got there in 1908. The name is doubly appropriate because the creek runs brown during the spring freshets.

COLD SHIVER: Col [2697 m]; 1953; N Purcells. We can just imagine how the members of Peter Robinson's party felt when they arrived at this high col in the midst of a wet snowstorm, not knowing what lay on the other side or when they would find warmth and shelter.

COLEMAN: Mount [3135 m], **Creek**; 1898; Cline. Arthur Philemon Coleman (1852–1939) was a professor of geology, mountaineer and explorer. He was president of both the Royal Society of Canada and the Geological Society of America. His brother, Lucius, owned a ranch in the Alberta foothills and served as outfitter for their trips into these mountains. Their principal journeys of discovery were made in 1888 to Kinbasket Lake; 1892 to Fortress Lake; 1893 to Athabasca Pass; and 1907 and '08 to the Mount Robson area. See Coleman's book *The Canadian Rockies, Old and New Trails* (Toronto, 1911).

COLIN: Mount [2687 m]; 1859; Jasper. There were two Colin Frasers in the service of the HBC. The elder (1805–1867) was piper (personal servant) for Sir George Simpson and travelled widely with the peripatetic governor.

COLLIE: Mount [3116 m]; 1897; Waputik. C.S. Thompson named this summit for his friend and contemporary John Norman Collie (1859–1942), one of the more distinguished British alpinists of the day. He was professor of organic chemistry at London University, elected president of the Alpine Club in 1920 and spent a total of six summers (1897, '98, 1900, '02, '10 and '11) climbing in the Canadian Alps. He had also been with Mummery in the Himalayas in 1895. Collie returned to Skye in his final years and is buried at Struan, beside John Mackenzie, the first professional mountain guide of Great Britain.

COLLIER: Mount [3215 m]; 1903; Bow Ranges. Joseph Collier (1855–1905) was a British medical doctor who climbed only one season in Canada. He was accompanied by his brother, George, and used the services of guide Christian Kaufmann in making ascents, including this peak.

COLONEL: Pass [1870 m], **Creek, The** [2786 m]; 1911; Robson. Named by the ABC in honour of Colonel Aimé Laussedat (1819–1907), French military officer and geodesist whose photographic surveying techniques, begun in 1849, were copied worldwide. He was a hero to the topographers of Canada.

COLOSSAL: Peak [2940 m]; 1948; Adamant. This name commemorates the climbing team of Ferris and Putnam, known as Colossal Enterprises. They, with Kauffman and Henry S. Pinkham (1946–1952), made the first ascents of this and a dozen other nearby peaks.

COLUMBIA: River, Icefield, Mount [3747 m], **Lake** [810 m]; 1792; Icefields. Capt. Robert Gray (1755–1806) of Tiverton, Rhode Island, having been the first American to circumnavigate the world, took his ship, *Columbia Rediviva*, across the bar at the mouth of the river in 1792. Like the salmon that once abounded in this river, the name travelled hundreds of miles upstream, ultimately reaching the hydrographic apex of North America. The lake of this name is on map sheet 82J/5 and is often erroneously referred to as the source of the river.

COLUMBIAD: Mountain [2815 m]; 1969; Cariboo. To alpinist Arthur Maki, the rock at this summit in Wells Gray Provincial Park resembled a 19th-century cannon.

COMMANDER: Mountain [3362 m], **Glacier, Group**; 1915; Purcell. This name, in the southern Purcell Range, originated with Stone after his first visit to this locale. The glacier, however, was "Tiger Claw" to Minnesota-native Dr. Cora Johnstone Best (d. 1930) when she saw it in 1922.

COMMITTEE PUNCH BOWL: Lake [1750 m]; 1824; N Rockies. The central of three small lakes at the height of Athabasca Pass. It drains both to the Arctic and Pacific oceans and was named by Simon Fraser for the governing committee of his employer, the Northwest Company.

COND: Peak [2810 m]; 1924; Kokanee. This was once called Apex,

Mt. Columbia. GLEN BOLES PHOTO

as it is the highest peak in its group but was renamed for Frederick Thomas Percy Cond (1886–1919), BCLS 1911, who did layout surveying for the CPR in this area. He was a victim of the great influenza epidemic of 1918.

CONDOR: Peak [2945 m]; 1920; Front. HMS *Condor* was a gunboat commanded by Capt. Lord Charles William de la Poer Beresford during the bombardment of Alexandria in 1882. Beresford (1846–1919) was subsequently aide-de-camp to Queen Victoria, a member of the House of Commons and commander in chief of the Mediterranean fleet.

CONE: Mountain [2910 m]; 1916; Sundance. Named for its shape when seen from the Spray Valley.

CONFEDERATION: Mount [2969 m]; 1927; Churchill. One might have thought this summit was ascended, or at least named, on July 1. But, alas, Ostheimer seems to have applied this on June 25, and he only reached 9,000 feet in his attempt to climb it two days later.

CONICAL: Peak [2840 m]; 1924; Murchison. Applied by the Topographical Survey, this is a purely descriptive name—and entirely accurate.

CONNAUGHT: Creek, Tunnel [1160 m]; 1916; Sir Donald. Renamed from Bear Creek at the request of the CPR for the official 1914 opening of the tunnel. This project, five miles straight under Mount Macdonald and saving some five hundred feet in elevation from Rogers Pass, was named for Arthur William Patrick Albert (1850–1942), third son of Queen Victoria. He was duke of Connaught and served as Governor General of Canada, 1911–16, having previously been inspector general of the Imperial Armed Forces.

CONNEMARA: Peak [2880 m]; 1971; Starbird. Professor West borrowed the name for this peak in the Irish Group from the barren mountain area of County Galway.

CONNOR: Mount [2938 m], **Lakes**; Italian. Ralph Connor was the pen name of Charles William Gordon (1860–1937), a Presbyterian clergyman turned novelist who wrote several popular stories about the miners who worked in this corner of Alberta and British Columbia.

CONRAD: Mount [3252 m], **Creek, Glacier, Group**; 1935; Bugaboo. Celebrated English alpinist and professor of literature Ivor Armstrong Richards applied this name. It is one of several place names in these mountains honouring Conrad Kain, the Austrian-born guide who led the professor and his wife on their ascent of this summit.

CONSOLATION: Lakes [1942 m and 1957 m], **Pass** [2472 m]; 1899;

Bow Ranges. Named by Wilcox in contrast to the nearby desolation, as he saw it, of the Valley of the Ten Peaks (Moraine Lake).

CONTINUATION: Col [2290 m]; 1972; S Purcells. This was the saddle where Wagner's party, which had made the first ascents of several peaks to the west, paused for lunch before undertaking the remainder of the Pioneer Peaks.

CONWAY: Mount [3100 m], **Glacier, Group, Creek**; 1901; Freshfield. Named by Collie to honour William Martin Conway (1856–1937), first baron of Allington and an art historian, alpinist and writer. He was elected president of the AC in 1902.

CONY: Peak [2847 m]; 1947; N Purcells. This peak above Silent Pass, was named by Hendricks for the family of these critters that his party came across as they ascended from their camp. *See also* Pika.

COOPER: Mount [3089 m], **Creek**; 1924; Slocan. James Cooper was a trader who attempted to compete with the HBC and was driven out of business by ruthless price warfare. In 1859, at age 38, he became the first harbourmaster of British Columbia and in time somewhat of a provincial folk hero.

COPELAND: Mount [2580 m], **Creek, Pass** [1670 m]; 1910; Monashee. Ralph Copeland (1837–1905) was a participant in the second German Arctic expedition, 1869–70. He was Astronomer Royal for Scotland after 1889 and had visited Revelstoke.

COPPER: Mountain [2795 m]; 1884; Ball. Macoun applied the name because of some copper prospects found near its crest by Dennis and Healy. The copper, however, was as ethereal here as the gold in Golden or the silver in Silver City. **Peaks** [2600 m]; 1905; Hermit. These were described by Thorington in 1916 as "two tiny summits." There is minimal copper here, too; but the area had been worked over by Corbin and his associates.

COPPERCROWN: Mountain [3114 m], **Creek**; 1911; S Purcells. Charles D. Ellis, who was involved in numerous mining ventures in the mountains west of Invermere, applied this name because of the colouring of the summit rocks. *See also* MacCarthy.

COPPERSTAIN: Mountain [2618 m], **Creek**; 1901; Dogtooth. The Topographical Survey crew noted traces of copper ore on this summit. The Dogtooth Range, a northerly extension of the more highly mineralized Purcells, quickly attracted prospectors. Another "Bobbie Burns" claim was filed just south of this mountain, but it was never exploited.

CORAL: Creek, Mountain [3125 m], **Pass** [2545 m]; 1892; Cline. This name was applied by Coleman because the Ordovician formations, outcropping extensively in this area, abound in fossil coral. Later this name was moved to Coleman's Cataract Creek and his "Coral" became "McDonald."

CORBIN: Peak [2712 m]; 1886; Hermit. *"Messrs Corbin, Kennedy, & Weed"* were reported to mine in the "Illecillewaet Subdivision" according to Gold Commissioner G.M. Sproat's report of January 2, 1888, to Provincial Secretary John Robson. It should be noted, though, that one Daniel Chase Corbin (1832–1913) was president of the Spokane International and Eastern British Columbia Railways, both fronts for the CPR in the bitter contest waged with Jim Hill's Great Northern Railroad for the mining trade of southern British Columbia and adjacent reaches of Idaho. Born in Newport, New Hampshire, and dying in Spokane, Washington, Jim Corbin is typical of many people who left the hardscrabble hillsides of New England and the Maritimes to make their fame and fortune in the North American West.

CORDONNIER: Mount [3021 m]; 1924; French. Gen. Emilien Victor Cordonnier (1856–1936) was commander of the French forces in Macedonia, assisting the local Serbian militia under Gen. Putnik, 1915–16.

CORNER: Peak [2972 m]; 1915; N Purcells. The highest point of the Spillimacheen Range, this peak stays consistently in view to the left as one ascends the Spillimacheen River and turns the corner into its tributary, McMurdo Creek.

CORNICE: Peak [3180 m]; 1967; Cline. **Mountain** [2850 m]; 1908; Sir Sandford. This is a common name in various mountain areas, in the latter case by Palmer.

CORNUCOPIA: Peak [3210 m]; 1970; Maligne. Putnam applied this name because an excess of fossils of this nature was found below the peak and en route to its summit.

CORNWALL: Mount [2970 m]; 1922; Opal. The light cruiser HMS *Cornwall* was engaged at the Battle of Jutland and, unlike many other vessels of the Royal Navy, survived intact.

CORNWELL: Mount [2972 m]; 1918; High Rock. Fifteen-year-old John Trevers Cornwell, Boy, First Class, was a member of a gun crew on HMS *Chester* and was posthumously awarded the Victoria Cross for his conspicuous gallantry in action during the Battle of Jutland.

CORONA: Creek, Ridge [2965 m]; 1973; Murchison. We don't know how the creek got its handle, but the name was carried onto the ridge above by the party making its first ascent.

CORONATION: Mountain [3176 m]; 1901; Freshfield. Named, but not climbed, by Collie on August 9, 1902, the day of the coronation of King Edward VII.

CORONET: Mountain [3152 m], **Creek**; 1923; Maligne. Named by Palmer for the shape of a snow formation near the summit.

CORY: Mount [2802 m]; 1928; Sawback. William Wallace Cory (1865–1943) was deputy minister of the interior from 1905 to 1930. The summit was once known as Hole in the Wall because of the large cave that can be seen from the west below its south ridge.

COSTIGAN: Mount [2980 m]; 1904; Palliser. John Costigan (1835–1916) of New Brunswick was in the Macdonald administration from 1882 to 1896 and lobbied for separate schools.

COUGAR: Brook, Pass [2149 m], **Mountain** [2393 m]; 1901; Hermit. This name is commonly applied because of cougar sightings. In this case it was Wheeler who spotted one of the big cats near this minor summit above the Nakimu Caves. There is another Cougar on map sheet 82J/10.

COURCELETTE: Peak [3044 m]; 1918; High Rock. This is the name of a village between Albert and Bapame, in northeast France, the scene of fighting by Canadian forces in 1916 and 1918.

COURSIER: Mountain [2646 m]; 1957; Gold. Henry Noble Coursier (1861–1938) started his career as a timekeeper for Andrew Onderdonk. Later, as a businessman in Revelstoke, he organized a town orchestra in 1892, became the first president of the Board of Trade and succeeded Sibbald as the local magistrate.

COWL: Mountain [3060 m]; 1972; Icefields. This name is similar in derivation to "Blackfriars," from the seeming resemblance to a hooded monk.

CRADOCK: Mount [3030 m], **Glacier**; 1918; Royal. Rear Admiral Sir Christopher George Francis Maurice Cradock (1852–1914) was commander of a British squadron that was soundly defeated by three superior German warships off Coronel, Chile. He went down with his ship, HMS *Good Hope*, on November 1, 1914.

CRAIGELLACHIE: Location [385 m]; 1884; Gold. Meaning "stand fast," the name comes from a rocky crag in Morayshire, Scotland, where Donald Smith, Lord Revelstoke and a CPR financial backer grew up. This is near the spot where the Last Spike was driven. *See also* Revelstoke.

CRANBERRY: Mountain [2886 m]; 1930; Gold. This summit was "Twin Peaks" to the CPR construction workers, but L.E. Harris, DLS, who

actually went up onto the mountain, named it for the mountain cran-
berries he found.

CRESCENT: Spire [2850m], **Towers** [2830m]; 1933; Bugaboo. Thorington was impressed with the shape of these smaller eminences
adjacent on the northeast of the massive Bugaboo Spire. **Mountain**
[3020m]; 1949; Premier. Hendricks applied this name just north of
David; a common choice for peaks with a fringe of snow cornice.

CRESWELL: Mount [2970m]; 1972; Icefields. William Nicol Creswell
(1822–1888) was an artist and painter who visited the Rockies.

CROMWELL: Mount [3330m]; 1972; Icefields; **Tower** [3215m];
Murchison. Both of these features are named after Oliver Eaton
Cromwell (1893–1987), an American alpinist who climbed frequently
in the Canadian Alps and made many first ascents in these mountains,
often guided by Ernest Feuz and in company with Georgia Engelhardt,
whom he later married.

CRONUS: Peak [3085m]; 1950; Windy. Fabergé chose this name.
Cronus (Kronos) was a pre-Olympian god, the son of Uranus, who
castrated his father and married his sister. He is the father of Zeus.

CROSSED FISH: Peak [2850m]; 1963; Bugaboo. Harvard Mountaineering Club member Bill Buckingham's first ascent party performed an ultimate in banality, naming this summit for a brand of
sardines they consumed there. At least they had a pre-labelled container for the summit record.

CROWFOOT: Glacier, Mountain [3050m]; 1959; Waputik. The
Blackfoot chief Crowfoot (1833?–1890), adoptive father of
Poundmaker, did not permit his people to partake in the 1885 Riel-led
uprising, despite his disillusionment with the Canadian government.

CROWSNEST: Mountain [2785m]; **Pass** [1357m]; 1858; S Rockies.
This name refers to the sighting of nesting ravens by ornithologist
Capt. Blakiston some 10 km northeast of the subsequently famous
pass. It was Palliser who finally labelled the mountain "The Crow's
Nest." The north and slightly lower half of this massif is known as
"Seven Sisters Mountain" because of its distinct high points.

CRYSTALLINE: Creek, Mountain [2850m], **Group**; 1899; N Purcells.
This name originated with a mining claim and was thence applied to
the creek flowing by the mine and to the principal mountain of the
area by Robinson.

CUESTAFORM: Peak [2758m]; 1953; N Purcells. Professor Robinson
based this name on a geomorphological term (from the Spanish *cuesta*,
meaning "slope") that refers to a ridge whose crest is determined by
the dip structure of local sedimentary bedrock.

CURRIE: Mount [2810 m]; 1924; Blue. Sir Arthur William Currie (1875–1933) rose to the rank of lieutenant-general commanding the Canadian Corps in the First World War. He later became president of the Canadian Legion of the British Empire Service League.

CURTIS: Peak [3051 m]; 1924; Bow Ranges. This is the south shoulder of Mount Biddle and was named for Rest Fenno Curtis (1850–1918), who taught mathematics at several New England institutions and visited these mountains frequently in the heyday of Appalachian Mountain Club exploration. He served as president of the AMC in 1889.

CYCLE: Peak [2700 m], **Pass** [2566 m]; 1948; Adamant. Given by the "Colossal" party, from the series of descending cirque-like basins, which they felt possibly indicated various stages of glaciation.

CYCLONE: Peak [3041 m]; 1910; Clearwater. When Professor Hickson and Edward Feuz Sr. and Jr. first studied routes on this summit, there was a thunderstorm around its crest.

CYPRIAN: Peak [3268 m]; 1902; Dawson. This name was given by Wheeler to the westerly peak of the Bishops Range, in conformity with the renaming of the Mitre. St. Cyprian was the widely admired Christian bishop of Carthage, beheaded for his faith in A.D. 258 by order of the Roman emperor Valerian. His feast day is September 16. *See also* Augustine.

Names and natures do often agree.

—John Clarke,
Paroemiologia Anglo-Latina, 1639

DAER: Mount [2960 m], **Creek**; 1914; Mitchell. Thomas Douglas (1771–1820), Lord Daer and fifth earl of Selkirk received a large land grant from the HBC in 1811, on which he founded Assiniboina.

DAG: Mount [2667 m]; 1970; Valhalla. This is the name of the Norse god who drives the Chariot of the Day. It was applied here by Robert Dean, a member of the Kootenay Mountaineering Club. This summit had earlier been called "Gimli II." There are a host of other Icelandic names in this area.

DAINARD: Mount [2658 m], **Creek**; 1968; W Rockies. **Lake** [2097 m]. Manuel Dainard (d. 1912) was a woodsman, prospector and outfitter of Golden who travelled the Columbia Valley from Brisco to Boat Encampment frequently in the years after 1890. Just a few months before his death, he was packing supplies for Palmer on the latter's final and successful trip to Mount Sir Sandford. The lake is on map sheet 82N1.

DAIS: Mountain [3300 m]; 1924; Chaba. The ABC applied this name because of the elevated platform upon which the actual summit appeared to stand.

DALHOUSIE: Mount [2974 m]; 1860; Maligne. Southesk named this summit for his friend James Andrew Broun Ramsay (1812–1860), the 10th earl of Dalhousie, at whose home he had first started planning his adventurous trip to the mountains of North America. The earl had distinguished himself as Governor General of India and his father, George (1770–1838), the ninth earl, had been governor-in-chief of Canada, 1819–28, and founded the Quebec Literary and Historical Society in 1824.

DALY: Mount [3152 m], **Glacier**; 1916; Waputik. Fay suggested this name in honour of his friend, Joseph Francis Daly (1840–1916), who had served many years as president of the American Geographical Society of New York. The name may have received approval partly because Reginald Aldworth Daly (1871–1957), a Canadian by birth and member of the International Boundary Commission, was one of the most famous geologists of his day. He spent 30 years on the faculty of Harvard University and became the world authority on the origin of igneous rocks.

DAMON: Peak [2740 m]; 1948; Adamant. On the west side of Friendship Col, this was named by Putnam in recollection of the devoted friends of Graeco-Roman history. *See also* Pythias.

DARRAH: Mount [2754 m]; 1916; Boundary. Capt. Charles John Darrah (d. 1871) of the Royal Engineers, a veteran of the Crimean War, was an astronomer assigned to the IBSC as assistant to Lt. Col. Hawkins.

DAVID: Mount [2780 m]; 1918; Lyell. This was applied by the ABC in honour of David Thompson, surveyor and explorer of the NWC. **Peak** [3110 m], **Pass** [2700 m], **Glacier**; 1927; Premier. The Board on Geographical Names, when engaging in its redesignation of major summits in the Premier Range, applied this name to replace Carpé's earlier "David Thompson." **Peak** [2820 m]; 1950; N Purcells. David Hope-Simpson, geologist and mining engineer, made the first ascent of this peak in 1946 while employed near the head of McMurdo Creek. His associates back at the Beverly Mine labelled it "David's Folly," a name that Professor West shortened for dignity. After service with the GSC, Simpson taught at St. Mary's University in Halifax.

DAWSON: Mount [3399 m], **Group, Glacier**; 1889; Central Selkirks. Named by Green for George Mercer Dawson (1849-1901), topographic surveyor of distinction and director of the GSC, for whom is also named the capital city of the Yukon. The major points of this massif have separate names. Dawson's father, Sir John William Dawson, was a noted geologist and principal of McGill College. A native of Nova Scotia, he studied briefly in Edinburgh and had worked with Charles Lyell in Canada in 1841. *See also* Feuz.

DEAD MAN: Flats; 1916; Front Ranges. In 1904, François Marret killed his brother, Jean, who owned a farm on this strath above the Bow River just east from the Three Sisters.

DEATH: Rapids; 1815. Known to the French-speaking voyageurs as the "Dalles des Morts," this stretch of the Columbia, south of the present Mica Dam, is now flooded behind the Revelstoke Dam, but not forgotten. In the year 1838 alone, 12 persons were drowned there, including the daughter and son-in-law of Governor Simpson.

DEATH TRAP: Location; 1894; Bow Ranges. This steep-sided slot seemed to be an especially dangerous place to Allen, as it is frequently swept by avalanches from both Mount Victoria and Mount Lefroy. He was prophetic in his nomenclature; many lives have been lost here.

DECEPTION: Mountain [2810 m]; 1925; Maligne. We are unsure who named this summit, but the fact that it is measurably higher than Southesk's Mount Lindsay, only barely 1 km distant to the southeast, may have some bearing on the name. **Pass** [2475 m]; 1929; Slate. Skiers heading into Skoki Lodge have been known to bear left over the nearer (west) half of this pass and find themselves trapped on dangerous terrain.

DEFENDER: Mountain [2790 m]; 1921; French. This point lies west of the divide but is nevertheless higher than Mount Onslow, of which it is a companion summit.

DE GAULLE: Mount [2952 m]; 1964; French. Charles André Joseph Marie de Gaulle (1890–1970) was an early advocate of mechanized warfare among French army officers. After the defeat of France in 1940 under the inept generalship of Weygand and Gamelin, he organized the "Free French" forces of the Second World War. De Gaulle later returned in triumph to his homeland where from 1944 to 1946 and from 1958 to 1969 he was its dominant political power. This point

Deltaform Mountain. GLEN BOLES DRAWING

is really a subsidiary of Mt. Nivelle, from which it is separated by a col of less than 150 metres (500 feet) depression.

DELPHINE: Creek, Mountain [3399 m]; 1911; Farnham. Harnden took this name for a mining operation on the mountain's lower slopes. The mine had been prospected by George Starke but was later transferred to Rufus Kimpton, a grubstaker of Golden. Starke then built a hotel at Wilmer, also named for his wife, Delphine (née Francour), who died in 1921.

DELTAFORM: Mountain [3424 m]; 1898; Ten Peaks. This is #8, or "Saknowa," on the 1896 Allen map. It was renamed by Wilcox because its northerly face reminded him of the shape of the Greek letter Delta.

DELUGE: Mountain [2789 m]; 1953; N Purcells. Robinson's party got thoroughly drenched and cold while camped across the valley from this mountain.

DE MARGERIE: Mount [3000 m]; 1924; Freshfield. The Topographical Survey suggested the name of Emmanuel Jacquin de Margerie (1862–1953), a contemporary and collaborator of Termier in French geology.

Having been taught by an English governess, he developed a proficiency in languages and translated many geological works in addition to his own original material. His fieldwork ranged from Spitzbergen to several areas in the Americas. He also wrote four volumes of memoirs.

DENNIS: Mountain [2539 m], **Pass** [2261 m]; 1902; Lake Louise. Suggested by Whymper for Lt. Col. John Stoughton Dennis (1820–1885), briefly surveyor general of Canada, who later became deputy minister of the interior. The high-handed and rigid attitude of his American-style system of surveys near the Red River settlements triggered the first Riel Rebellion. In his last years, Dennis dabbled in some mineral prospects near what was briefly called Silver City, southeast of Laggan (now Lake Louise).

DENNY: Mount [3000 m]; 1973; Opal. In the centennial year of the RCMP, Boles named this summit after Sir Cecil Edward Denny (1850–1928), inspector of the Northwest Mounted Police until 1881. Thereafter Denny served as an officer in the Indian Department and as archivist of Alberta. There are two peaks to this massif, the northern one designated as "Sir Cecil" and the southern as "Edward."

DENT: Mount [3267 m]; 1899; Freshfield. This is another of Collie's names and honours his friend, Clinton Thomas Dent (1850–1912), a distinguished British surgeon, physiologist and alpinist who became president of the AC in 1887.

DENVER: Mount [2758 m], **Glacier**; 1917; Valhalla. Many of the place names associated with mining activities in southern British Columbia reflected the national derivation of those who bestowed them. In this light, the work of Begbie in holding the province to the British Crown takes on added historical significance.

DE SMET: Range, Roche [2539 m]; 1846; Jasper. Pierre Jean De Smet (1801-1873) was a Belgian Jesuit missionary who travelled a great deal among the First Nations of the Pacific Northwest and Missouri. Several of the locals named the prominent rock near Jasper in his honour on April 25, 1846, by discharging their muskets in the direction of the highest mountain. There is also a lesser mountain, east of Columbia Lake, which was another stopping point on the priest's travels through these mountains.

DES POILUS: Mount [3161 m], **Glacier**; 1916; Waputik. This was "Hidden Peak" on the map prepared in 1896 by Jean Habel, a German geographer who travelled extensively in these mountains. It was renamed in Habel's honour by Collie in 1900, then changed by order-in-council during the Great War, when it was felt improper for anything good to be named after a German. The present name honours all the lowly privates of the French army, of whom a million and a half were killed in that conflict.

DEVILLE: Glacier; 1889; Dawson. **Mount** [2924 m]; Van Horne. Edouard Gaston Deville (1849–1924), a native of Nièvre in central France, retired from the French navy to become surveyor general of Canada in 1885. He achieved worldwide distinction for his use of photogrammetry and the excellence of the results achieved by his parties in the field.

DEVILS COUCH: [2728 m]: 1964; Valhalla. In the past, this point had been called King Tut's Couch and also Ski Jump Mountain. Members of the Kootenay Mountaineering Club named several points in the **DEVILS RANGE**; 1976, including **DEVILS DOME** [2789 m]; 1971; **DEVILS HORN Mountain** [2637 m]; 1971; **DEVILS SPIRE** [2636 m]; 1974; **DIABLO Mountain** [2667 m]; 1971.

DEVILS HEAD: Mountain [2997 m]; 1840; Palliser. According to Governor Simpson, the mountain's profile bore a resemblance to an upturned but not pleasing face.

DEVILS: Thumb [2458 m]; 1894; Bow Ranges. Allen gave this minor spire its overstated name. The summit is west across Lake Louise from Mount Fairview.

DEVON: Mountain [3004 m], **Lakes** [2286 m±]; 1919; Clearwater. Named by Bridgland for the Devonian bedrock formations that outcrop extensively in this area.

DIABLERET: Glacier; 1924; Waputik. This name migrated from an area of Switzerland lying west of the Bernese Oberland. The original place is now a ski resort and occasional climbing centre. The Swiss guides who worked for the CPR often chose names from their homeland.

DIADEM: Peak [3371 m], **Creek**; 1898; Icefields. The summit was named by Collie for the fringe of snow adorning its crest.

DICKEY: Mountain [2525 m]; 1955; Clachnacudainn. William Earl Dickey (1893–1954) was electrical superintendent for Revelstoke, a photographer, and publicity chairman for the Revelstoke Board of Trade. 8 Mile Mountain was renamed for him after his death.

DIMSDALE: Lake [1360 m], **Mountain** [2810 m]; 1923; N Rockies. Officially named by the ABC for Henry George Dimsdale, a location engineer employed on the construction of the Edmonton, Dunvegan & British Columbia Railway, which later became part of the CNR.

DIP SLOPE: Mountain [3125 m]; 1968; Clearwater. This undistinguished peak near the head of Clearwater River was named by Putnam for the obvious stratigraphic control of its topography.

DISASTER: Point [1005 m]; 1874; Jasper. Deville gave this name because, while exploring with Sandford Fleming along the Athabasca River, the latter's brandy flask was crushed against a rock by one of their packhorses while passing this point.

DISMAL: Glacier, Pass [2270 m]; 1956; Moloch. The first party to set foot on this glacier below Mount Moloch was led by Putnam. Its four members were wet and weary from travelling through a two-day snowstorm. Their dog nosed her way into their already soggy tent, shook herself free of the damp and refused to budge, thereby compounding the party's attitude. Renamed Fridolin in 1990.

DIVERGENCE: Peak [2827 m], **Creek**; 1921; Whirlpool. The peak marks an angle on the interprovincial boundary, which prompted the ABC to give it this name.

DIVISION: Mountain [3030 m]; 1919; Lyell. This name was suggested by Walcott, who noted that it stands out in the icefield.

DOCKING: Mount [2853 m]; 1966; Mitchell. Pte. 2 John H. Docking, of Cranbrook, was killed in action in the Second World War.

DOGTOOTH: Range; 1892. McArthur applied the name, noting the number of small but sharp peaks in the range across the Beaver River from Sir Donald. The area has never been popular with alpinists because of the vastly more exciting terrain to the south, east and west, but prospectors spent a lot of time there in years past. The first gold discovery was reported in 1883 by Edward Kelly at Cannon [sic] Creek, about 10 miles above where the Canadian Pacific Railway crosses the Columbia. On Topham's map of 1890 this range is shown as "Prairie Hills."

DOLLY VARDEN: Mountain [2662 m]; 1893; Slocan. The mountain was named from a mining claim on its lower southwest slope, which was in turn named after the trout (char). The miner was also an angler, and from the results of his diggings he appears to have had better luck at fishing. The fish shows bright reddish orange spots and can be found in the streams of British Columbia.

DOLOMITE: Creek, Peak [2782 m], **Pass** [2393 m]; 1924; Murchison. The typical chemical composition of dolomite is $CaMgCO_3$. Much of the rock in the vicinity is of this type, first analyzed by the French mineralogist Deodat de Gratet de Dolomieu (1750–1801), for whom a range in the Italian Alps was named. There is also some similarity between the outline of these summits and the original Dolomites.

DOLPHIN: Peak [3026 m]; 1951; Windy. Fabergé followed the nautical motif already established in this portion of the Windy Group.

DOME: The [2736 m]; 1891; Sir Donald. This name was given by Fay because of the summit's shape when seen from the north, near Mount Abbott. **The** [3090 m]; 1908; Robson. This is a point just below Mount Robson, named by Coleman for its shape as seen from the bend in Robson Glacier near the Extinguisher. It has occasionally been referred to as, and confused with, the Helmet.

DOMINION: Peak [3125 m], **Pass** [2050 m]; 1952; Monashee. Hendricks' party made the first ascent of this summit on Dominion Day.

DONARD: Mountain [3011 m]; 1969; Starbird. Professor West and his friends took this name from the highest point of County Down in Northern Ireland and set it upon the landscape as a centrepiece of the Irish Group.

DONEGAL: Peak [2850 m]; 1961; Starbird. Borrowed by Professor West from the county and town in Ulster.

DONKIN: Mount [2940 m], **Pass** [2548 m]; 1889; Dawson. William Green named this after a fellow member of the AC who had disappeared on a high traverse in the Caucasus Mountains the year before. William Frederick Donkin (1845–1888) was accompanied by Harry Fox and two highly regarded Swiss guides, Kaspar Streich and Johann Fischer. Their bodies were never found.

DORMAN: Mount [2798 m]; 1950; Harrison. This seems to have been named for the English-American marine paleobiologist George Lockwood Dorman, some of whose studies included fossil types found in the rocks of this area.

DORMER: Mountain [2766 m], **River**; 1928; Front. This name is descriptive of the appearance of a series of minor ridges from this peak that have been truncated by glacial scouring along the main valley.

DOROTHY: Mountain [3063 m]; 1928; Commander. This name was applied by participants at the 1928 ACC encampment not far from the base of this mountain. We are unsure who the original Dorothy was—there were three ladies with that name attending the camp.

DOUAI: Mountain [3120 m]; 1918; Alexandra. This comes from a town in northeast France that was the seat of a university started by Philip II of Spain to house English Catholic refugee scholars. The famous Douai version of the Bible was prepared here, in opposition to that being promoted under the aegis of England's King James I. In October 1918 the city was retaken from the collapsing German army, and Canadian troops were in on the action.

DOUGLAS: Mount [3235 m]; 1898; **Creek, Lake**; 1905; Clearwater. This commemorates David Douglas (1798–1834), the Scots botanist whose name is on the most famous timber tree of North America (not actually a fir, but a member of the hemlock family). His first crossing of the Athabasca Pass was in 1827, when he named Mounts Brown and Hooker after two of his patrons. He is the best known, but not the first, to state an erroneous height for that pass. Douglas made several other exploratory and botanizing trips in North America before meeting his death in an accident on Hawaii. This summit was at one time known as "Black Douglas" to distinguish it from the more snow-covered St. Bride.

DOWNIE: Creek, Peak [2926 m], **Lake**; 1866; NW Selkirks. William Downie (1819–1893) was a native of Ayrshire but brought up in the Maritimes. In 1849 he joined the gold rush to California, where his name is on the town of Downieville. During the American Civil War he became a major in the Union Army, but went north to British Columbia as soon as that conflict was over. He led a group up the Columbia River in 1865, but after two unsuccessful years he drifted down to Panama and ultimately back to California. Downie undertook one final trip to B.C. in 1885, along the coast to Kitimat, reporting optimistically to Minister of Mines John Robson. Assigned to survey wagon roads to the placer mining camps that Downie and others had established in the upper Goldstream Valley, Walter Moberly was the actual name-giver. *See also* Carnes.

DRAGON: Peak [2940 m]; 1928; Fryatt. So named by the ABC for the appearance of some of the summit rocks.

DRAWBRIDGE: Pass [2575 m], **Peak** [2720 m]; 1920; Ramparts. A bridge-like area between two higher peaks, Redoubt and Bastion, this was part of the ABC's fortification pattern of nomenclature in the area of the Ramparts.

DREWRY: Cairn [2733 m]; 1906; Dogtooth. Here, Wheeler commemorated a pioneer surveyor of the Canadian west, William Stuart Drewry (1859–1939) of Belleville, Ontario, one of the instigators of the geodetic survey of Canada. His cairn was a prime triangulation point in the mountain surveys being extended by Wheeler. Unfortunately, subsequent mapmakers have let Drewry down, not only by 8 m, but no official status, either.

DRUMMOND: Mount [3148 m], **Glacier**; 1884; Clearwater. This summit was named by Dawson for Thomas Drummond (1780–1835), a naturalist with the second Franklin Arctic expedition. He had ascended the Athabasca River and spent the winter of 1825–26 in this area.

DRY: Ranges. A guidebook writer's term of convenience, it fittingly describes the ranges at the eastern edge of the Canadian Rockies. Most of the moisture coming in from the Pacific Ocean has been wrung out of the air by the time it reaches the peaks that overlook the plains. *See also* Front.

DRYDEN: Mountain [2758 m]; 1961; Vermilion. Named for Lt. John R. Dryden of Golden, who was killed in action during the Second World War.

DRYSDALE: Mount [2932 m]; 1924; Ottertail. Charles Wales Drysdale was a vigorous member of the GSC who was killed in action during the third year of the Great War, at age 32. He had been an assistant and later successor to Leroy in mapping the Slocan mineralized area.

DUBLIN: Mountain [2758 m]; 1969; Starbird. Since this summit is some distance west of those peaks named for vessels participating in the Battle of Jutland, Professor West must not have had the light cruiser in mind when he entered this name among the Irish Group of peaks.

DUCHESNAY: Mount [2927 m], **Creek, Pass** [2666 m]; 1902; Bow Ranges. Acting on Outram's suggestion, CPR vice-president McNicoll named this summit after Edward J. Duchesnay, the assistant general superintendent of the CPR's western division, who had surveyed a line for the CPR to the Yukon and had recommended the use of lake steamers. In 1901 he was killed by falling rock that had been loosened by fire in a tunnel under construction at Spuzzum, B.C.

DUCHESS: Peak [2912 m]; 1931; S Purcells. Named by Dr. Thorington for the first vessel owned by Capt. Armstrong. A truly ramshackle affair, it was built in 1886, the original rivercraft of the upper Columbia. It capsized two years later and was replaced by a much finer version.

DUFFY: Peaks [2814 m]; Monashees. We, like TV's Sgt. Schultz, know nothing.

DUNCAN: Lake [552 m], **River, Glacier, Mount** [3202 m]; 1890; Battle. John Duncan was an early prospector in southern B.C. who spent many years working claims in the vicinity of the lake and lower reaches of the river that now bear his name. Duncan was a witness at the murder trial of John Sproule. The mountain and glacier were named by Topham from the river. It should be noted, though, that on David Thompson's map of 1812, the Kootenay River is shown as "McGillivray's River" and the mountains along its upper reaches are labelled "Duncan's Mountains." *See also* Hamill.

DUNGEON: Peak [3130 m]; 1916; Ramparts. More evidence of the ABC's lexicon of ancient castlery.

DUNKIRK: Mount [3030 m]; 1940; Monashee. When Henry Hall and Ed Feuz Jr. climbed this previously unnamed mountain in midsummer, the English-speaking world was replete with admiration for the success of the heroic withdrawal of British forces from Dunkirk the previous June.

DUPLICATE: Mountain [3150 m]; 1919; Icefield. The ABC considered the two summits of this mountain similar in outline and appearance.

DURRAND: Peak [2759 m], **Glacier**; 1963; Moloch. Putnam applied this name to remember Kauffman's friend, William Durand (1883–1963), an eccentric Scot and poacher/warden stationed at Flat Creek in Glacier National Park. He was always of great and enthusiastic assistance to backpacking alpinists. A native of Wick, Durand had served in the Boer and Great wars; he then joined the park's staff, retiring in 1948. Somehow an extra "r" was added to the name in the course of it becoming official.

*Where a man calls himself by a name which is
not his name, he is telling a falsehood.*
—LORD ESHER; JUDGMENT IN *REDDAWAY V. BANHAM*, 1895

EAGLE: Pass [561 m]; 1865; Gold. Moberly was the first white man to record his passage through this pass, during the course of which he was accompanied by an eagle soaring overhead. A wagon trail was laid through here four years later, and as the high point of the Canadian Pacific Railway in 1885 was labelled "ClanWilliam." Not to be confused with a similarly named feature in the coastal waters of the province, for the widening of which the HBC petitioned the sum of $2,500 from the legislative council in 1868. **Peak** [2846 m], **Glacier**; 1887; Sir Donald. Named by Perley for the appearance of a prominent gendarme on its southwest ridge. This peak became one of the standard climbs from Glacier House, although on an early AMC ascent a party of alpinists managed to get benighted on this very ridge. There are other Eagles in these mountains, one in the Front Ranges of the Rockies, a **Spire** [2780 m], 1969, in the Purcells, and even a **Crest** among the Leaning Towers that McCoubrey named in 1933 because an eagle's nest was observed upon it.

EARLGREY: Pass [2278 m], **Mount** [3124 m]; 1910; SW Purcells. Albert Henry George (1851–1917) the fourth Earl Grey, was descended from a long line of English public officeholders (and connoisseurs of fine tea). He served as Governor General of Canada from 1904 to 1911, one of the most popular persons to hold that office. During a summer camping trip up the Toby Valley in 1909, he and Lady Grey crossed the Purcell Range via a route that had previously been called Wells Pass after Wilmer "Fred" Wells, a local prospector and politician who had used it in his travels. By this time Wells had established himself profitably at the Giant Mascot mine in the Spillimacheen Valley. Even earlier, this route had been known as Kinbasket's Trail.

EAST: Peak [3231 m]; 1910; Adamant. This was named by Palmer for its position east of a group of mountains to which he had given various names from Gothic mythology. Palmer described the peak as "nothing but a thin wall," which, seen end-on, looked like a steeple. **Peak** [3000 m]; 1918; Lyell. The ABC applied this one on the easterly point of Division Mountain. **Creek, Peak** [3063 m]; 1939; Bugaboo. Engelhard used this mundane name in accordance with those she applied to a whole series of nearby peaks. *See also* North.

EASY: Glacier; 1956; Alphabet. When Putnam submitted other nearby names, like that of the OK Glacier, his marginal notes on the preliminary map sheet were taken literally in Ottawa.

EASTPOST: Spire [2697 m]; 1933; Bugaboo. Thorington named this outpost of the Bugaboo Group, overlooking his campsite, from its location relative to the main mass of this startling granitic uplift.

EBON: Peak [2910 m]; 1917; Waputik. The ABC named this peak for the dark, almost black, Ordovician formations of which this summit is largely composed.

ECHO: Glacier; 1948; Adamant. The first party to ascend this glacier included Dr. Ferris, who was struck by the symphonic dimensions of the echoes reverberating off the face of Quadrant Mountain, which marks the east edge of this sadly dwindling glacier.

EDELWEISS: Village; 1912. This location on the gravelly hillside north of Golden was selected by the CPR as a permanent home for its then highly touted Swiss guides. The guides, however, were unhappy with their ersatz Swiss chalets and in time, most moved their families down to the more congenial life in town.

EDEN: Mount [3180 m]; 1927; Icefields. Ostheimer suggested this name, but gave no reason.

ED FALLS: Mount [3013 m]; 1937; Windy. N.E. McConnell, BCLS, applied this name in honour of Edward Falls (1868–1943), a fur trapper from Golden whose franchise line was in the Windy River Valley below this summit.

EDITH: Mount [2554 m], **Pass** [1945 m]; 1886; Sawback. This popular rock climb north of town was named for Mrs. John Fosbery Orde (née Edith Cox), who visited Banff in company with Lady Macdonald when the town was first being platted.

EDITH CAVELL: Mount [3363 m], **Lake**, **Creek**; 1916; Jasper. Edith Louisa Cavell (1865–1915) was an English nurse, serving in 1914 as matron of a Belgian Red Cross hospital in Brussels. She was accused of espionage and aiding Allied prisoners to escape to rejoin their units—a charge she admitted, claiming only that it was her sworn duty to save lives. Under German military law those actions constituted treason, and after a quick trial she was shot, despite the vigorous intercession of the American ambassador. To the British, Edith Cavell became a symbol of heroism and was so honoured. *See also* Leval and Angel.

EDWARD: Peak [3514 m]; 1972; Lyell. This highest summit of Mount Lyell is named in honour of the senior of the five Swiss guides who became residents of Edelweiss Village. In time, Edward Feuz (1884–1981) also became the patriarch of alpine guides in North America. *See also* Walter.

E E O R: This entry was not suggested by A.A. Milne, but pertains to the East End Of Rundle, where a number of challenging high-angle routes have been developed.

EGYPT: Lake [2027 m]; 1922; Ball. Surrounding this lake are several points with Egyptian-sounding names, all applied by the Topographic Survey. *See also* Scarab, Pharaoh, etc.

EGYPTIAN: Peaks; 1973; S Purcells. This refers to the massif extending north from Jumbo Pass. The theme started in 1909 with Earl Grey, who applied a few names nearer the main stem of Toby Creek. After being extended by others, the overall name was applied by Wagner. *See also* Amon-Ra and Karnak.

EIFFEL: Tower [3080 m], **Peak** [3084 m], **Lake** [2249 m]; 1908; Bow Ranges. Alexandre Gustave Eiffel (1832–1923) was a celebrated French engineer who designed many steel structures, of which his most famous was for the Paris Exposition of 1889. The sharp, tower-like aspect of this rock suggested a similarity. Eiffel had warmed up for his tower job by designing the framework for the Statue of Liberty four years earlier.

EISENHOWER: Tower [2752 m]; 1979; Sawback. Since late 1979, this name has applied only to the east tower of Castle Mountain, the entire mass of which had its name officially changed to Eisenhower in 1946.

The argument had to do with the appropriateness of naming a mountain after a living person, though this was by no means the only time such had been done, and, more credibly, to replacing a longstanding and most appropriate name with one that had little relevance to these mountains.

ELBOW: River, Lake [2097 m]; Opal. This name dates from early days of white settlement in Alberta and is alleged to have been derived from the Elbow River south of Calgary.

ELDON: Location [1643 m], **Formation**; 1884; Lake Louise. This was originally a whistle stop (not even that, now) west of Castle Mountain. The derivation of the name is unclear. More noteworthy than the name's origin, though, is the rock formation that derives its name from the location. The Eldon, here at its thickest, and the Cathedral formation (both of Cambrian age) are separated by the relatively thin Burgess Shale and make up some of the most durable limestone/dolomite cliff lines in the Rockies. They each range in thickness up to 180m and extend as unbroken walls, often for miles.

ELEPHAS: Mountain [2940m]; 1922; Ramparts. The ABC felt that some of the massive summit rocks had the aspect of an elephant, for which creature this is the Latin name.

ELK: Pass [1891 m], **Lakes** [1737 m], **Range, River**; 1915; French. The ABC made it official when they demarcated the boundary between the provinces, but "Elk" had long been used to denote this wide, low pass over the main range of the Rockies.

ELKAN: Mount [2760 m]; French. This is a package name, part Elk and part Kananaskis—appropriate under the circumstances, as this summit drains into those two rivers.

ELLIOTT: Peak [2872 m]; 1907; Cline. Elliott Chappel Barnes Jr. (1898–1914) was eight years old when he climbed this peak. His father's ranch, Kadoona Tinda (Stoney for "windy plains"), lay at its foot. This is the prominent peak near the present upper end of Abraham Lake, which Mary Schäffer had named "Kadoona" the year before.

ELLIS: Mount [2970m]; 1972; Icefields. Respectful members of the ACC, led by Boles, named this summit after their friend, Derrick Ellis, a Bow Helicopter pilot who had been killed earlier in the season.

ELPOCA: Mountain [3029 m], **Pass** [2088 m]; 1960; Opal. This mountain lies between the heads of the Elbow River and Pocaterra Creek. George Pocaterra once owned the Buffalo Head Ranch and was nicknamed "El Poca."

EMERALD: Lake [1302 m], **Glacier, Pass** [2712 m], **River**; 1885;

Waputik. Given this name by the CPR for its colour, the lake then derived much of its water from glacial sources. The name spread to other features around and above (*see also* President). Later this name was relocated and finally settled on an obscure lesser peak some 500 m lower and much closer to the lake. The CPR operated a chalet at the lake after 1902.

EMPEROR: Mountain [3124 m]; 1967; SW Purcells. Wagner named this for Beethoven's "Emperor Concerto in B flat." It is actually the west summit of Archduke Mountain, also named for one of Beethoven's compositions.

EMPIRE STATE: Peak [2603 m]; 1936; W Rockies. This summit in the Top of the World area is slightly higher and somewhat to the south of Chrysler, as things also stand on Manhattan Island. Named by Ben Rosicki.

END: Mountain [2420 m]; 1884; Front. McArthur noted that this peak is at the southeast end of the Palliser Range and overlooks the prairies of southern Alberta.

ENDLESS CHAIN: Ridge [2867 m]; 1907; Maligne. Anyone who has seen this long unbroken line rising to the east above the lower Sunwapta River, let alone attempted to hike along it, understands why Mary Schäffer labelled this ridge as she did.

ENGADINE: Mount [2970 m]; 1917; Kananaskis. This name refers to the forest of Graubunden (Grisons), made famous by Walter Scott and home of St. Moritz and the Romansch language. It was also the name of a British seaplane tender, converted from a cruiser, that took a limited part in the Battle of Jutland.

ENGELHARD: Mount [3270 m]; 1966; Icefield. Tower [3210 m]; 1973; Murchison. Both of these features honour Georgia Engelhard (1906–1986), a vigorous alpinist and photographer who climbed frequently in these mountains with Ernest Feuz. She made the first ascent of the tower in his company.

ENGLISH: Mountain [2680 m]; 1965; Gold. Twenty-six-year-old Sgt. George Melville English, of Revelstoke, died in an automobile accident during the Second World War.

ENNIS: Mount [3133 m]; 1901; Ottertail. Whymper allegedly applied this name to honour an official of the Allen Steamship Lines. Perhaps he got a free ride out of it somehow. Ennis was subsequently involved with the emigration of settlers from Iceland to western Canada. *See also* Valhalla.

ENTERPRISE: Peak [2870 m]; 1948; Adamant. This peak, the southernmost of the sedimentary summits adjacent on the north of the

Adamant pluton, has occasionally been referred to as Yellow Mountain because of the colour of its summit rocks. *See also* Colossal.

EON: Mountain [3310 m], **Creek**; 1901; Assiniboine. This name appears to have been given by Sir James Outram, who was the first to ascend the dominant peak of the area, Mount Assiniboine. This lesser peak was the scene of a famous mountain fatality when Dr. Winthrop Ellsworth Stone (1861–1921), president of Purdue University and brother of U.S. Supreme Court Justice-to-be Harlan Fiske Stone, fell to his death while making its first ascent. His wife Margaret spent eight days alone on a high ledge before being rescued by a party led by Rudolph Aemmer.

EPAULETTE: Mountain [3095 m]; 1961; Waputik. This name was derived from the shape of the folded strata exposed in the mountain's cliffs. Previously it had been known as Pyramid Mountain, a banal name with numerous other applications.

ERASMUS: Mount [3265 m]; 1859; Lyell. Peter Erasmus (1834–1931), of a Danish father and a Metis mother, became a noted fur trader and guide. His services were used by Hector in 1858–59. He was later honoured for his role in the Riel uprisings.

EREBUS: Mount [3119 m]; 1916; Ramparts. This was the name of one of the two ships used by Sir John Franklin on his 1845 expedition, the last of his explorations of the Canadian Arctic. Erebus is the Greek god of darkness, so it's not a bad name for a place in or near which to spend the long Arctic night.

EREMITE: Mountain [2910 m], **Glacier**; 1916; Ramparts. This name, a term for a religious hermit, was applied by the ABC because this is a solitary peak.

ERMATINGER: Mount [3060 m]; 1920; Whirlpool. Named by the ABC for Edward Ermatinger (1796–1876), born on Elba and an employee of the HBC for 10 years from 1818. He served at York Factory, then Red River and finally in the Columbia. The mountain had previously been known as "Horn."

ERNEST: Peak [3511 m]; 1972; Lyell. This is the central and divide peak of the Lyell massif and was named for Ernest Feuz (1889–1960), third of the five sons of Edward Feuz, the original Swiss guide employed by the CPR. With his older brother Edward Jr. and younger brother Walter, he helped establish the family's prominence in the mountaineering history of western Canada. *See also* Walter.

ERRATUM: Peak [2818 m]; 1987; Westfall. Less than 1 km south of Wrong Peak, the derivation of this name is self-evident.

ERRIS: Mount [2820 m]; 1916; Highrock. This name was transported across the ocean from the famous headlands of County Mayo on the northwest coast of Ireland.

ESCALADE: Peak [2953 m], **Glacier**; 1947; Battle. The Kauffmans and Brewster considered this peak, which they did not climb, a difficult one and therefore conferred on it the name of the Genevan celebration of the defeat of the Savoyards in 1601. The name is from the French word for climbing; the insurgents hoped to scale the walls of Calvin's city of Geneva and restore it to the control of the papacy and themselves.

ESCARPMENT: Peak [3121 m]; 1956; Windy. Some 3 km southwest of Neptune. Aptly named by Hendricks, its south face overlooks—and in some places overhangs—the headwaters of Bigmouth Creek. **River**; 1957; Clearwater. The west side of this valley is dominated by a series of spectacular cliffs, rising sheer in excess of 300 m each. The east side is impressive too, but with the entire area being on the drier side of the Rockies, there are few glaciers and the region is not much frequented by alpinists.

ESMERALDA: Peak [2789 m]; 1958; Kokanee. This was the name of a mine below the peak and is Spanish for "emerald." It is also the name of the beautiful gypsy girl in Victor Hugo's *The Hunchback of Notre Dame*.

ESPLANADE: Range; 1908; Sorceror. With a number of named high points scattered along it, this was the "Boardwalk" of Herbert Ives (1882–1953) in 1907, so named because of its flat appearance. The next year, Percy Carson of the Topographical Survey gave it a more appropriate handle, for though the crest is very easily travelled, it is completely above timberline and boards are scarce. Ives' *Ill-fated Summer in British Columbia* included a lengthy saga of one Merkle Jacobs who broke his leg while hiking north along the Boardwalk. He was then ensconced in a tent for several weeks, from which his leg, set in a tension cast, protruded into the weather. When summer was nearly over, he was evacuated by litter to Beavermouth, where he attended a dance the following evening. See *The Great Glacier and Its House*, 1982, for a fuller account.

ETHELBERT: Mount [3158 m], **Group**; 1886; Bugaboo. This was the religious name of the first nun to visit the Kootenay, who died in 1886 on Capt. Armstrong's *Ptarmigan* en route to her mission. She was buried on the banks of the Columbia within sight of the mountain, which the skipper thereupon named for her.

ETHERINGTON: Mount [2877 m], **Creek**; 1924; High Rock. This name was applied in honour of Colonel Frederick Etherington, a medical doctor from Ontario who treated wounded members of the Canadian army in the Great War.

EVANS: Mount [3210 m]; 1935; Whirlpool. Capt. Sir Edward Ratcliffe Garth Russell Evans (1880–1957) was an explorer and served as second-in-command to Capt. Robert Falcon Scott in 1912. He is more noted for his exploits in the Great War when he was in command of the English destroyer HMS *Broke* and managed to sink two German ships in one encounter while holding four others at bay. He later became Admiral Lord Mountevans.

EVAN-THOMAS: Mount [3097 m], **Creek**; 1922; Opal. Rear Admiral Sir Hugh Evan-Thomas (1862–1928) was commander of the Fifth Battle Squadron at the Battle of Jutland. He retired as a full admiral in 1924.

EVENING: Mountain [2949 m]; 1959; Battle. This summit is slightly higher than the nearby Mount Nemo and was climbed via the ridge connecting the two. Silverstein applied the name due to the lateness of his party's arrival at the summit.

EXCELSIOR: Mountain [2770 m]; 1916; Maligne. This name was applied by Hinton, who was anxious to develop patronage for his railway, using here the Latin word for "greater." *See also* Sirdar.

EXSHAW: Locality [1296 m]; 1905; Fairholme. This name was chosen by the CPR in honour of William Exshaw (1866–1927), managing director of the cement factory that furnished much traffic to the railway. Most of a century later this operation continues to gnaw away at the local limestone hillsides, which still seem largely unaffected. Exshaw was the son-in-law of Sir Sandford Fleming, having married the great man's daughter, Lily.

EXTINGUISHER: Tower [2393 m]; 1907; Robson. Actually, this is not a tower, but rather the abrupt end of a sharp ridge that rises to the south. Situated at the bend of the lower Robson Glacier, this prominent landmark has the steep conical shape of a candle extinguisher, a resemblance readily noted by Coleman. Five years later, Walcott commented to the Board on Geographical Names: "That particular rock carries a very important bed of Cambro-Ordovician fossils and will be referred to many times in the future in literature. It may be that I shall suggest a shorter and more euphonious name for it." However, he never did.

EYEBROW: Peak [3353 m]; 1910; Starbird. "Owing to two broad rock scars near the summit," wrote Wheeler, "and their arrangement in connection with the snow surrounding, giving them the appearance of gigantic eyebrows, we named it 'Eyebrow Peak.'" This was Harnden's "Unnamed 11,090" of 1913 and Stone's "Mount Bruce" in 1916. Wheeler's visit to the Bugaboo Pass area, his only mapping trip to the Purcells, was marred by frequent cloudiness and he was seldom able to verify his sightings with second observations. Professor Robinson avers that the true Eyebrow is actually today's Mount Farnham and today's Eyebrow is Wheeler's Aurora. Robinson's photographs are convincing.

> *When fate writ my name it made a blot.*
> —HENRY FIELDING, *AMELIA*, 1752

FABLE: Mount [2702 m]; 1947; Front. A Calgary party set out for this peak and returned very late, having spent the day floundering in the bush. A second group, consisting of Bob Hind, Lawrence Parker and Jim Tarrant, reached it very easily and decided this name was appropriate to the story told by the earlier group.

FAFNIR: Mount [2819 m]; 1947; Battle. Kauffman recalled the dragon in Wagner's *Der Ring des Niebelungen* who was killed by Siegfried— another part of the battle motif.

FAIRHOLME: Range; 1860; Front. Capt. Palliser applied the married name of his sister Grace, Mrs. William Fairholme of Berwickshire. Her husband bankrolled Palliser from time to time, both before and after the expedition to western Canada.

FAIRVIEW: Mountain [2744 m]; 1894; Bow Ranges. Allen was among the first to enjoy the view from this easily ascended point south of and overlooking Lake Louise. However, on his first map he called it Goat Peak.

FAIRY MEADOW: Locality [2030 m]; 1946; Adamant. This lovely spot at the head of Swan Creek was named by Hendricks, recalling published descriptions of an idyllic mountain valley and timberline location in the Karakoram used as a campsite by the 1932 German-American Nanga Parbat expedition. A mountain cabin was built here for the ACC in 1966 and renamed in 2003 for one of these authors.

FAITH: Peak [2961 m]; 1966; Albert. Lying east of the high point named

Virtue, this is the first of its subsidiaries. Professor West noted that it lay 2 km west of Charity and was considerably less in altitude. *See also* Fortitude.

FANG: Rock [2836 m]; 1902; Moloch. Bridgland was highly impressed with the dramatic appearance of this peak, which is readily visible from many high points in the Central Selkirks. Members of his party built one of their distinctive barrel-shaped cairns on the lower west flank of this summit.

FARBUS: Mountain [3150 m]; 1918; Alexandra. This name commemorates a small village on the eastern slope of Vimy Ridge where many Canadians fought and died in the Great War.

FARM: Creek; 1900; Sorceror. This west-flowing tributary to Tangier Creek is blessed with a large, grassy meadow [1112 m] at its confluence, which was the site of a trapper's cabin until the mid-1950s. There is no record of whether there ever was a real farm, though the nearby terrain might lend itself well to such use.

FARNHAM: Peak [3468m], **Tower** [3353m], **Creek, Group**; 1911. Named by Harnden in recognition of Paulding Farnham, a prominent member of the local Windermere mining fraternity, some of whose claim locations were in this massif. Farnham was in and out of mining deals with Starbird, Stark(e) and others over a 20-year span after 1900. *See also* Eyebrow.

FARQUHAR: Mount [2905 m]; 1919; High Rock. Major Francis Douglas Farquhar (1874–1915), DSO 1900 for his service in the Boer War, commanded a battalion of the Coldstream Guards and was killed in the Great War.

FARRAR: Mount [3240m]; 1923; Icefields. John Percy Farrar (1857–1929) was a British traveller and alpinist. He served in the Boer War, achieving the permanent rank of captain. He visited the Canadian Rockies in 1899, but was an authority on the Alps. Farrar was elected president of the AC in 1917 and served many years as editor of its journal. The name was applied here by Schwab.

FATIGUE: Pass [2310m], **Creek, Mountain** [2959m]; 1916; Bow Ranges. We hiked up the trail to see if we could figure out what would cause anyone to choose such a discouraging name, but we ran out of steam and never found out.

FAY: Mount [3234m], **Glacier**; 1902; Bow Ranges. Charles Ernest Fay (1846–1931) was the most distinguished and influential North American alpinist of his day. As editor of *Appalachia*, for over 30 years the only mountaineering journal of consequence on the continent, his views were important. He was four times president of the AMC and

Mt. Fay. GLEN BOLES DRAWING

served three terms as president of the AAC. Fay made annual visits to the mountains of western Canada. He was professor of modern languages at Tufts University for most of his life. The mountain is "Heejee," #1 of Allen's Ten Peaks.

FAYS: Peak [2817 m]; 1903; Badshot. This lesser peak lies at the south end of the Badshot Range and was named by Reginald Walter Brock (1874–1935), then of the GSC field staff and five years later to become its head.

FEATHER: Spire [2932 m]; 1959; Battle. Anger applied this handle to the most delicate-looking of the pinnacles along his Iron Ridge.

FELINE: Peak [2910 m]; 193?; Monashee. Noel McConnell, in his surveying work, had the habit of giving simple one-syllable names to his triangulation stations, which were only occasionally on high points. Near this summit he used a station labelled "Cat" on his map, and not far distant was "Hat." Years later, Dr. Wallerstein came along and climbed some of the high points. Knowing the names of McConnell's original station points, he simply enhanced the names.

FELUCCA: Mountain [2765 m]; 1924; W Rockies. A small sailing vessel of Mediterranean design, often towed behind a larger ship and equipped with oars. The larger Frigate Mountain, somewhat to the east, may have influenced the choice of name.

FERNIE: City [1010 m]; 1904; S Rockies. William Fernie (1837–1921) came to Vancouver from England in 1860. He served as gold commissioner in the East Kootenay for 10 years after 1873. Later, having undertaken construction of a trail through Crowsnest Pass, he discovered the area's massive coal formations and in 1898 established the town, which was formally incorporated in 1904.

FERRITE: Peak [2911 m]; 1971; Nemo. This is a part of the Iron Ridge, at least toponymically.

FERRO: Pass [2270 m]; 1924; Mitchell. This name derives from the nearby presence of iron-rich springs. This was Allen's "Wallandoo Pass" of 1893.

FETHERSTONHAUGH: Creek, Pass [1805 m]; 1925; N Rockies. Named by the ABC after W.S. Fetherstonhaugh, a location engineer for the Grand Trunk Pacific who worked the Tête Jaune Pass area in 1907. Capt. Albany Fetherstonhaugh was a member of the British contingent in the survey and demarcation of the 49th parallel from the Red River west to the crest of the Rocky Mountains.

FEUZ: Peak [3350 m]; 1899; Dawson. Given by Professor Fay to honour Edward Feuz Sr., his guide on a trip across the Asulkan Pass during which the party made the first ascent of this second peak of Mount Dawson. *See also* Häsler. **Tower** [3140 m]; 1973; Murchison. At the time of its second ascent, this tower was named by Putnam after Ernest Feuz, who found a way up its nearly vertical ridge in 1941, while engaged as guide to Georgia Engelhard and her future husband, Mr. Cromwell.

FIDDLE: River, Range, Peak [2243 m]; 1858; Jasper. Father Pierre Jean De Smet had previously called it "Violin," but on the Palliser map of 1956 it was translated to "Fiddle."

FIELD: Town [1273 m], **Mount** [2643 m]; 1883; Waputik. William Cornelius Van Horne was always running out of construction money while pushing his CPR through the mountains. In 1883, he inveigled Cyrus West Field (1819–1896), promoter of the first Atlantic cable, to visit the "end of steel" just west of Kicking Horse Pass. As a spur-of-the-moment inducement to invest, Van Horne named the division point then being established there after his guest. Field refused the bait, but later must surely have wished he had taken it. The mountain is not much, but it does overlook the town.

FIFI: Mount [2621 m]; 1921; Sawback. Joseph Hickson chose this name at the time he made its first ascent. He hinted at a relationship to the neighbouring and more impressive Mount Louis.

FINDHORN: Peak [2881 m]; 1902; Purity. Wheeler named this north-west peak of Mount McBean after the river in Banffshire on the banks of which lies the village—and distillery—of Tomatin, then owned by the McBean family. The first ascent of this mountain group was the sole objective of a small expedition from the Scottish Mountaineering Club in 1914.

FINDLAY: Mount [3162 m], **Creek, Glacier, Group**; 1898; S Purcells. This name generally appears as Finlay after John (Jaco) Finlay (1774–1833), a partner in the NWC in charge at Lake Athabasca. He had laid out a trail over the Howse Pass in 1806—before Howse was given credit for it. He and his brother James came by their status in the fur trade through their father, who was one of the original "pedlars" operating out of Montreal in competition with the Bay-based HBC.

FINGER: Mount [2545 m]; 1935; Sawback. Grassi, who made an early ascent, named this for its shape, with the southerly crest pointing upwards.

FINGERBOARD: Peaks [2880 m]; 1967; SW Purcells. Had Bruce Beck been a more accomplished musician he would probably have named this group, including his Archduke Mountain, the Keyboard.

FISHER: Range; 1859; Opal. This name appears on the Palliser Map and, though the narrative is silent on the topic, was likely given in honour of Reverend George Fisher (1794–1873), a British astronomer and Arctic explorer. He was an authority on the magnetic pole and aurora borealis. **Peak** [3053 m]; 1920; Fisher. John (Jacky) Arbuthnot Fisher (1841–1920), the first Baron Kilverstone, served many years as First Sea Lord of the British Admiralty and was largely responsible for the modernization of the British fleet, preparing it for action against the burgeoning German High Seas Fleet in the Great War. He resigned in 1915 as a protest against initiation of Churchill's controversial and ill-fated Dardanelles campaign.

FIST: The [2630 m]; 1973; British. This name was applied by guide Bernie Schiesser, not in reference to the border castle and natural strongpoint that was originally part of the ancient Wall of Hadrian across Great Britain, but rather because it too looked very much like a clenched fist.

FITZSIMMONS: Mount [2880 m]; 1969; SW Purcells. This name commemorates one of the pioneers of the nearby settlement of Argenta. Wagner noted that Charles Fitzsimmons, a logger from Alberta, was a friend of the Lakes.

FITZWILLIAM: Mount [2907 m]; 1863; Jasper. This is the south buttress of Yellowhead Pass and was labelled by Dr. Cheadle to commemorate the family name of Viscount Milton, his medical patient and fellow traveller across these mountains.

FLAT: Creek, Pass [1600 m]; 1884; Albert. An undistinguished location in its own right, this whistle stop on the CPR down the Illecillewaet valley from Glacier became a well-known jumping-off place for climbing trips. The valley to the south is indeed flat, with little rise to the pass where it heads with the Incomappleux River.

FLATHEAD: Range, River; 1924; Boundary. This range takes its name from the First Nations tribe that originally lived mostly in the area of northwestern Montana and the Idaho panhandle. The name is often said to derive from the flat skull produced by binding infants' heads with boards. In fact, the Flathead people did not do this, so their skulls were not pointed like those of neighbouring tribes who did practise head-binding. The Flathead were forced onto reservations in 1855, but they still exist today.

FLATTOP: Peak [3063 m]; 1930; Bugaboo. This lesser summit of the Bugaboo Group was aptly named by Cromwell after he made its first ascent in company with the Grindelwald guide, Peter Kaufmann, nephew of the brothers Hans and Christian Kaufmann, who had been party to many climbs in the Rockies a generation earlier.

FLEANCE: Mountain [2910 m]; 1960; SW Purcells. West applied this name in keeping with the Macbeth theme used for the others of this group. Fleance was the son of Banquo and ancestor of the Stuart line of Scottish (and later English) kings.

FLEMING: Peak [3100 m]; 1901; Hermit. Named by Wheeler of the Topographical Survey for Sir Sandford Fleming, first engineer-in-chief of the Canadian Pacific, principal formulator of Standard Time and first honourary president of the Alpine Club of Canada. *See also* Sir Sandford.

FLINTS: Peak [2950 m], **Park**; 1959; Front. This name was applied in honour of a local landowner, and was given the possessive form to avoid any geological connotation.

FLOE: Lake [2027 m], **Creek**; 1930; Vermilion. The lake nestles into a steep north-facing cliff that has sheltered a glacier within recent years; the glacier fed into the lake, and its recessional moraine now dams a slightly higher lake level.

FLORENCE: Mount [2970 m]; 1928; Maligne. In 1924 Florence Ferratti married Max Maurice Strumia, who later made the first ascent of this crest in company with W.R. Hainsworth. Dr. Strumia thereupon named it for his wife. *See also* Hawley.

FOCH: Mount [3180 m], **Glacier, Creek**; 1918; French. Ferdinand Foch (1851–1929) was professor of strategy at the St. Cyr École Militaire in the years before the Great War. During that conflict he became one of the most successful of the Allied generals and was the supreme allied commander in France at the close of the war.

FOLK: Mount [3087 m]; 1964; S Rockies. Corporal Andrew Folk, of nearby Cranbrook, was killed in action during the Second World War.

FOOTSTOOL: The [3100 m]; 1910; Sir Sandford. This name was applied by Palmer to the prominent high-level snow crest lying just east of the monarch of the Northern Selkirks, Mount Sir Sandford.

FORBES: Mount [3612 m], **Creek, Glacier, Group**; 1859; Lyell. This striking summit was named by James Hector for Edward Forbes (1815–1854), a leading figure of the Scottish Enlightenment, professor of natural history at the University of Edinburgh and one of Hector's instructors. *See also* Rosita. **Glacier**; 1948; Adamant. Putnam named this feature for James David Forbes (1809–1868), a student of Louis Agassiz, the Scots physicist and glaciologist whose most notable work was in the transmission of heat. This small glacier displayed remarkably well the dirt bands that Forbes studied.

FORDING: River, Pass [2310 m]; 1884; High Rock. This river was crossed repeatedly by Dr. Dawson in his early explorations, hence the name. The pass is a connection to the Elk River.

FORECASTLE: Peak [2915 m]; 1961; Battle. Silverstein applied this name in extension of the literary Melville theme that had been introduced to the area by his friend, Anger, two years earlier. This peak, whose eastern aspect is often dominated in the summer by a huge cornice, stands between Pequod and Typee.

FOREMAST: Peak [2697 m]; 1972; Battle. Named by Kauffman in conformity with several nearby summits of the Battle Range and in particular as the forward unit of a series of peaks that, viewed from a distance, reminded him of a four-masted ship sailing west. *See also* Schooner.

FORGETMENOT: Pass [1770 m]; 1963; N Rockies; **Ridge**; Front. Both of these names were derived by the ABC from a local abundance of this flower.

FORKS: Peak [2868 m]; 1924; Premier. Named by Carpé, this peak lies in the south headwaters forks of what he called Mica (now Tête) Creek.

FORSTER: Creek, Mount [2474 m], **Pass** [2270 m], **Group**; 1924; Starbird. Harold Ernest Forster (1869–1940) was a young companion of Harold Topham on the latter's visit to the Selkirks in 1890. He stayed in the Canadian West and in 1912 married Meda Hume. That same year he took up a ranch, Firlands, in the upper Columbia valley and became a provincial legislator. Forster was involved in many mining ventures in the Purcells, mostly by having grubstaked others

Mt. Forbes. GLEN BOLES PHOTO

through his Peterborough Trading Company. Forster was killed by Natives who were seeking liquor and then burned Firlands to cover their crime. The mountain, small as it is, and totally devoid of ice, was "Mount Highball" to Harnden in 1913. In early mining records, the creek was the third—after Toby and Horsethief—to flow into the upper Columbia from the west, downstream from Invermere.

FORSYTHE: Mount [2993 m], **Creek**; 1916; SW Rockies. White avers that this name was that of an employee of the CPR.

FORTALICE: Mount [2840 m]; 1919; Jasper. This is an outwork (an outer strong point not connected directly to the main structure), as its name implies, also considerably north of the main uplift. Apparently the ABC applied the name as an afterthought.

FORTITUDE: Mountain [2746 m]; 1890; Albert. This was the name of a mineral prospect on its lower slopes and became the first among Professor West's numerous virtues, which he scattered over the near-by landscape. *See also* Charity, Faith, Hope, Justice, Prudence and Virtue.

FORTRESS: Mountain [3020 m], **Lake** [1336 m], **Pass** [1335 m]; 1892; Fryatt. Coleman visited the area and was impressed by the mountain dominating this high lake. The lake is geomorphologically interesting, having recently drained to the east and the Arctic Ocean rather than via its present outlet to the Wood River and the Pacific. **The** [3002 m]; 1957; Kananaskis. This one is very impressive, complete with Tower and, according to Canada's greatest mountain guide, Hans Gmoser, who led its first ascent, also very hard to conquer.

FORTUNE: Mount [2633 m]; 1922; Sundance. This was the name of a 965-ton British destroyer of the Fourth Flotilla, sunk near midnight on May 31, 1916, during the Battle of Jutland. *See also* Wintour.

FOSSIL: Mountain [2946 m], **Creek**; 1906; Slate. The geological formations of the Canadian Rockies are many and varied. Some of them are quite barren of fossils; others, as Bridgland found in this area, are not.

FOSTER: Peak [3204 m]; 1932; Vermillion. This feature was named for Sir George Eulas Foster (1847–1931), statesman and diplomat. He was the Canadian delegate to the Versailles Treaty negotiations and also served as acting prime minister during Sir Robert Borden's absences.

FOUR SQUATTERS: The; 1910; Bugaboo. This collective name was originally applied by the exploring quartet of Harmon, Kain, Longstaff and Wheeler. Sixty years later Kruszyna decided to become more specific and christened their separate high points: Aloof [3069 m], Humble [3002 m], Reposing [3002 m] and Crouching [2972 m].

FOX: Mount [2973 m]; 1860; French. This name is on the Palliser map, but not mentioned in the text. It might well have been given to honour Sir Charles Fox (1810–1874), a British engineer and designer of railroads. Fox had built rail lines in many parts of Europe, Africa, Asia and in eastern Canada. His name is primarily associated with the introduction of the parallel switch. **Mount** [3196 m]; 1889; Dawson. This name was given by William Green in honour of Harry Fox (1856–1888), who had lost his life in the Caucasus the preceding year. *See also* Donkin.

FRANCES: Mount [3038 m]; 1902; Cline. This point bears the given name of Mrs. Lucius Quincy Coleman, whose husband made its first ascent while she stayed down in camp near timberline at the head of Coral Creek and did the cooking. Her husband Lucius was a brother of the distinguished A.P. Coleman.

FRANCHÈRE: Peak [2829 m]; 1916; Jasper. This name was given by Deville in honour of Gabriel Franchère (1786–1863), a clerk in the employ of the Pacific Fur Company, who crossed the Athabasca Pass eastward after his original employer was absorbed by the NWC.

FRANKLIN: Peaks [2892 m]; 1858; Harrison. Palliser gave this name in honour of Sir John Franklin (1786–1847), who led three expeditions in search of the Northwest Passage and to explore the Canadian

Arctic coast. He never returned from the third, and his widow Jane (née Griffin) spent most of her remaining 29 years organizing and abetting searchers to determine his fate. Almost 50 such parties went out, from both England and the United States. Franklin's remains were not found until over a century later, but the essential story of his party's fate was learned in 1859. In 1927, Ostheimer named a peak west of the Columbia Icefield in his honour as well.

FRASER: River, Pass [2010m]; 1808; Ramparts. The river was first descended by Simon Fraser (1776–1862), a native of Vermont who became one of the most notable explorers and fur traders in the history of the Canadian West. Variations and derivations from his name are scattered all around map sheet 83D/9.

FRAYNE: Mount [2914m]; 1928; Front. Born in Scranton, Pennsylvania, Hugh Frayne (1869–1934) was a child labourer in coal mines and later an official of the Amalgamated Sheet Metal Workers International Alliance. As such, and representing the American Federation of Labor, he travelled extensively in the United States and Canada assisting in local union organizing efforts. He became widely respected as a far-sighted and public-spirited citizen.

FRED LAING: Ridge [2696m]; 1939; Windy. N.E. McConnell named this ridge after Frederick William Laing (1869–1948), a schoolteacher in Revelstoke who later served as secretary to various provincial ministers of agriculture and, in 1938, compiled the *Geographic Naming Record* of British Columbia.

FRENCH: Mount [3234m], **Creek**; 1918; British. Sir John Denton Pinkstone French (1852–1925) was field marshal and commander in chief of the British Expeditionary Force in France during the first year of the Great War. **Glacier, Creek, Peaks** [2810m]; 1968; Monashee. *See also* Frenchman Cap. *See also* Remillard.

FRENCHMAN CAP: Mountain [2897m]; 1885; Monashee. This is a prominent peak across the Columbia valley from Downie Creek and not far up from Death Rapids. Its name seems to have derived from a guide used by Coleman in his 1888 trip upriver from Revelstoke to the abandoned mining towns of the Goldstream. The guide was referred to only as "Frenchie."

FRESHFIELD: Mount [3336m], **Icefield, Creek, Group, Lake** [1658m]; 1897; W Rockies. Douglas William Freshfield (1845–1934) was a born alpinist, having accompanied his mother on her many extended hiking trips through Switzerland. He became editor of the *Alpine Journal* in 1872 and president of the AC in 1893. His services were no less noteworthy to the Royal Geographical Society. The mountain and associated glacial system west of Howse Pass were named in his honour by Collie. In 1920, his 75th year, Freshfield visited western Canada but was too feeble to make any climbs and did not even see the group of peaks bearing his name. Glacial recession in recent years has created a large lake where the lower Freshfield Glacier once extended.

FRESNOY: Mountain [3240 m]; 1919; Alexandra. This name commemorates another of the towns in northeast France where Canadian troops performed heroic action in the Great War. In 1902, Outram called the summit "Consolation" after he failed to attain the summit of the higher Mount Alexandra, but he was able to make this one.

FRIA: Mount [2915 m], Col [2820 m]; 1910; Adamant. Palmer named this summit, along with nearby Wotan and Thor, on the second of his four visits to the region around Mount Sir Sandford. He, like many other alpinists, was taken with Norse mythology.

FRIDOLIN: Peak [2810 m]; 1990; Moloch. Named by Ruedi Beglinger; this point was occupied by Ley Harris as Gwynn Survey Station. To Putnam it had been "Dismal."

FRIENDSHIP: Col [2720 m]; 1948; Adamant. Given by Kauffman and Putnam because this col was the route by which their party planned to exit the Fairy Meadow region to rendezvous with a Hendricks-led party approaching the Sir Sandford area from Tangier Summit. The two groups had cooperated in joint air drops and were well acquainted personally.

FRIGATE: Mountain [2880 m]; 1924; W Rockies. The name first appears in the famous 18th Report, but there is no indication of why this name was applied, although the snow-flecked aspect of these peaks, seen from the west against the darker line of the Rockies' main ranges, suggests the outline of a sailing ship. The slightly lower Felucca is not far distant.

FRIGG: Glacier, Tower [2520 m]; 1984; Badshot. This name was tidied up from its original (and slightly longer) submission. Frigg was the wife of Odin in Norse mythology.

FRONT: Ranges. This is a term of geographical convenience for the first ranges of the Canadian Rockies to be seen as one approaches the mountains from the east. A similar appellation is used in a comparable geographic situation in Colorado. *See also* Dry.

FRY: Creek, Pinnacles; 1924; S Purcells. This was the original name for the creek draining the Leaning Towers. The group at its head inherited the name because they were approached by a party, led by Gilbert Wilson of the GSC, coming up Fry's Creek from Kootenay

Lake. Richard Fry (1838–1898) was of a family well known in the area, a sometime miner and ferry operator who took up land on Kootenay Lake.

FRYATT: Mount [3361m], **Creek, Group**; 1920; Rockies. The ABC named this summit at the northwest of the Columbia Icefield for Charles Algernon Fryatt (1872–1916). He was the Capt. of the unarmed merchant ship *Brussels*, which was captured by German U-boats. Fryatt was accused (not without justification) of having attempted the unsportsmanlike manoeuvre of ramming a submarine and was summarily shot by his captors. In 1913 Mumm had called the mountain "Patricia."

FUHRER: Mount [3063 m]; 1972; Clearwater. Putnam named this peak for Hans Fuhrer (1897-1957), the elder of two brothers from Innertkirchen, Switzerland, who worked as guides for the CNR.

FULGURITE: Peak [2669 m]; 1966; Albert. Dr. West found this in the sandy terrain near the summit of the peak. Fulgurite is fused silicate material left in sand or small rock fragments by a lightning strike.

FULLERTON: Mount [2728 m]; 1940; Fisher. Charles Percy Fullerton (1870–1938), a lawyer by training and a jurist, became chairman of the Canadian Board of Railway Commissioners in 1931 and later served as chairman of the CNR.

FURY: Pass [2185 m]; 1964; Monashee. This is the pass leading from Storm Creek over the height of land to Mud River, and its name records the kind of weather endured by Arthur Maki and his party during its passage. The name is common in mountaineering literature.

FUSILADE: Pass [2484 m]; 1963; Moloch. The party first traversing the pass included John Edward Williamson, long-time editor of the annual safety report of the AAC and ACC, who climbed nearby Mount Anstey and was met with a fusillade of loose rocks while making the approach.

FYNN: Creek; 1918; British. Valere Alfred Fynn (1870–1929), whose father had laid out portions of the Trans-Siberian Railway, attended technical schools in Switzerland and became a prosperous electrical inventor and manufacturer. After moving to St. Louis in 1908, he travelled to the Rockies south of Banff by pack train for several seasons, approaching via this valley. He made numerous first ascents on these trips.

*I cannot conclude without mentioning how sensibly I
feel the dismemberment of America from this empire,
and that I should be miserable indeed if I did not feel
that no blame on that account can be laid at my door, and
did I not also know that knavery seems to be so much a
striking feature of its inhabitants that it may not in the
end be an evil that they will become aliens to this kingdom.*

—George iii, letter to Earl Shelburne, 1782

GABLE: Mountain [2928 m]; 1916; Front. The name for this lesser summit was first applied by Collie in 1898, used again by Schäffer in 1906 and finally made official by the ABC. It is descriptive of the shape of the mountain as seen on the approach up Alexandra River.

GAGNEBIN: Mount [2905 m], **Creek**; 1917; SW Rockies. In this area of widespread sedimentary rock, a summit just had to be named for Elie Gagnebin (1891–1949), the notable Swiss stratigrapher and structural geologist.

GALATEA: Mount [3185 m], **Creek**; 1922; Kananaskis. This name comes from the sea nymph of Greek mythology, but refers more immediately to a British cruiser that was heavily engaged in the Battle of Jutland. Its lookout had made the first sighting of the dreaded German High Seas Fleet on the afternoon of May 31, 1916.

GALLO: Peak [2641 m]; 1967; Slocan. This peak, once known as Spyglass North, was named for a native of Czechoslovakia, Joseph Ficek Gallo (1882–1973). He had worked for the CPR at Field before turning to prospecting around these hillsides during the 1920s.

GALLOWAY: Mountain [2972 m]; 1966; N Purcells. New Zealand-born mining engineer John Davidson Galloway (1886–1938) was assistant to and then the B.C. provincial mineralogist from 1913 to 1932.

GALTON: Range, Pass [1903 m]; 1916; Boundary. Sir Francis Galton (1822–1911) was an English scientist and writer on scientific topics who founded *Meteorographica* in 1862, thereby establishing the basis for modern weather maps. He was also a student of heredity and wrote a commentary on cats.

GALWAY: Mountain [3002 m]; 1969; Starbird. Renamed by West, this had been known as Killarney Mountain.

GARGOYLE: The [3090 m]; 1948; Adamant. This lesser summit of the

Gothics Group was named by Kauffman and Putnam for then prominent overhanging block of rock that graced one edge of its otherwise flattish top.

GANSNER: Mount [3011 m]; 1960; Starbird. This lesser summit lies southwest of Birthday Peak and was named by Arthur Maki and Professor West. But for whom?

GARNET: Col [2775 m]; 1951; Windy. **Creek, Mountain**; Ottertail. This name has been applied frequently by wandering hikers and alpinists because of the presence of these dark red semi-precious stones in the native schist. Gem quality is rare, however, in these mountains. **Peak** [2876 m]. This is the highest point in Wells Gray Provincial Park.

GARTH: Mount [3030 m]; 1924; Freshfield. John MacDonald (1774–1860), referred to as "of Garth" to distinguish him from others of similar name also in the employ of the NWC, built Rocky Mountain House in 1799 and was at several other posts before his most notable assignment to Astoria in 1813.

GASS: Mount [2866 m]; 1928; High Rock. Lawrence Henderson Gass, DLS 1914, a native of Iroquois, Ontario, was killed in action in 1917.

GATES: Peak [2778 m]; 1928; Gold. Edwin B. Gates (1904–1973), a one-time American chemical engineer, bought the St. Leon property from the estate of Mike Grady and revived it. He operated the hotel from 1945 to 1968, when it burned to the ground.

GEC: Mount [3130 m]; 1948; Icefields. This monster pile of trilobites was climbed for the first time by a party whose members' first names were George, Ellen and Chuck. After initially putting her husband, Chuck (Wilts), at the head of the list, Ellen decided that that came out too much like a beer container and rearranged the letters.

GEIKIE: Glacier; 1888; Dawson. There were two Scots brothers Geikie, Sir Archibald (1835–1924) and James (1839–1915). They both became famous in the study of glaciology; Archibald was also director of the British Geological Survey. Reverend Green gave this name to the southwest outlet of the Illecillewaet Icefield into the Incomappleux River. **Mount** [3270 m], Creek, Meadows; Ramparts. James McEvoy of the GSC chose the name here, also in honour of the Geikie brothers.

GENDARME: Mountain [2922 m]; 1911; N Rockies. This is a generic mountain term and applies to a prominent rock or other obstacle to the progress of a climber on a ridge. The term is from the French military police and in this instance was applied by Wheeler.

GEOTHITE: Peak [2919 m]; 1971; Nemo. Not being in our OED, we aren't sure what is meant by this name, and the people who ought to know don't recall using the name.

GEST: Tower [3170 m]; 1973; Murchison. Lillian Gest (1898–1986) was an indefatigable lover of the Canadian Alps. From a well-to-do Philadelphia family, she devoted most of her life to social causes, but was introduced to these mountains by Caroline Hinman (1884–1960), whose summer pack trips for young ladies were an annual event after 1917. In her later years Gest wrote several monographs on points of interest near Lake Louise.

GHOST: Mountain [3204 m], **Glacier**; 1920 Chaba. The ABC gave this name because the mountain showed a white and "spectral appearance." **Lakes** [1494 m], **River**; 1966; Front. The river was called "Deadman's" by Hector in 1858. The lakes have been largely assimilated into a Minnewanka diversion, for stabilization of Calgary's water and electric power system.

GIANTS KNEECAP: Summit [2758 m]; 1925; Kokanee. This is an unusual item to find next to a Battleship, but with a little imagination, this summit does look like an overgrown patella.

GIBBON: Pass [2300 m]; 1959; Ball. John Murray Gibbon (1875–1952) was for many years in charge of the CPR's public relations. Subsequently he wrote an authoritative history of Canada's great national enterprise. He became the first president of the Canadian Authors Association and a fellow of the Royal Society of Canada.

GIBRALTAR: Mountain [2665 m], 1928; Highwood. **Peak** [289 m]; 1910; Adamant. These names are almost commonplace, taking their origin in each instance from a supposed resemblance to the famous rock and British naval base overlooking the Bay of Algeciras in southernmost Spain. Such likenesses are not always strong; for instance, the original [426 m] is composed of relatively soft limestone, whereas the one named by Palmer in 1910 is of very hard granite.

GIEGERICH: Creek, Overlook [2910 m]; W Purcells. Edward Francis Giegerich (d. 1951) of Kaslo was a store operator who grubstaked a number of miners. His brother, Henry, was smart enough to have for his law partner a man who went on to become B.C. Commissioner of Lands in 1903. The name was officially acknowledged in Ottawa much later than in Victoria; Robinson's designation of the overlook did not occur until 1954.

GILGIT: Mountain [3090 m]; 1898; Freshfield. The market town of this name in northern Kashmir is one of the traditional staging points for expeditions into the Karakorum Range. The name here, however, was given by Collie in association with Mummery and Nanga Parbat.

Mummery's ill-fated expedition to Nanga Parbat in 1896 last saw civilization at Gilgit.

GILMOUR: Glacier; 1916; Cariboo. Andrew James Gilmour (1871–1941) of New York was a dermatologist. He made many trips into the mountains of Canada, several in company with Holway and Butters. One of his trips was the first into what has since become known as the Premier Range, and he was twice near the Battle Range, where he made the first ascent of Mount Butters in 1914. But his most noteworthy trip was that to Mount Sir Alexander in 1929.

GIMLI: Peak [2758 m]; 1937; Valhalla. This is of Icelandic derivation and was an alternate name for New Iceland, the pioneer settlement of Icelanders in Manitoba. In Norse mythology it is the abode of the righteous dead who have passed the judgement of Ragnarok. Gimli is described as "a hall fairer than the sun, and covered with gold."

GIROUARD: Mount [2995 m]; 1904; Fairholme. Colonel Sir Edward Percy Girouard (1867–1932) was born in Montreal and was a British public servant who became Imperial High Commission for various African colonies. During the Great War he served as director of munitions supply, charged by the War Cabinet with coordinating the overlapping armament demands of His Majesty's armed forces. His father, Desiré, had been a judge of the Canadian Supreme Court.

GLACIER: Location [1250 m]; 1885; Sir Donald. This (now relocated) station stop took its name from the most spectacular sight around, the Great or Illecillewaet Glacier, which tumbled down in those cooler years to an altitude of about 1520 m, not far from the station and its adjoining hotel, Glacier House. The area became a notable tourist attraction for the CPR until a series of wintertime disasters and the need for reliable train operation forced construction of the Connaught Tunnel. At the same time, much of the glacier had melted. The melting has continued so that today hardly any of the glacier is visible from where the famous hotel once stood. *See also* Vaux. **Lake** [1433 m], **River**; 1858; Lyell. This name was given by Hector to the valley north of Mount Forbes for what were then obvious reasons. **Peak** [3283 m]; 1894; Lake Louise. Allen observed there was a small glacier lying in the shadow area north of this peak.

GLACIER CIRCLE: Valley [2000 m]; 1890; Dawson. Harold Topham was the first to camp in this isolated but interesting valley. At that time the Deville Glacier swept grandly through its southern portion and out between the North and South Sentinels (now Mounts Macoun and Topham) toward the Beaver River. It was and still is difficult of access and dominated by mosquitoes in summer. Despite these drawbacks, the place was so scenic that the CPR built a log hut there in 1922 for the benefit of climbers, which was rehabilitated and expanded in 1972 but has since fallen again into disrepair.

GLACIER CREST: Viewpoint [2237 m]; 1895; Sir Donald. Named by members of the AMC for its position between the Illecillewaet and Asulkan glaciers. It was a popular and easy day trip for guests at Glacier House.

GLACIER DOME: Mountain [3000 m]; 1928; Commander. This summit lies west of the Lake of the Hanging Glaciers and is easily reachable from almost any direction. During most of the summer season its crest is a gently rounded mound of snow. It was first called Mount Starbird and then labelled The Dome by the AAC party of 1928.

GLACIER VIEW: Peak [2758 m]; 1924; Kokanee. That's what one gets from this peak, particularly when looking down to the north. But you'd better hurry.

GLADSHEIM: Mount [2820 m]; 1900; Valhalla. The words mean "glittering home" in Norse and refer to the shimmering effect of an icebound lake.

GLASGOW: Mount [2944 m]; 1922; Opal. This was the name of a cruiser engaged in the Battle of Jutland that neither sank nor played a distinguished role. It is also a city in Scotland, the second largest urban centre in the United Kingdom.

GLORIA: Mount [2908 m], **Lake** [1877 m]; 1913; Assiniboine. This name is part of the pattern of superlatives applied by Wheeler's ABC team to the features that surround Mount Assiniboine. *See also* Marvel, Wonder.

GOAT: Range; 1860; S Rockies. **Peak** [2810 m]; W Rockies. **Glacier**; 1948; Sir Sandford. The first of these was a Palliser translation of a Native name; it is, however, a common name in many alpine regions, invariably given because of the presence, at one time or another, of *Oreamnos montanus* or some of his relatives.

GOBI: Pass [2240 m]; 1980; Battle. So named by Putnam and Laurilla because to obtain water, they had to hike quite a distance from their otherwise pleasant campsite on the crest of the pass.

GOG: Lake [2243 m]; 1913; Assiniboine. Here the name was applied by the ABC. Gog is generally referred to in Holy Scripture as an enemy of the faithful. **Pinnacle** [2621 m]; 1948; Adamant. This pinnacle is one of a pair (as is usually the case when this name is applied), named in this instance by Putnam when he, with his friends Kauffman and Ferris, first visited the Shoestring Glacier of the Adamant Range. *See also* Magog.

GOLD: Range; 1860. Some has been found here, but no real rush; the name was optimistic. **River**, 1868; Sir Sandford. This name or one of its variants, like many others, often represented a large amount of wishful thinking. The river, which flows eastward to the Columbia, shares common headwaters at Moberly Pass with the west-flowing Goldstream, which has actually shown entrancing bits of colour for well over a century.

GOLDEN: City [782 m]; 1883. The promoters of this location, which was once known as Kicking Horse Flats, went one better than Silver City, below Castle Mountain. The town had been platted in part by an assistant to the famous Major Rogers, Frederick Aylmer, whose suggestion determined the town's name. The first mayor, elected in 1957, was George Marrs, son-in-law to the famous guide Edward Feuz Jr.

GOLDEN EAGLE: Peak [3060 m]; 1917; Lyell. This name was given by Bridgland because he saw an eagle's nest high on this peak.

GOLDSTREAM: River, Mountain [2825 m]; 1867; NW Selkirks. Walter Moberly appears to have been the first to apply this name to the major tributary of the Columbia flowing west from the heart of the Northern Selkirks. It is appropriate, for from his day to this there have been intermittent gold-mining operations in its basin. *See also* Remillard.

GONG: Lake [1759 m], **Peak** [3120 m]; 1919; Churchill. The lake was named by the ABC because of its shape. Because he was there, the peak has also been called "Thorington Tower."

GOODAIR: Peak [2810 m]; 1934; Jasper. Percy Hamilton Goodair (1877–1929) was a warden of Jasper National Park. He bears the unfortunate distinction of being the only park warden in Canada to have been killed by a grizzly bear, right outside his cabin.

GOODALL: Mountain [2820 m]; 1965; Cariboo. Trooper Walter H. Goodall, of McAlister, B.C., was killed in action on April 1, 1945.

GOODRICH: Mount [2829 m]; 1959; Battle. The first ascent party of Sterling Neale, Charles Plummer and Sam Silverstein collectively named this summit for Nathaniel Lewis Goodrich (1880–1957), distinguished cartographer, alpinist and librarian of Dartmouth College.

GOODSIR: Towers [3562 m], **Creek, Group**; 1859; Ottertail. There were two Goodsir brothers, both medical doctors, just as there are two towers (the lower north one being 3524 m). John (1814–1867) was a professor of anatomy at Edinburgh University, where Hector had studied medicine. His younger brother, H.D., was surgeon with the final Franklin expedition. Hector named these striking peaks of the Ice River area in their collective honour.

Stegasaurus Ridge of the Gold Range. ROGER LAURILLA PHOTO

GORDON: Mount [3203 m]; 1916; Waputik. Alexander MacLennan Gordon (1875–1965) was a native Canadian and persistent climber who studied for the Presbyterian ministry in Europe. Over the years he served flocks in several provinces and was an armed forces chaplain in both world wars.

GORDON HORNE: Peak [2885 m]; 1930; Monashee. Angus Patrick Horne of Blue River, B.C., for whom a lake is named only a few miles to the west, prospected this region in the early 1920s, and Tom Horne was drowned nearby in 1900. But we haven't been able to get a handle on Gordon.

GOTHICS: Glacier, Group, Col [3190 m]; 1910; Adamant. Given by Palmer as he, with Holway and Butters, first saw the extent of this large icefield, some of whose rimming summits they climbed. *See also* Fria.

GOULD: Dome [2894 m]; 1858; High Rock. This name was applied by Lt. Blakiston (before he was dismissed from the Palliser expedition) after the British naturalist John Gould (1804–1881). Blakiston applied the name to the more prominent point, now called Tornado Mountain, whence it was relocated in 1915 to a lesser summit some 5 km to the south.

GRADY: Mountain [2880 m]; 1963; Gold. This is the west twin summit of Mount Burnham and is named for Michael Grady (d. 1944), who was the proprietor of the St. Leon Hot Springs Hotel on the shores of the Upper Arrow Lake. Grady was a prospector who found the Silver

Queen Mine and located the hot springs in 1892. He built the hotel there 10 years later—the same year he brought in the Standard Mine near Silverton.

GRAHAM: Mount [2957 m]; 1929; Moloch. This name was applied by the Topographical Survey to honour Ernest Graham, an early member of the Revelstoke City Council.

GRAND: Glacier, Mountain [3297 m]; 1890; Dawson. Harold Topham first saw this glacier from the Beaver Valley when it was a far grander sight than it is after subsequent years of warming and melting. After viewing the spectacular icefall Topham then named the mountain at its head.

GRANITE: Peak [3094 m]; 1928; Commander. There are plutons all over the Columbia Mountains, a far different geological condition than is exposed in the Rockies. **Glacier**; 1946; Adamant. Hendricks' party was the first to explore this glacier at the head of Swan Creek, where it finds most of its sources in the northward drainage of the Adamant pluton.

GRANT: Peak [3120 m]; 1902; Hermit. The Topographical Survey gave this name to honour George Monro Grant (1835–1902), Presbyterian minister and principal of Queen's University, who accompanied Sir Sandford Fleming, as amanuensis, on Fleming's epic 1872 journey across Canada. See Grant's book *Ocean to Ocean* (London, 1873).

GRASSI: Ridge; 1962; Bow Ranges. Lawrence Grassi (1891–1980) was a popular guide and warden of the Banff National Park. Some of his trail work around Lake Oesa, below this ridge, is extremely impressive for the quality of its drywall masonry. He pointed out the climbing possibilities of this long dry ridge of the Wiwaxy Peaks.

GRAVEYARD: Flats [1437 m]; 1907; Cline. Schäffer named this location for the quantities of bones strewn on the gravel flats of the North Saskatchewan River, where her "Nashan" entered. This was a popular campsite in the half-century after 1885 for pack-train parties going north from Lake Louise to the summits of the Columbia Icefield and adjacent groups. *See also* Alexandra.

GRAY: Peak [3180 m], **Pass** [1356 m]; 1927; **Icefields.** There were, amazingly, two fathers of Confederation with identical names—John Hamilton Gray. However, the one from P.E.I. (1812–1887), having been premier of the province, found himself unable to lead his constituents effectively and retired from active politics in 1868. The one from New Brunswick was the more interesting. Born in Bermuda in 1814, he represented Saint John in the House of Commons until he resigned to become judge of the B.C. Supreme Court, where he stayed until his death in 1889. Ostheimer applied the name, but did not express either rationale or preference. **Mount** [3000 m]; 1951; Vermilion. Maybe the other one is honoured here. However, it should be noted that B.C. land surveyor John Hamilton Gray died in 1941.

GRAYS: Peak [2755 m]; 1963; SW Rockies. Once known as Haystack Mountain, this peak was renamed to honour Robert Hampton Gray, VC, and his brother, Jack, who were both killed in action during the Second World War.

GREAT CAIRN: Location [1890 m]; 1953; Sir Sandford. This is the present site of the ACC's Ben Ferris Hut, overlooking the dwindling snout of the Sir Sandford Glacier, which was built in 1964 by Paul Thomas Doherty (1919–2000), Dr. Ferris and certain of the ladies in their lives. For a quarry the builders used a 20-foot cairn that had been built in 1953 by members of the Harvard Mountaineering Club. When Palmer had visited this locale in the years 1909–12, it was covered by more than 100 m of ice. As recently as 1948, the site, across the valley to the north of Mount Sir Sandford, was still ice covered to a considerable depth.

GREEN: Mount [2692 m]; 1901; Sir Donald. Named by Wheeler for William Spotswood Green (1847–1919), Episcopal clergyman, who climbed in these mountains in 1888 and wrote the first book about the Selkirks. He was under commission from the Royal Geographical Society, which had been impressed with his prior work in New Zealand. Green later became commissioner of the Irish fisheries. As the pioneer alpinist of British Columbia, if not the entire Canadian Alps, he faced a number of what became familiar problems: a pack horse fell into a stream, crushing "... *your society's instrument t...*" and "... *some beast with a most depraved taste had breakfasted off my alpine rope* ..." He also found a novel use for the wine cellar at Glacier House: it became his "impromptu darkroom." See his book *Among the Selkirk Glaciers* (London, 1890). *See also* Terminal.

GRENDEL: Peak [2785 m]; 1947; Battle. This name was applied by Kauffman in continuance of the "battle" motif of the area. Grendel was the name of the monster slain by the warrior Beowulf in the Anglo-Saxon epic poem (he tore off the monster's arm in an all-night battle).

GREY DIKE: Peak [2728 m]; 1966; Albert. Professor West again spoke the truth; this summit is marked by a dike of greyish aplite, intrusive into the country rock.

GREY FANG: Mountain [2845 m]; 1956; Moloch. Named by Putnam for its lighter colour and its association to the west of Fang Rock, along with the adjacent, but lower White Fang.

GRIFFITH: Mount [2767 m]; 1966; N Purcells. This summit had once been known as "Ice Dome" and was called "Plumley Peak" by Robinson in 1952, but was officially named for John Edgar Griffith, who had been gold commissioner (mining recorder) at Golden in the East Kootenay from 1897 to 1908.

GRISWOLD: Peak [2941 m]; 1931; S Purcells. Thorington put this third name on the map in a one-day frenzy of climbing activity with his friend, Julian Hillhouse. The other two names were Katherine and Christine, and they all referred to the lady to whom Thorington was married. This was Harnden's "Toby Peak" of 1911.

GRIZZLY: Mountain [2757 m]; 1901; Hermit. This point, northeast of Ursus Minor, was previously called Sifton. Its present name was given by Norwegian-born Dr. August Severin Eggers (1862–1936), physician and surgeon of Grand Forks, North Dakota, after he met a few of the locals while on a climbing trip from the Glacier House.

GROTTO: Mountain [2706 m]; 1858; Fairholme. Bourgeau named this summit in reference to the large, high-arched cave on its flank.

GUARDSMAN: Mountain [3000 m]; 1910; Sir Sandford. Palmer named this one in keeping with his general motif for the peaks surrounding Mount Sir Sandford, that they represented outer defences of his principal objective, since three years of amateur attacks had failed to gain him the summit. It was only when, in desperation, he engaged the services of Edward Feuz Jr. and Rudolph Aemmer that he was able to stand on the summits of the two highest peaks of the region.

GUARDSMEN: The [3277 m]; 1915; Commander. Stone applied this name because of the position of this linear peak south of Commander Mountain.

GWENDOLINE: Mountain [3149 m]; 1937; Starbird. With a slightly different spelling, this was the name of a riverboat that was the principal asset of Capt. Armstrong next to his favourite *Duchess*. It was named for the young daughter of the earl of Stadbroke, and when it was wrecked in 1899, Armstrong went on a two-year hiatus to the Yukon. Thorington applied this name on the land, as he did with several other Columbia River boats. This peak, however, had been occupied by the GSC in 1912 and was consequently, but briefly, called "Survey Peak" by Robinson in 1952.

GUNBOAT: Mountain [3000 m]; 1924; Cariboo. Despite its fearsome name, Carpé found this to be an easy climb, but noted that it seemed to be "the hub of a wheel-like series of ridges" in the eastern part of what is now called the Premier Range.

GUNNARSEN: Mountain [2610 m]; 1960; Gold. Hans Gunnarsen, of

Norwegian birth, became a celebrated local skier in the Revelstoke area, competing at age 27 in the 1936 Olympics and becoming the Dominion champion in 1940. Like his compatriot, Torger Tokle, he was killed in action during the Second World War.

GUSTY: Peak [3000 m]; 1972; Kananaskis. Boles complained that when he made the first ascent of this peak it was under severe winter conditions, though done in midsummer.

GWYN: [2780 m]; 1963; Hermit. This was one of N.E. McConnell's survey points. It was also the stage name of an actress friend of King Charles II, born Margaret Lymcott, from whom are descended several famous Fitzroys.

GYDOSIC: Mount [2789 m]; 1964; S Rockies. Joseph S. Gydosic of Fernie was killed in action in the Second World War.

GYR: Mountain [2857 m]; 1987; Westfall. The Kootenay Mountaineering Club party making its first ascent told us they sighted a gyr falcon during the climb.

Generally things are ancienter
than the names whereby they are called.
—RICHARD HOOKER, *LAWS OF ECCLESIASTICAL POLITY, V*, 1597

HABEL: Creek; 1907; Icefield. Jean Habel (1839–1902) was a German mathematician and geographer, famous mostly for his exploratory work in the Andes, but who also made two lengthy visits to the Canadian Rockies, mapping parts of the range. On his first trip, in 1896, he went up the Yoho valley to its glacial sources. On the second, in 1901, he went up the creek still bearing his name to a mountain he called "Chaba," which is presently an officially unnamed peak north of the present locus of the name. In 1985 the Committee on Geographic Names undertook a belated rehabilitation of Habel, applying his name to the previously undesignated north peak of Mount Rhondda. *See also* Des Poilus.

HADDO: Peak [3070 m]; 1916; Bow Ranges. This name comes from the ancestral estate, Haddo House, of the earls of Aberdeen. In this instance it commemorates the eldest son of the Marquess of Aberdeen,

George, Lord Haddo, who became the eighth earl in 1934. The summit is the next one north of Mount Aberdeen and some 80 m lower. The seventh earl, John Campbell Hamilton-Gordon (1847–1934), was Governor General of Canada 1893–98.

HADIKEN: Mount [2886 m]; 1964; SW Rockies. Sgt. Alexander A. Hadiken was killed in action in the Second World War.

HAEMATITE: Peak [3000 m]; 1979; Nemo. This name is the beginning of a lot of iron, applied here by Silverstein to the northeast point of the Iron Ridge.

HAGEN: Peak [2627 m]; 1961; Van Horne. Pte. 2 Alfred G. Hagen, of Field, B.C., some 30 km south of the peak, was killed in action on March 9, 1944.

HAIDUK: Peak [2910 m], **Lake** [2057 m], **Creek**; 1922; Ball. Nearby are such names as Scarab, Sphinx and Mummy lakes, all dominated by the Pharaoh Peaks, in this corner of Canada "Egyptianized" by the Topographical Survey. Unfortunately, this particular name is not Egyptian at all; it refers to a class of Balkan rebels who were resentful of Turkish rule, and also to a group of Hungarian mercenaries.

HAIG: Mount [2610 m]; 1862; Boundary. This lesser summit near the 49th parallel was named to honour Capt. Robert Wolseley Haig (d. 1872) assigned to the IBSC. Haig had originally been commissioned an artillery officer in 1848 and ended his days commanding the Bombay sappers. **Glacier**; 1918; British. This name goes along with the summit from which it flows, but here honouring Sir Douglas Haig.

HALIA: Mountain [2760 m]; 1951; Windy. Influential members of the first ascent party had attended Phillips Exeter Academy in New Hampshire, en route to the Harvard Mountaineering Club, and applied their school's name to this point. However, the more erudite David Jones got approval for the name of the wife of Poseidon, which goes better with the surrounding toponymy.

HA LING: Peak; 2004. *See* Chinaman's Peak.

HALL: Peak [3040 m]; 1961; S Rockies. Pte. 2 John H. Hall of Marysville was killed in action in the Second World War. **Tower** [3215 m]; 1973; Murchison. This name was applied by Putnam to the southernmost unit of the Murchison Towers in recognition of its 1940 first ascent by Henry Snow Hall Jr. (1895–1987), a generous and tireless contributor to alpinism worldwide, long-time official and first honourary president of the AAC and a great supporter of the ACC.

HALLAM: Peak [3128 m], **Glacier**; 1950; Monashee. This name was given in memory of William Hallam Jr. (1889–1930), BCLS, who drowned on Kinbasket Lake while returning from the summer's surveying trip in the Wood River area. Two of his assistants, Gordon Nixon and Allan Game, died with him when their canoe capsized during a squall on the chilly lake. The name is now officially placed slightly to the east of the highest point of this range.

HALSTEAD: Pass [2758 m]; 1970; Clearwater. This is hardly a pass, being much higher than nearby low points between the peaks north of the Bonnet Snowfield, but perhaps this is all a minor American diplomat deserves. Albert Halstead (1867–1949) travelled this area with Wilcox and Alfred Castle in 1916. He was a sometime newspaperman who became the U.S. commissioner in Vienna after the Great War and subsequently served as consul general in Montreal, 1920–28, and in London, 1928–32.

HALVORSON: Mountain [2781 m]; 1965; Cariboo. Trooper Frank Halvorson, of McBride, some two dozen kilometres to the east, was killed in action on October 29, 1944.

HAMBER: Park; 1941; W Rockies. Eric Werge Hamber (1880–1950) was lieutenant-governor of British Columbia for five years beginning in 1936, thereafter serving as chancellor of the University of British Columbia. This provincial park was designated in his honour in the year of his retirement. Its dimensions have expanded and contracted from time to time, but it still contains some of the most beautiful mountains in Canada.

HAMILL: Mount [3243 m], **Creek, Glacier, Formation**; 1911; S Purcells. Harnden was the first to set this name into the literature. It derives from Thomas B. Hamill (d. 1885), a Welsh-born mining scout who came north from California in 1883 and developed mining properties across Kootenay Lake for the then owners of the famous Bluebell Mine. He was murdered by American-born Robert Evan Sproule, a fellow prospector who felt Hamill had jumped one of his prior claims. Sproule became exasperated with seemingly interminable and unsatisfactory legal process and took more drastic action. He was hanged in Victoria in 1886, per order of Judge Begbie, despite considerable public sympathy and intervention by influential Bostonians. The formation is a durable quartzite which outcrops extensively in the southern Purcells and near Rogers Pass in the Selkirks, offering unanimously excellent climbing.

HAMILTON: Mount [2795 m]; 1987; Westfall. Applied to honour a deceased member of the Kootenay Mountaineering Club.

HAMMOND: Mountain [3368 m]; 1910; Farnham. This one is complicated. It has variously appeared as "Mt. Thompson," "Thumb" and "St.

Thomas." But, as our Aunt Lulu learned, "That ain't all." As time went on scholars determined that this must have been David Thompson's Mount Nelson. However, by 1910 it had yet another handle, given by Charles Ellis for the late Herbert Carlyle Hammond of Toronto, who owned some land nearby and had bankrolled the Parridice Mine. Ellis (1874–1951) had much to do with subsequent local mountain nomenclature and owned the Ptarmigan Mine. Despite all of this, Harnden gave the mountain yet another name in 1913, calling it "Sir Charles." Nobody knew why. The original Nelson is back to Nelson again, and "Hammond" is on a lesser peak just west of the Farnham massif.

HANBURY: Peak [2911 m], **Glacier**; 1901; Ottertail. Whymper suggested this name in honour of David Theophilus Hanbury (1864–1910), a British-born explorer of the Canadian Arctic. See his book *Sport and Travel in the Northland of Canada* (London, 1904).

HANGING GLACIERS: Lake of the [2150 m]; 1928; Commander. This spectacular lake was originally christened by Starbird in 1911, calling it after his wife's preferred given name, Maye. Others came by and started calling it Glacier Lake, and finally the ACC provided the present very descriptive name at the time of the annual camp near its shores.

HANNINGTON: Mount [2576 m]; N Rockies. This name recalls Charles Francis Hannington (1848–1930), a companion of Edward Jarvis's on their 1874 exploratory trip for the CPR, in the course of which Hannington barely made it. Later he surveyed the Crowsnest Pass for the CPR and in the Great War became a major in a railway construction battalion. The summit is north across the pass from Mount Jarvis. See Jarvis's segment in Sandford Fleming's 1887 *Report on Surveys & Preliminary Operations on the Canadian Pacific Railway* (Ottawa, 1977).

HANOVER: Peak [2768 m]; 1970; Battle. Kruszyna applied this name in keeping with nearby Big Green, for the town in New Hampshire where the "Big Green" (Dartmouth College) is located.

HARDISTY: Mount [2700 m], **Creek**; 1958; Maligne. James Hector applied this name to express his thanks to Richard Hardisty (1831–1889), who rose through the ranks of the HBC to become chief factor at Fort Edmonton and subsequently a senator of Canada. Hardisty was also brother-in-law to Sir Donald Smith.

HARKIN: Mount [2980 m]; 1923; Mitchell. Bridgland suggested this to honour the Dominion Commissioner of Parks, 1911–36, James Bernard Harkin (1875–1955), a noted conservationist who had been personal secretary to Sifton.

HARMON: Mountain [2941 m]; 1952; Starbird. Byron Harmon (1875–1942) was the prime photographer of the Canadian Alps. Arriving in Banff in 1903, he soon became an active participant in ACC climbs and visited the Purcells in 1910 and 1911. His negatives currently form one of the greatest and most informative treasures of the Peter and Catherine Whyte Foundation (Whyte Museum of the Canadian Rockies). His name was applied here by Robinson.

HARPOON: Peak [3092 m]; 1970; Battle. Kruszyna stuck with the Melvilleana initiated by Anger in the major nomenclature of the Battle Range in this reference to Moby Dick.

HARRIS: Mount [3299 m]; 1957; Clearwater. Ley Edward Harris, DLS 1918, of Calgary, worked for the Topographical Survey in the area around Sorceror Mountain in 1929. He surveyed this peak in the Rockies and climbed some of its neighbours in the course of his work.

HARRISON: Mount [3359 m], **Group**; 1964; S Rockies. Francis A. Harrison, of the RCAF and Cranbrook, was killed in action during the Second World War. This peak, exceeding 11,000 feet in altitude, was the last in the Rockies to be climbed.

HÄSLER: Peak [3377 m]; 1899; Dawson. This easterly point of Mount Dawson was named by Professor Fay in honour of one of his two guides on its first ascent. Christian Häsler (1857–1924) was a native of Gsteigwiler, a small town south and above Interlaken in the Oberland. He came to Canada for the summer seasons from 1899 through 1911, returning later to live out his life in Golden at the home of his only son, Christian Jr. *See also* Feuz and *The Guiding Spirit*.

HAT: Peak [2882 m]; 1937; Monashee. This name started out as a surveyor's reference name, applied by N.E. McConnell. With the passage of time, and a little help from Wallerstein, who used the name in an article he wrote on climbing there, it stuck.

HATTERAS: Mount [2941 m], **Glacier, Creek, Group**; 1954; N Purcell. Having tentatively called it "Wedge" for its shape, Robinson settled instead on the fictional Arctic explorer Capt. Hatteras, whose exploits were described by Jules Verne in 1866. Robinson drew his inspiration for this by looking west across the Duncan River toward the recently named Mount Nemo.

HAULTAIN: Mount [2737 m]; 1916; Jasper. Sir Frederick William George Haultain (1857–1942) served in the legislature of the North-West Territories for Macleod from 1888 and was president of its executive council 1897–1905. When the province of Saskatchewan was established in 1905, he joined its legislature and became chief justice of its Superior Court in 1912, where he served for the next 26 years.

HAWKINS: Mount [2694 m]; 1860; Boundary. Palliser shows this name on his map, presumably after Sir John Summerfield Hawkins (1812–1895), who, as colonel of the Royal Engineers, was in charge of the British IBSC team. This boundary delineation exercise was almost contemporaneous with the British North American Expedition under Capt. Palliser, and the two parties met on several occasions. Hawkins retired as a major-general in 1881.

HAWLEY: Mount [3000 m]; 1928; Maligne. Hawley LaFitte married William Richard Hainsworth in 1919. But she stayed down in camp near Maligne Lake when her husband made the first ascent of this summit. *See also* Florence.

HAWORTH: Glacier; 1948; Sir Sandford. Charles C. Haworth Jr., a budding authority on the spectroscopy of water, was killed by a fall from the summit of nearby Mount Citadel in 1946. Putnam later gave his name to a body of "permanent" snow that had been called the Silvertip Neve by Palmer in 1910, a western tributary of the Silvertip Glacier. Glacial recession, a result of the warming climatic trend of the last century, had made it a completely separate entity by 1953. In subsequent years, David Peter Jones found a number of preserved tree trunks on the north edge of the glacier, which indicated an earlier period of considerably warmer climate.

HAYNES: Mount [2941 m]; 1924; SW Rockies. John Carmichael Haynes (1831–1889) was gold commissioner at Osoyoos from 1861 until 1865, after which he became a judge and member of the legislative assembly.

HEAD: Mount [2782 m]; 1859; Highwood. Palliser himself applied this name in gratitude for the support given his expedition by Sir Edmund Walker Head (1805–1868), Governor General of Canada from 1854 to 1861. Head was greatly in favour of the concept of confederation and worked to this end. He later served as governor of the HBC. It is interesting that Canada had two governors of the same last name, but who left such different impressions of their tenure. Francis Bond Head (1793-1875), though a professed Liberal, was roundly disliked. His callous unresponsiveness brought on the ill-managed Rebellion of 1837, which was fomented in great part by William Lyon Mackenzie, grandfather of Canada's longest-tenured prime minister.

HEALY: Creek, Pass [2330 m]; 1898; Ball. Allen called it "Heely's Creek," but this stream, which drains northeastward from Simpson Pass east of Mount Bourgeau, was named for Capt. John Jerome Healy, a former Montana sheriff who became an intermittent mining prospector in the Rockies, at one time in company with J.S. Dennis. Healy ended his days as manager of operations in Dawson City for the North American Telephone and Telegraph Company. *See also* Helena.

HEART: Mountain [2149 m]; 1957; Front. The rationale for the name of this minor elevation is best observed by looking southeast from the vicinity of Exshaw.

HECTOR: Mount [3394 m], **Lake** [1648 m], **Glacier**; 1884; Murchison. Doctor (afterwards Sir) James Hector (1834–1907) was surgeon and geologist of the Palliser Expedition and turned out to be its most vigorous member, naming many landmarks of the Canadian Rockies. In 1861 he went to New Zealand as director of both the Meteorological Institute and Geological Survey. His name was officially placed on this prominent summit by Dawson. In 1904 Hector returned to Canada as a guest of the CPR, but the untimely death of his youngest son, Douglas, by appendicitis in Revelstoke, caused his trip to be cut short and he never returned to the area he had explored. It should be noted that Hector received his appointment to New Zealand very shortly after returning to England from western Canada, and, as the reports and maps were printed without his proofreading, there were a number of errors. The lake was "Lower Arrow" on Collie's map of 1897. *See also* Andromache.

HELA: Peak [2717 m]; 1917; Valhalla. This is the name for the Norse goddess of the dead, daughter of Loki and Angurboda, whose castle was called Helheim. The word has come into the English language with only minor abbreviation.

HELEN: Lake [2368 m]; **Creek**; Murchison. Named for a daughter of Reverend H.P. Nichols. *See also* Katherine.

HELENA: Ridge [2862m]; 1886; Sawback. This name belongs most famously to the daughter of King Coel, a British chieftain (Old King Cole) whose son became the Roman emperor Constantine and whose fervour for Christianity earned her sainthood. The name migrated here from Montana, however, in company with Sheriff Healy.

HELLROAR: Creek, Mountain [2900m]; 1963; Monashee. This is a generic name that has frequently been given to rushing mountain streams. In this case it migrated up to a nearby summit.

HELMER: Mount [3030 m]; 1924; Freshfield. Origin uncertain. Ronald Helmerow Helmer (1875–1967), born in Ceylon and educated in Russia, was a resident of Nicola, B.C., and president of the B.C. Stock Breeders' Association. Brig. Gen. Richard Alexis Helmer (1864–1922) was a professional soldier and became Dominion Inspector of Musketry. His only son, Alexis Hannum, an artillery officer, was killed early in the Great War.

HELMET: The [3420m]; 1908; Robson. Coleman declared this to be "a striking point of rocks on the north flank of Robson." There are other Helmets, as follow: **Mountain** [3138 m] on map sheet 82N/1 and **Mountain** [2882 m] on 83C/14, named in 1925.

HENDAY: Mount [2820 m]; 1954; Jasper. Anthony Henday (d. 1762) was born on the Isle of Wight and served 14 years in the employ of the HBC. He undertook the company's first intentional inland explorations—an obligation of its royal charter—in 1754–55.

HENNESSEY: Mount [2816 m]; 1964; Hermit. This name was irreverently applied by Kruszyna and other members of the party making its first (and trying) ascent. They did not report if their laboriously backpacked supplies contained anything with this name on the label, or if they were merely influenced by the adjacent and more impressive Mount Shaughnessy.

HENRY MACLEOD: Mount [3288 m]; 1902; Maligne. Coleman gave this name to honour Henry Augustine Fitzgerald MacLeod, a surveyor working on CPR locations for Sandford Fleming who reconnoitered the Maligne River in 1875 and was the first white man to report on its scenic and now famous lake.

HERCHMER: Mountain [2606 m]; 1916; S Rockies. William Hornaday indicates that he applied the name to this summit, which lies some 8 km north of Hornaday Pass, to honour Harry Herchmer, Esq. of Fernie, who was the head of the local game protective association. Another well-known Herchmer in Canada was Lawrence William (1840–1915), a native of Oxfordshire who had seen service in India and was commissioner of the RCMP for 14 years from 1886.

HERCULES: Mount [2893 m]; 1975; Windy. Near Jason and the Argonaut, Putnam's party applied this name as they wandered by on their tedious way across the high country of the Northern Selkirks. Pondering their descent into the uncomfortable and mosquito-filled depths of Norman Wood Creek, none of them felt too strong.

HERMIT: The [2597 m], **Mountain** [3050 m], **Glacier, Range**; 1887. Originally applied by Perley to the prominent peak on the north side of Rogers Pass, later renamed Tupper. The name was moved by Wheeler to the more massive, though less scenic, summit to the north, but remains on a prominent gendarme [2711 m] on the west ridge of Mount Tupper. The present recipient of the name "Hermit Mountain" was originally called "Stony," along with the creek draining its east slope, which the CPR spanned in 1884 with a spectacular wooden railway trestle. A mountain hut, periodically rehabilitated and relocated ever since, was established by the CPR in the alps below this massif in 1902.

HICKSON: Peak [3080 m]; 1969; Clearwater. Putnam suggested the name because this area had first been visited in 1930 by Joseph

William Andrew Hickson (1873–1956), professor of metaphysics and logic at McGill University and a persistent exploratory alpinist of the Canadian Alps. He served as president of the ACC and editor of its journal. He was also a lifelong patron of Edward Feuz Jr.

HIGH ROCK: Range; 1919; S Front. This name was given because of the cliffy nature of these ranges as seen from the east—out toward the Plains. The Highwoods are a companion group.

HIGHWOOD: River, Range, Pass [2210 m]; 1858; High Rock. This river appears with differing Native names on several early maps. The present handle was given by Blakiston because the wooded area along its banks extended to a much higher level above the watercourse than did most others he had noted.

HILDA: Creek, Mount [3060 m]; 1938; Icefield. The mountain is actually a part of the Athabasca massif overlooking the head of Hilda Creek. This name belonged to the maiden wife of Grim in the legend of Dietrich, but no one seems to know how it got applied in the Rockies.

HILLMAN: Mount [2861 m]; Badshot. Origin unknown.

HITCHHIKER: Peak [2717 m]; 1971; Windy. This name was given by David Peter Jones of Revelstoke, a member of the first party of alpinists to visit the Remillard Group. The prominent "thumb" on this otherwise forgettable peak's skyline ridge suggested the seeking of a ride—out—via Stitt Creek.

HOD: Mount [2775 m]; 1998; S. Purcells. This long dry ridge south of Baldr commemorates the blind god of Teutonic mythology.

HOLWAY: Mount [3043 m]; 1912; Moloch. Palmer gave this name to honour his sturdy climbing associate, Edward Willett Dorland Holway (1853–1923). A native of Michigan, Holway had for many years Holway had run the Winnishiek County State Bank in Decorah, Iowa, before taking a professorship in botany, specializing in rust fungi, at the University of Minnesota, where one of his colleagues was Professor Butters. He took up alpinism late in life, becoming proficient in 1906 as a student of Jacob Müller, Swiss guide at Lake Louise. Alpinism soon became Holway's obsession—and a productive one. He led the first ascent of this peak and numerous others. He was a fervent patron of Glacier House, and his ashes were scattered in the beautiful Asulkan Valley.

HOOD: Mount [2903 m]; 1922; Opal. Sir Horace Lambert Alexander Hood (1870–1916) was commandant of the Naval College, rear admiral and commander of the Third Battle Cruiser Squadron at Jutland. He went down with his flagship, *Invincible*. In his honour was subsequently named the largest battle cruiser ever built: 42,500 tons and the pride of the British Navy. *Hood*, however, went down in the next war, near Iceland, with all hands save one, after the third salvo fired against it by the more heavily armoured and almost equally swift German battleship *Bismarck*. *See also* Inflexible.

HOOGE: Mount [3206 m]; 1920; Lyell. This is the south summit of Monchy Mountain and bears the name of a small village east of Ypres where Canadian forces saw much action in the Great War.

HOOKER: Mount [3286 m], **Icefield**; 1827; Whirlpool. David Douglas named this summit (and ascribed its erroneously exalted altitude) after one of his patrons, Sir William Jackson Hooker (1785–1865), the famous English botanist and director of the Kew Museum and Gardens. *See also* Brown.

HOPE: Peak [2999 m]; 1966; Albert. Professor West, by coincidence or otherwise, serendipitously placed this name on the summit of that of his various "virtues" which lies nearest to Tomatin, eastward across the Incomappleux River.

HOREB: Mountain [2972 m]; 1915; Bugaboo. This is an alternate name for Mount Sinai and is the place referred to in Psalm 106 where the golden calf was worshipped. Stone suggested the name as a "scriptural allusion to the stream of water which ... appears to gush out of the solid rock high up on its face."

HORN: The [3012 m]; 1946; Adamant. This is the more prominent westerly point of Mount Unicorn and was applied by the first ascent party, led by Dr. Hendricks.

HORNADAY: Pass [1690 m]; 1905; S Rockies. William Temple Hornaday (1854-1937), American zoologist, was director of the New York zoological park and a sometime alpinist. He wrote *Camp-Fires in the Canadian Rockies* (1916), describing with loving concern the fauna of these mountains. His attitude toward wildlife stands in marked contrast to that of his contemporary, William Baillie-Grohman, whose obituary noted that a great regret of his life must have been that he had only killed 499 chamois. *See also* Canal.

HORNICKEL: Mount [2987 m]; 1910; Harrison. George Hornickel, a native of Cleveland, Ohio, was the first superintendent of the Elk Valley Coal and Coke Company, Ltd. In 1930, this name was abortively also suggested for a peak in the Purcell Range.

HORSEMAN: Spire [3002 m]; 1960; N Purcells. This was named by the West party because of a spectacular belay stance (straddling a ridge *au cheval*) that was required for the final pitch of the spire's first ascent.

HORSESHOE: Glacier; 1898; Lake Louise. Wilcox gave this name to the remnant glacier lying in the shadow of the five peaks at the head of Paradise Valley—Lefroy, Glacier, Ringrose, Hungabee and Wenkchemna. **Peaks**; 1969; SW Purcells. These are six summits around the north-facing basin near Truce Mountain, including names like Quibble, Tranquility, Squabble and Covenant, all close to 3155 m. **Mountain** [3090 m]; 1973; Cline. Tony Daffern, alpine bibliophile, found a horseshoe high on this peak while making what he had hoped would be its first ascent.

HORSETHIEF: Creek; 1885; Starbird. According to Harnden, an American and a Swede rustled some ponies belonging to an itinerant illegal-whiskey peddler. Apparently, after the dust settled on the "misunderstanding," there was a huge party at Fort Steele. Earlier, according to Mrs. St. Maur, the stream had been known as Slade Creek, after a local prospector, and in many early mining records it is simply referred to as #2 Creek.

HORSEY: Mount [2850 m]; 1961; Van Horne. This summit had been known as Drewry Tower and Buttress Mountain, but was officially renamed after George Frederick Horsey (1881–1960), a senior engineer for the national parks in B.C., 1916–46, who had been superintendent of Glacier National Park during the Second World War.

HORUS: Mount [2725 m]; S. Purcells. This peak, 2.7 km north of Jumbo Pass, was named for the principal deity of lower Egypt, often depicted as a falcon, with its two eyes being the sun and the moon. This summit has sometimes been referred to as Thoth.

HOUDINI: Needles [2663 m]; 1948; 82N/13; Adamant. When first seen from below on the Echo Glacier by Ferris, Kauffman and Putnam (the first ascent party), they could not imagine how this crest could be climbed. They soon found, however, that the back side (SE), as in so many similar cases, offered an easy route. The name, however, had already been given in recognition of their putative difficulty. Harry Houdini (1874–1926) was an American magician of Hungarian extraction (born Ehrich Weiss), known for his ability to get out of tight situations.

HOUND'S TOOTH: Mountain [2820 m] 1960; Bugaboo. This is a forepeak of the higher Marmolata and received its present name because it appeared clean of any means of ascent—until Layton Kor arrived on the scene.

HOUSTON: Creek, Glacier, Pass [2393 m]; 1930; Bugaboo. John Houston (1850–1910) was a dedicated member of the press who followed mining boom towns in B.C. He published the *Truth* in Donald

and Golden in 1888, then moved on to Nelson, where he brought out the *Miner*. Elected a member of the provincial parliament, he was soon faced with a motion calling for his expulsion—for appearing in the chamber drunk. (He defended himself by contending that if sobriety were a legislative requirement, there would never be a quorum.) He abandoned his office as mayor of Nelson in 1897, when two aldermen switched political sides on him.

HOWARD: Mount [2777 m]; 1939; Fisher. Edward Howard of the Alberta Forest Service retired in 1928. The summit had previously been known by as Moose Mountain.

HOWARD DOUGLAS: Mount [2820 m], **Creek**; 1922; Front. Howard Douglas (1852–1929) was commissioner of the national parks of Canada after 1911, having previously been superintendent of the Rocky Mountain (Banff) National Park from 1896. Meanwhile, he found time to serve as the first chairman of Calgary's school board, and at the time of his death was chief censor of theatres and motion pictures for the province of Alberta.

HOWSE: Pass [1530 m], **Peak** [3290 m], **River**; 1814; Waputik. Joseph Howse (1773–1852) was an explorer and fur trader for the HBC. Though not the first to do so, he crossed this pass (lower than the Kicking Horse by 100 m and easier) in 1810, and thereafter it was known by his name. He also wrote a grammar of the Cree language.

(Pages 126-127) Looking south from the summit of Mt. Oates. Serenity Mountain at left; Mt. Bowers in left centre foreground; Mt. Ermatinger at right centre and Mt. Hooker at right. GLEN BOLES PHOTO

Professor Eliot Coues says that Howse and Jasper Hawse are the same person. The name first appears on David Thompson's map.

HOWSER: Location [555 m], **Creek, Spires** [3399 m], **Peak** [3094 m]; 1900; Bugaboo. This name has a unique derivation, starting with the settlement on Duncan Lake, originally called Duncan City. The residents' mail having frequently been misdirected to Duncan on Vancouver Island, it was changed to Hauser, after a local prospector, and then anglicized. After Wheeler's 1910 foray into the Central Purcells with Longstaff, Kain and Harmon, the name was extended from the creek up to some of the high points near its head. The east ridge of the peak is adorned by several minor points, all named (and ascended) in 1946. The spires, however, have been a significant mountaineering challenge for many years, their west faces being among the most spectacular granite walls in North America.

HUBBARD'S ROOST: Ridge [2492 m]; 1992; Battle. Putnam named this easily ascended ridge just south of Schooner Pass and east of Omoo after his friend Donald Hubbard (1900–2000), American scientist and student of tectites, who would frequently absent himself

Howser Spires. GLEN BOLES DRAWING

from wood-splitting and other duties at the nearby Battle Abbey and go off in solitude to various high points.

HUBER: Mount [3368 m]; 1903; Bow Ranges. This summit, southwest of Mount Victoria, was named by Wilcox for Emil Huber (1865–1939), the Swiss alpinist from Zürich who was a member of the team that made the first ascent of Mount Sir Donald. See *The Great Glacier and Its House.*

HUESTIS: Mount [3063 m]; 1969; Clearwater. Eric Stephen Huestis, a native Albertan, was an ardent conservationist who served many years in the Alberta Forest Service. In 1963 he became deputy minister for lands and forests of Alberta until his retirement three years later.

HUGHES: Range [2846 m]; 1917; S Rockies. This was on Palliser's map as the Stanford Range. A half-century later it became the haunt of George Washington Hughes, a local miner and packer (at $90 per ton) who was a contemporary of Farnham and McMurdo. **Peak** [2624 m]; 1965; Gold. Walter F. Hughes, of the RCAF and Revelstoke, was killed in action during the Second World War.

HUGH NEAVE: Mount [2829 m]; Monashee. East of Hobson Lake, this was originally ascended as a survey point called Hobson Station.

HUGIN: Mount [2778 m]; 1999; Kokanee. Steven Horvath applied this name for one of the two ravens that sit on the Norse god Odin's shoulder (the other is Munin). Ravens are frequently seen in the Selkirks.

HUME: Creek, Pass [2410 m]; 1952; N Purcells. Here, Robinson honoured Horace Duncan Hume (1882–1945), a native of New Brunswick who ran Golden's Kootenay House after the turn of the 19th century. He was an occasional prospector and persistent grubstaker whose hostelry was quite popular with the miners from McMurdo and Bobbie

Howser Spire, west face. ROGER LAURILLA PHOTO

Burns creeks. His brother, J. Fred Hume, bought a hotel in Nelson after some years in the CPR dining car service. *See also* Forster.

HUNGABEE: Mount [3492 m], **Glacier**; 1894; Bow Ranges. This is from the Stoney word for chieftain and was given by Allen because of the dominating aspect of this peak relative to its neighbours.

HUNTER: Mount [2615 m]; 1859; Van Horne. Hector named this summit, which lies some 18 km east of Golden, after someone he admired; of that there seems to be little doubt. But for whom? Archdeacon James Hunter (1817–1882) was an Anglican missionary among the Cree who translated the Bible and other religious works into their language. John Hunter (1728–1793), a notable Scots anatomist and surgeon, was one of the most famous figures of the Scottish enlightenment, and taught Hector at the University of Edinburgh.

HUNTINGTON: Glacier, Creek; 1935; Cline. These features were named for Harvard mathematician Edward Vermilye Huntington (1874–1952), who was a member of a pack trip in this vicinity with Outram in 1924. Prior to the widespread use of computers, Huntington's tables of logarithms and trigonometric functions were standard items in schools and engineering offices. He also devised the politico-mathematical formula by which the 435 congressional seats are reapportioned every 10 years among the various United States.

HURD: Mount [2993 m], **Pass** [2635 m]; 1904; Ottertail. The Topographic Survey applied this one at the suggestion of guide and packer Tom Wilson. Major M.F. Hurd was a CPR layout engineer off and on from 1871, when he had begun a survey of the left bank of the Thompson River toward Eagle Pass. In the area where his name is applied, he was assistant to Major Rogers. This mountain was featured on a 10-cent stamp, issued in 1928 and taken from a painting by Canadian landscape artist Frederic Marlett Bell-Smith (1846–1923), himself a regular visitor to Glacier House and these mountains.

HYAK: Mountain [2870 m]; 1937; S Purcells. This was once called Chip Mountain, but was renamed at the suggestion of Dr. Thorington, who also moved the names of most of the vessels that had operated on the upper Columbia River from their graves along its banks to the high points of the southern Purcells. Hyak was another of the ramshackle riverboats that plied the stream from Golden to Invermere between the opening of the CPR main line in 1886 and the completion of the Kootenay Central branch in 1914, an event that effectively put the boats out of business.

Mt. Huber. GLEN BOLES PHOTO

*Admiral: That part of a warship which does
the talking while the figurehead does the thinking.*
—AMBROSE BIERCE, *THE DEVIL'S DICTIONARY*, 1906.

ICE: River, Pass [2665 m]; 1884; Ottertail. This name was applied by Dawson, who might well have found it chilly. **Dome** [2910m]; 1949; Cariboo. Hendricks' party found this summit to be well and fittingly described.

ICEFALL: Peak [3210m], **Brook**; 1918; W Rockies. This is the north summit of the Bush Mountain massif and is endowed with a spectacular icefall, as noted by the ABC. The name is somewhat generic and has been applied by other parties in other areas, most notably in 1977 to a **Mountain** [3221m] in the Clearwater area by distinguished Canadian alpinist Scipio Merler (1928–2004).

ICONOCLAST: Mountain [3236m]; 1902; Sorceror. This little-visited summit was named by Wheeler in recognition of its "black precipitous face." It took two women, Cora Best and Audrey Shippam, to summon up the fortitude to make its first ascent. *See also* Commander.

IDA: Mount [3180m]; 1912; Alexander. This name was transposed by S.P. Fay from the highest peak on Crete, famous in Greek mythology, to the more prosaic wilds of the Sir Alexander area.

ILLECILLEWAET: River, Glacier; 1865; Sir Donald. Walter Moberly, accompanied by several Shuswap guides detailed by the chief at Upper Arrow Lake, ventured up this river in his search for wagon routes and named it with his guides' word for "swift water". Unfortunately for his place in the history of Canadian transportation, Moberly followed the river's more northerly fork (Tangier Creek) to its headwaters pass with a northward-flowing stream (Sorceror Creek). Returning to try the east fork, Moberly was faced with a strike. It was late in the season, he was told; winter was coming, the other valley was inhospitable, with steep mountains down which tumbled many avalanches; they would surely be weathered in, if not killed. Reluctantly, he returned to the more hospitable terrain around the lake and his winter camp at Wildhorse Creek [Ymir], leaving Rogers Pass undiscovered for another 18 years. The glacier was the first in North America to be measured with scientific precision. *See also* Vaux, Ram, Peyto and *The Great Glacier and Its House.*

Mt. Ida. GLEN BOLES PHOTO

ILLUSION: Peak [2772 m]; 1947; Battle. This is the westerly point of the three summits making up Battle Mountain and was so named by Kauffman because he first thought it to be the entire mountain as he approached from the depths of the Incomappleux Valley. When he attained the summit, he realized he still had quite a way to go.

INADVERTENT: Peak [2963 m]; 1982; SW Purcells. Kruszyna meant to be climbing Mount Hamill, but got lost in the fog on the glacier approach and found himself making a first ascent—inadvertently. *See also* Intended.

INCISOR: The [2854 m]; 1974; Dawson. This is an excellent name for the "tooth" that marks the southerly high point of Mount Topham.

INCOMAPPLEUX: River; 1865; Battle. This is the Shuswap word for a variety of fish that was not comprehensible to Moberly. Nor was it to many others, for the stream often appears in early writings as simply "Fish Creek."

INDEFATIGABLE: Mount [2670 m]; 1917; British. This was the name of one of Britain's newer battle cruisers during the Great War. It was also the first ship sunk during the Battle of Jutland, on the afternoon of May 31, 1916, taking 1,015 men to their deaths.

INDIAN: Peak [2992 m]; 1912; Mitchell. This is a variation on the Red Man/White Man nomenclature also found nearby and was noted by White to have been in common usage at an early date.

INFLEXIBLE: Mount [3000 m]; 1917; Kananaskis. This was the name of a battle cruiser that fought in and survived the Battle of Jutland. Battle cruisers were warships in which armour protection was sacrificed in the interests of speed and armament. While the concept seemed meritorious, British speed was only rarely able to overcome the accuracy and devastating effectiveness of German gunnery. The cruisers' promotion to prominence as a class of fighting ship was due in great part to the advocacy of Winston Churchill, though toward the close of his eventful tenure as First Lord of the Admiralty he was pruning expenditures for them and reducing new construction. *See also* Hood.

INGLISMALDIE: Mount [2964 m]; 1887; Fairholme. Named by George Stewart, first superintendent of Rocky Mountain (Banff) National Park, to honour the ancestral home of the earl of Kintyre, a visitor in western Canada at the time.

INGRAM: Mount [2749 m]; 1960; SW Rockies. Frank Ingram of Fernie was killed in action in 1941.

INTENDED: Peak [3063 m]; 1985; S Purcells. When the sky cleared on Inadvertent Peak, Kruszyna realized where he was and decided that he would see about climbing this other nearby point another time. Unfortunately, someone else beat him to it.

INTERNATIONAL: Mountain [3053 m], **Basin**; 1888; N Purcells. This was originally the name of a mining claim filed by McMurdo on May 28, 1888, in an area of the Spillimacheen drainage he referred to as the Bobbie Burns Basin.

INTERSECTION: Mountain [2452 m]; 1924; N Rockies. Given by the ABC for the summit that marks the point whence the interprovincial boundary follows close to the 120th meridian, due north, rather than the northwesterly meanders of the Continental Divide.

INVERMERE: City [795 m]; Purcells. This was once called Peterborough, but it was frequently confused with a larger place of the same name in Ontario. The town's name was subsequently changed to one transplanted from the English Lake District, meaning "at the mouth of the lake."

INVERNESS: Peaks [2651 m], **Glacier**; 1911; Clachnacudainn. Wheeler applied this handle to some items in the Clachnacudainn Group, which seems sort of backwards, inasmuch as in Scotland, the "Stone of the Tubs" is but one feature within the City of Inverness.

INVINCIBLE: Mount [2730 m]; 1917; British; RS. This was the inappropriate name of one of the ill-fated battle cruisers whose speed, though great, was insufficient to save them from accurate German gunnery at the Battle of Jutland. It was Admiral Hood's flagship, but that did little to protect it when straddled by enemy fire at 5:34 on the evening of May 31, 1916. The ship's magazines exploded, and it broke in half, sinking with her entire manifest of 1,025 men.

IRISH: Creek, Peaks; 1967; Starbird. This was named by West in keeping with its proximity to the Scotch and Welsh peaks.

IRON: Ridge [2970 m]; 1959; Battle. Anger applied the name because of the immense quantities of climbing "iron" that were deemed necessary in order to make any progress toward an ascent. Subsequent alpinists have tended to agree with this judgement.

IRONMAN: The [3233 m]; 1946; Adamant. This name was bestowed on the north shoulder of Mount Austerity by the companions of Sterling Hendricks to commemorate one of his countless demonstrations of outstanding mountaineering proficiency. This one occurred during the climb on which he led his companions up the Granite Glacier to the second ascent and a new route on this prominent peak.

IRVINE: Mount [3060 m]; 1927; Icefields. Ostheimer suggested this name in honour of Andrew Comyn Irvine (1902–1924), the younger companion of George Leigh Mallory, Britain's climbing ace, on

Mount Everest in 1924. The success of the pair has never been determined. They were last seen above the 28,000-foot level by Noel Odell "going strong," and only Mallory's body has been recovered—far down on the north face.

ISABELLE: Peak [2938 m]; 1906; Ball. C.S. Thompson named this peak after his sister.

ISHBEL: Mount [2908 m]; 1956; Sawback. Ishbel Maria Marjoribanks (1857–1939), a staunch advocate of women's rights, was the daughter of the first Lord Tweedsmuir and wife of John Hamilton Gordon, the seventh earl of Aberdeen, who wrote with great concern about the peasants of Ireland.

ISIS: Mountain [2819 m]; 1973; Commander. This is the southernmost of the Egyptian Peaks of the Purcell Range, named by Wagner, and lies just north of Jumbo Pass. Isis was the moon goddess and mother figure in the Egyptian religion, and the consort of Osiris. *See also* Amon-Ra.

ISOLATED: Peak [2845 m]; 1916; Waputik. Outram and Whymper climbed this summit in 1901. Then located in the middle of a wide glacier, it was neither part of the Yoho peaks to the west nor the Balfour Group to the east. Whymper also used the name "Insular" for this peak.

ITALIAN: Group; 1920; S Rockies. A term of convenience initiated by guidebook editors to designate a group of mountains in the Southern Rockies of which the majority of the peaks' names are derived from prominent Italian figures of the early 20th century, mostly pertinent to Great War activities.

*See what it is to have a nation take its place among
civilized states before it has either gentlemen or scholars.
They have in the course of twenty years acquired a
distinct national character for low, lying knavery.*
—ROBERT SOUTHEY, LETTER TO W.S. LANDOR, 1812

JACKPINE: River, Pass [2040 m], **Mountain** [2560m]; 1913; N Rockies. This part of the Rockies is all jackpine country; *Pinus banksiana* is the predominant tree of the region. The pass was named by Mary

Jobe (Akeley) (1886–1966) on the second of her several expeditions to Mount Sir Alexander.

JAMES WALKER: Mount [3035 m]; 1959; Kananaskis. Colonel James Walker (1848–1936), Mountie, rancher, businessman and civic leader, was named Calgary's "Citizen of the Century" in 1975, the centennial of the city he helped found.

JANUS: Peak [2952 m]; 1989; Argonaut. Named by members of the Kootenay Mountaineering Club for the Roman god of doorways, and new beginnings.

JARVIS: Pass [1955 m], **Mount** [2152 m], Lakes, Creek; 1906; N Rockies. Edward Worrell Jarvis (1847–1894) came west in 1871 as a CPR location engineer under Sandford Fleming. With his rodman, Hannington, and other companions, he left Quesnel in early winter of 1874 and went east by dogsled from Prince George, trying to locate a suitable pass for the proposed transcontinental rail line. They covered a lot of ground and endured considerable hardship before finally emerging on the east—foodless, dogless and almost barefoot—at Lac Ste. Anne near the end of March 1875. Jarvis became a major in the Winnipeg field artillery in 1879, was officer #73 in the RCMP and ended his days as superintendent of the Regina post. The name was applied by R.W. Jones, a surveyor for the Grand Trunk Pacific.

JASON: Peak [2833 m]; 1975; Windy. This name was suggested by Putnam, after the mythological leader of the Argonauts and in keeping with this peak's proximity to Argonaut Mountain.

JASPER: Town [1054 m], **Park**; 1910. Jasper Hawse was an employee of the NWC and in charge of its Brûlé Lake post in 1817. The post was relocated some years later to a spot some 20 km northeast of the present town, where it served as an important staging point for the final voyageur move across the Athabasca Pass. Jasper House was abandoned in 1884 and settlers occupied what is now the present townsite in 1900, when it was briefly known as "Fitzhugh." *See also* Howse.

JELLICOE: Mount [3246 m]; 1919; British. Admiral John Rushworth (1859–1935), first Earl Jellicoe, was commander of the British Grand Fleet during the Great War and in direct charge at the Battle of Jutland. Though substantially outnumbered and outgunned, the German High Seas Fleet unknowingly inflicted many more severe losses than it suffered. Yet when the smoke cleared away, Britannia still seemed to rule the waves, even if inept reporting and leadership had enabled Admiral Tirpitz's fleet to get safely away. As the truth became apparent, the German "victory" greatly enhanced morale in Germany and helped to keep the war effort going for another two years. Jellicoe, however upstaged by his flamboyant subordinate, Beatty, was nevertheless supported by the British establishment and became Governor General of New Zealand after the war.

JERICHO: Wall [2910m]; 1960; Slate. This name has been around quite a while and belongs well in these mountains where many "walls come a-tumbling down," occasionally inspired by rams' horns, blown or otherwise.

JERRAM: Mount [2996m]; 1922; Opal. Vice-Admiral Sir Thomas Henry Martyn Jerram (1853–1933) was in charge of the China Station until 1915. He was then recalled to England and commanded the Second Battle Squadron of the Grand Fleet at Jutland. This unit consisted of eight battleships based in Cromarty Firth; they arrived too late to see much action in the conflict.

JIGGER: Peak [2728 m]; 1971; Battle. Putnam decided that this name belonged at the aft end of the Battle Range's westward-sailing schooner, of which Foremast is at the bow.

JOB: Creek, Pass [1494m]; 1892; Cline. Coleman named the pass and creek after an "enterprising Stoney Indian" named Job Beaver, his guide on his first trip to check on the elevated heights ascribed to Mounts Brown and Hooker.

JOFFRE: Mount [3449m], **Creek, Group**; 1918; French. The ABC named the highest peak of this area after Joseph Jacques Césaire "Papa" Joffre (1852–1931), commander in chief of the French army at the opening of the Great War. He received credit for French victory at the first Battle of the Marne in September 1914, where the German advance was halted. Students of military history have tended to agree that Joffre's generalship (despite the well-publicized use of Parisian taxis for military transport) was less responsible for checking the German drive than was the failure of the Imperial General Staff to adhere closely to the famous Schlieffen Plan. Joffre was greatly assisted by the efforts and initiative of the aging Gen. Joseph Simon Gallieni (1849–1916), recalled from retirement to be military governor of Paris, who appreciated better than anyone the degree to which the Germans had become overextended. Gallieni was posthumously made a marshal of France, but got no mountain in Canada.

JOHN LAURIE: Mount [2393 m]; 1961; Fairholme. This lesser but prominent summit, lying north of Exshaw and west of Morley, was named for John Laurie (1895–1959), of distinguished east Canadian ancestry who devoted his life to assisting First Nations in the Canadian West. He founded the Indian Association of Alberta and was elected an honourary chief of the Bloods, Sarcees and Stoneys. In addition, he received

Mt. Joffre. GLEN BOLES DRAWING

an honourary degree from the University of Alberta. The notable east-facing cliff of this mountain is commonly known as "Yamnuska" and is a popular shoulder-season high-angle climbing area.

JOHN OLIVER: Mount [3093 m]; 1928; Premier. "Honest John" Oliver (1856–1927) was a rancher and Liberal politician who served the last 10 years of his life as premier of British Columbia. In 1924 this summit was Carpé's "Aspiration Peak."

JOHNSTON: Creek, Canyon; 1882; Sawback. This was the name of an early prospector who assured Dawson there was gold in these mineralogically barren hills of the eastern Rockies. **Mount** [3093 m]; 1973; S Purcells. This, with Meden Agan and Atlung, was "Jackass Ridge" to Harnden in 1913. It was subsequently and officially named for Sir Harry Hamilton Johnston (1858–1927), a colonial administrator and explorer in Africa.

JONAS: Pass [2270 m], **Creek**; 1893; Maligne. Jonas was a chief among the Stoney people of Morley who furnished very helpful trail information to Professor Coleman and his brother.

JONES: Mount [2990 m]; 1952; 82N/10; Freshfield; RN. Kauffman gave this name for his sometime companion in these mountains, guide Kenneth Jones, who knew the ways of the upper Blaeberry River in the days before roads and who suggested ascending this heretofore unnamed summit. See *The Guiding Spirit*.

JORDAN: River, Range; 1965; Monashee. There are several rivers of this name in the world; the original translates to "the river of Dan" and flows into the Dead Sea.

JOSS: Mountain [2393 m], **Pass** [1356 m]; 1912; Gold; CW. This is the English term for a Chinese household deity and is also applied to for-

Justice Mountain and Justice Glacier. ROGER LAURILLA PHOTO

tune-telling items. While the mountain is sufficiently unexalted as to be below our "cut" for inclusion herein, it is home to a forestry lookout and is one of the few celestial names in this region.

JOUST: Mountain [2833 m] 1987; Westfall. Members of the Kootenay Mountaineering Club may well have had to tilt with crumbling rock fragments while making the ascent of this "rotten" peak.

JOWETT: Mount [2880 m]; 1945; Badshot. Alice Elizabeth Jowett (1853–1955) ran the Windsor Hotel in the town of Trout Lake for many years after 1903, keeping it open long after the local mining boom had subsided. She was a single parent as well as the owner of several profitable claims in the Badshot Range.

JULIAN: Mount [2760 m]; 1928; Maligne. Julian was the second son of Leopold Amery. The mountain was named by the father during his climbing trip through this area in company with guide Ed Feuz Jr. Julian followed the steps of his distinguished father in a career of public service. See *The Guiding Spirit.*

JUMBO: Mountain [3399 m], **Creek, Pass** [2279 m]; 1911; Commander. This summit derives its name (thanks to Harnden) from a mining claim encompassing 20.66 acres on Toby Creek, which was staked out October 25, 1890. Under the ownership of Daniel Corbin some of its ores were sent to England for processing. It was hoped the mine would be a big one, and its name was derived from that of Phineas Taylor

Barnum's massive elephant, which hit the North American scene in 1882 but met its match a few years later in the form of a Canadian locomotive.

JUPITER: Mount [2786 m]; 1902; Sir Donald. Named by Wheeler as encompassing its constituent summits, the previously named Castor, Pollux and Leda. This point sometimes appears in the mountain literature as Jove.

JUSTICE: Mountain [2879 m], **Glacier**; 1966; Albert. Professor West named this summit after one of the four cardinal virtues. *See also* Fortitude.

JUTLAND: Mount [2417 m]; 1918; Boundary. This summit, while not very high, commemorates the battle that could have lost the Great War for the British had it gone otherwise. On the other hand, had Jellicoe brought the Grand Fleet into action more effectively, it could have been a resounding victory. The mountain has a spectacular north-facing cirque with a charming tarn.

*Men are the constant dupes of names, while
their happiness and well-being mainly depend on things.*
—James Fenimore Cooper,
The American Democrat, xlvi, 1838

K2: Mount [3090 m]; 1938; Icefield. No, this handle was not transposed by Gibson from the Karakorum. Though invited to K2 in 1939, he never went there. Instead, he used this name to identify an outlying subsidiary summit of Mount Kitchener.

KAHL: Peak [3170 m]; 1967; Clearwater. Heinz Kahl (1933–1966), a native of Nurnberg, Germany, was a popular guide in the Rockies in the years after 1955. A generous and joyful man, he was never in the Escarpment Creek area, but his friends were—including us. His ashes, however, were scattered from the summit of Mount Temple.

KAIN: Mount [2880 m]; 1934; Robson. Conrad Kain (1883–1934) of Nasswald, Austria, came to Canada in 1909 and was employed for many years by the ACC. He is probably best known for his 1913 first ascent of Mount Robson, where the "Kain Face" is still regarded as a taxing but classic route. Kain was widely believed, in his time, to be the finest alpinist on the Canadian scene. He was a philosopher, friend and teacher, loved by all who knew him. In 1935, Dr. Thorington edited Kain's autobiography, *Where the Clouds Can Go*, and he abetted the process of putting Kain's name on the Canadian landscape.

KANANASKIS: Pass [2210 m], **River, Range**; 1858; British. Capt. Palliser named the pass after a Native man who was famous for surviving an axe attack.

KANE: Mount [3090 m], **Glacier**; 1920; Whirlpool. Wheeler suggested this name after Paul Kane (1810–1871), an early Canadian artist who travelled across the continent 1845–48, sketching as he went. His book *Wanderings of an Artist Among the Indians of North America* was influential in demonstrating the beauty, culture and possibilities of the great Canadian West. Walter Moberly clearly ascribed his decision to go there to having read this book. **Peak** [2789 m]; 1930; Kokanee. The brothers Kane, George Thomas (1862–?) and David Prosser (1871–1937), were pioneer landowners around Kaslo. They also had mineral rights, which assured them of prosperity. Natives of eastern Canada, they arrived in Kaslo in 1887, where George (the elder by nine years) was elected mayor in 1894.

KARAKAL: Mount [2966m]; 1952; Freshfield. Kauffman gave this name, recalling the dazzling pyramid at the entrance to Shangri-La from James Hilton's 1933 book *Lost Horizons*.

KARNAK: Mount [3399 m]; 1910; Commander. This name for an Egyptian temple was applied on the Canadian landscape by Stone and MacCarthy following the example of Earl Grey the preceding year.

KASLO: Town, River, Lake [1966 m]; 1889; S Purcells. This is an anglicizing of the name of the first prospector in this area, John Kasleau, who was sent here by the HBC in 1840 to obtain lead for bullets. He stayed on to look for gold and named the river for himself. Kasleau was the forerunner of the horde of miners that flooded the area a generation later.

KATHERINE: Lake [2373 m]; 1898; Murchison. Harry Pierce Nichols (1850–1940) was rector of Holy Trinity Church in New York, an indefatigable White Mountain hiker and a member of several first-ascent teams in the Canadian Alps. He also served as president of the AAC and was extremely popular with all who knew him. On one trip into the Rockies, C.S. Thompson named several alpine lakes after the ladies in "Uncle" Harry's life. Alice was his wife, and his three daughters were Katherine, Helen and Margaret. **Mountain** [2941 m]; 1929; S Purcells. Thorington christened this summit, only half a kilometre north of Christine, with his wife's middle name. *See also* Griswold.

KAUFMANN: Peaks [S 3110 m, N 3095 m]; 1902; Waputik. Christian (1872–1939) and Hans (1874–1930) Kaufmann were strong, handsome members of an old Oberland guiding family. Their father, Peter, had been employed by the CPR in 1903 and the sons worked summers for the CPR until 1906. See *The Guiding Spirit* for details of their employment and subsequent termination. Whymper named these two peaks in their collective honour. There is also a **Lake** [2057 m] in the Bow Ranges (82N/8) named for their father.

KELLIE: Peak [2820 m]; 1936; Gold. This point and the creek on 82K/13 were named for James Michael "Pothole" Kellie (1848–1927), a prospector and politician of Nelson and Revelstoke. He served as MPP for the West Kootenay 1891–96. His nickname was derived from his unique (and erroneous) assumption that gold was most likely found in the depths of waterfall-scoured potholes.

KELSEY: Mount [2482 m]; Jasper. In the years 1690–92, Henry Kelsey (1667–1724) made the first inland trip of any consequence for the HBC. After a period during which his value to the company was questioned, he was made governor of York Factory in 1717. He deserves a more prominent peak than this one, for it was on the strength of his one trip that the HBC managed to hang on to their charter when subjected to pointed questioning by a committee of the House of Commons.

KELVIN: Mount [2910 m]; 1953; N Purcells. Professor Robinson named this summit for William Thompson (1824–1907), first Baron Kelvin, the outstanding British man of science of his day. Primarily a mathematician, he was known worldwide for his research into esoteric physical issues, such as absolute zero. He was an original member of the Imperial Order of Merit. Lord Kelvin took his titled name from a river that enters the Clyde at Glasgow, where he taught at the university.

KEMMEL: Mountain [3120 m]; 1918; W Rockies. The ABC applied this name in keeping with the widespread practice of naming summits in these mountains after places in France where Canadians had seen extensive military action in the First World War. Kemmel is a small village 8 km south of Ypres.

KENT: Mount [2635 m]; 1917; Kananaskis. HMS *Kent*, a destroyer, was involved (but not sunk) in the Battle of Jutland.

KENTIGERN: Mount [3176 m]; 1928; Clearwater. Cautley applied this name after the patron saint of Glasgow, sometimes referred to as Mungo (518–603). After numerous tribulations Kentigern succeeded in converting the North Britons to Christianity, becoming known thereafter as the "apostle of Strathclyde."

KERKESLIN: Mount [2950 m]; 1858; Maligne. This name appears on Hector's map, north of Moberly and east of Christie, but since his narrative is silent on any derivation, this may well have been another gratuitous offering from mapmaker Edward Stanford.

KERR: Mount [2863 m]; 1907; Waputik. Robert Kerr (1845–1916) was passenger traffic manager of the CPR and largely responsible for the popularization of visits by Whymper and other dignitaries. Whymper also applied this patron's name to the pass connecting this peak to Mount Marpole.

KEYHOLE: The [2713 m]; 1910; Kokanee. This high and narrow pass is aptly named as it provides access to the Kokanee Glacier from the west.

KICKINGHORSE: River, Pass [1625 m]; 1858; Waputik. Dr. Hector was kicked by a recalcitrant pack horse when his exploring party was moving up this valley in the vicinity of present-day Leanchoil. The blow rendered him senseless for some time. In fact, his companions had almost given him up for dead when Hector awoke and recovered. The event gave rise to the name of the river, and then to the pass at its head, which Hector's party crossed a few days later.

KIDD: Mount [2958 m]; 1953; Kananaskis. There were two brothers of this name who ran the general store at the town of Morley. John Alfred Kidd did so from 1902 to 1907, but the summit was named for his brother Stuart (1883–1956), who ran the store for the next four years before moving on to Nordegg. Stuart was elected Chief Tah-Osa of the Stoneys in 1927.

KILLARNEY: Peak [2941 m]; 1969; Starbird. This name comes from a district in County Kerry, applied here in the Irish Range by Professor West.

KILPATRICK: Mount [3234 m]; 1904; Purity. Wheeler named this one for Thomas Kilpatrick (1857–1916), CPR superintendent at Revelstoke and founder of the Revelstoke Club. In 1901 he had been elected alderman and a dozen years later became mayor, the same year that the Donald station was closed and his responsibilities for the railway increased dramatically.

KINBASKET: Lake [max 754 m], **River**; 1865; W Rockies. According to Walter Moberly in his book *The Rocks and Rivers of British Columbia*, "[Paul Ignatius] Kinbaskit was a very good Indian." Moberly had negotiated with the Kootenay chief for the use of some canoes and guiding service. They went downstream, running some rapids, but wisely portaging around the worst, Surprise Rapids, until they "came to a lake [674 m] which [Moberly] named Kinbaskit Lake, much to the old chief's delight." The name, which translates to "touch the sky," was briefly lost in 1973 after the construction of Mica Dam and its cremation of the briefly named McNaughton Lake. Popular demand prevailed, however, and the old chief's name was returned in 1980 to the much enlarged body of water. The river, which drains westwards from the Clemenceau Icefield to the Columbia, was formerly called Middle, as it entered the chief's original lake at the middle.

KING: Mount [2892 m]; 1886; Van Horne. This was named by Klotz "after my confrere," William Frederick King (1854–1916), who followed Klotz as chief astronomer of Canada and then served as inspector of surveys. King was also the Canadian member of the International Boundary Commission from 1908 until his death. **Mountain** [3115 m]; 1978; Icefields. This was the highest point and centrepiece of Kruszyna's chess set, but he found it "very easy to conquer."

KING ALBERT: Mount [2981m]; 1918; Royal. King of the Belgians, Albert I (1875–1934) was an accomplished alpinist whose relaxation and recreation was rock climbing, although he died in a fall at Marche Les Dames. During the Great War his heroic stand, staying constantly with his troops, won him the admiration of the Allies and the respect of the Germans. This summit appears to be that named "Robinson" by Palliser in 1859, after the British astronomer and meteorologist Thomas Romney Robinson (1792–1882), who invented the cup anemometer in 1840.

KING EDWARD: Mount [3490m]; 1906; Icefields. Mary Schäffer applied this name in honour of Edward VII (1841–1910), who came to the British throne in 1901 following the death of his long-lived mother, Queen Victoria. A point [2810m] on the Kishenina Ridge near Waterton Park was also named for him.

KING GEORGE: Mount [3422 m]; 1916; Royal. This is the centrepiece of the group, and the ABC named it for George V, king of Great Britain and Ireland, emperor of India, Defender of the Faith, etc., who saw his nation through the Great War and the uncertain peace that ensued. The remaining summits are named for the members of his immediate family. *See also* Prince Albert.

KINNEY: Lake [984m]; 1912; Robson. Reverend George R. Brown Kinney (1872–1961), a native of New Brunswick but then resident in Victoria, made a last try at ascending Mount Robson from the Emperor Falls in 1909 with guide Curly Phillips. It was a valiant attempt, and years later Ed Feuz went so far as to state that Kinney, not Kain, had made the first ascent of Mount Robson. The lake is a prominent landmark along the trail up to the Robson Glacier, just below the point where the trail steepens to pass the impressive waterfalls. Kinney, who had been in the forefront of ACC climbers, retired from alpinism when his claimed ascent was disbelieved and finished his clerical career with the United Church of Canada at missions on Kootenay Lake.

KITCHEN: Range [2970 m], **Glacier**; 1958; W Rockies. This minor group at the western edge of the Rockies is prominent in the view down Swan Creek from the Adamant Range and highly visible from the kitchen window of the Bill Putnam Hut at Fairy Meadow. After repeatedly being asked for the name of "that bunch of mountains, over there," the builder of the cabin, in exasperation and after prompting by Hendricks, decided to name them. In 1979, several of the high points became official—**Stovepipe, Lid** and **Poker.** Lifter and Leg were rejected in favour of **Sophist** and **Solitude.** In 1902, Collie had named this group after Fred Stephens (1864–1928), a native of Michigan who had been his packer in 1900 and 1902 and later achieved great fame and admiration as a Canadian Rockies trail guide and outfitter.

KITCHENER: Mount [3480 m]; 1919; Icefields. Horatio Herbert (1850–1916), first Earl Kitchener, became the foremost British military figure since the Duke of Wellington. He first came to public attention in the campaign to relieve "Chinese" Gordon at Khartoum in 1885 and then served as governor of the Sudan. He was later commander in chief of India, became field marshal in 1909 and was lost at sea when the cruiser HMS *Hampshire* struck a mine while taking him on a mission to assist the military efforts of the Russians.

KIWA: Creek, Glacier; 1962; Cariboo. This is the Shuswap word for "crooked" and referred to the river. *See also* Sir John Abbot.

KIWETINOK: Peak [2902 m], **River, Pass** [2455m]; 1901; Waputik. This is the Stoney word for "on the north side" and appears to have been applied here by Klotz.

KLAHOWYA: Mount [2911 m]; 1931; S Purcells. This was another of Armstrong's riverboats that navigated the upper Columbia. Built in 1910, it boasted a summer schedule in 1911 of three round trips a week, leaving Golden at 7 a.m. on Tuesdays, Thursdays and Saturdays. The name, in Kootenay, allegedly means "greetings, friend."

KLOTZ: Mountain [2628 m]; 1886; Hermit. German-born Otto Julius Klotz (1852–1923) was astronomer to the Topographical Survey of the Selkirks, then chief astronomer to what was then called the Department of Mines and Technical Surveys. In 1917 he became director of the Dominion Observatory. He had worked on preliminary surveys of the Railway Belt.

KNIGHT: Mount [2906 m]; 1954; Jasper. Richard H. Knight (1877–1931),

DLS 1904, of Bruce Mines, Ontario, was superintendent of Jasper National Park after 1929. **Peak** [3060 m]; 1978; Icefields. This is one of the lesser pieces of Kruszyna's chessboard peaks.

KOALA: Peak [2941 m]; 1972; Starbird. This is the northerly part of Mount Sally Serena. Wagner avers that he applied the name because of the speckled appearance of the summit from the east.

KOKANEE: Park, Peak [2789 m], **Lake, Glacier, Group**; 1890. This is the Kootenay word for "red fish," referring to the landlocked salmon. It was also applied to a well-known sternwheeler that plied Kootenay Lake from 1896 to 1923.

KOOTENAY: Lake [532 m], **River**; 1845. The name comes from the Kootenay First Nation (called the "Lake Indians" by Father De Smet) from their words for water (*co*) and people (*tinneh*). Thompson, in 1808, had named the river after McGillivray. **Plain** [1345 m]; 1858; Cline. This location was known to Hector as a meeting place for an annual "fair" between the First Nations people of the intermountain region and those of the Plains. The locale is now mostly flooded by Abraham Lake. This was just downstream from the grassy bottomland later known as Wilson's Ranch for Tom Wilson, who bred horses there after 1910.

KRINKLETOP: Peak [2789 m]; 1954; N Purcells. This was known as Barrier to Robinson until he found that that name was already taken. He then derived a name from the distinctive chevron folding of the Horsethief Creek Formation displayed in this ridge.

I detest the American character as much as you do.
—Walter Savage Landor, to Robert Southey, 1812

LA CLYTTE: Mountain [2910 m]; 1920; W Rockies. The ABC suggested this to recognize the town used as a divisional reserve point by many Canadian units in the Great War.

LADY GREY: Mountain [3155 m]; 1910; S Purcells. This mountain was named in association with Earl Grey (1851–1917). His lady, Alice (née Holford), was with him when the popular Governor General visited this area.

LADY MACBETH: Mountain [2880 m]; 1960; W Purcells. This is the next peak south of Macbeth and was named by Professor West in accordance with his theme for this group of peaks.

LADY MACDONALD: Mount [2605 m]; 1886; Fairholme. This name was given at the time of Lady Macdonald's visit to Banff National Park soon after its initially small extent was designated, though then with a different name. Susan Agnes Bernard was the second wife of Sir John and outlived him by many years with the title of Baroness Macdonald of Earnscliffe. *See also* Agnes.

LAGGAN: Location [1540 m]; Lake Louise. This was the original name for what is now called Lake Louise Village and was derived from a location in the Great Glen of Scotland, which was the site of the bloody defeat of Clan Fraser by Clan Macdonald in 1655.

LAGRACE: Mount [2766 m]; 1925; Maligne. This was the name of one of the HBC's Native hunter-guides employed by the earl of Southesk during his 1859 trip through the northern frontal ranges of the Canadian Rockies. LaGrace was a colourful and distinctive character who seems to have had no other name or record beyond his service with the HBC. Principal Grant referred to him in 1872 as "Legrace" and "an old mummy."

LAKE: Mount [2911 m]; 1969; W Purcells. This name was given by Wagner after Stanley and Ethel Lake, a dry-humoured homesteading couple of Johnson's Landing. He was an occasional prospector in the area above Trout Lake.

LAKES: Peak [2850 m]; 1953; N Purcells. Peter Robinson applied this name because the peak rises some 600 m above a pair of alpine lakes in the basin to the north. However, it should be noted that Arthur and Harold Lakes owned the Wesko Exploration Company which had significant mineral interests in this area in the 1930s.

LAMBE: Mount [3181 m], **Glacier**; 1918; Freshfield. This name was applied by the ABC to honour Lawrence Morris Lambe (1863–1914), a paleontologist on the staff of the GSC.

LANCASTER: Mount [3155 m]; 1918; Italian. This was the name of a British warship engaged (but not sunk) in late spring 1916 at the Battle of Jutland.

LANGUEDOC: Glacier; 1975; Windy. Putnam suggested this name for the southern part of the French Glacier, Languedoc being a region in southern France. When his party was traversing this portion of the Northern Selkirks, he noted that the warming climate had caused the glacial mass to diminish and become two separate and distinct features.

LAPENSÉE: Mount [3106 m]; 1921; Fryatt. Olivier Roy Lapensée was a member of the NWC party moving eastward from Astoria in 1814. He was drowned while crossing the Athabasca River below Brûlé Lake.

LARDEAU: River, Location, Formation [539m]; 1912; S Selkirks. There used to be a post office, initially designated as "Lardo," on Kootenay Lake (it was established in 1899). The name appears to have been a linguistic corruption from that of an HBC voyageur. The formation is widespread in the Columbia Mountains and largely shunned by climbers because of its "incompetence."

LAST CHANCE: Peak [2941 m]; 1956; Bugaboo. This insignificant snow bump does not deserve a name at all; one descends to it from Mount Malloy. However, this name has always been popular with miners and was once the name of the present capital city of Montana, whence a number of the prospectors who roamed these hills had come.

LAUSERHUE: Mount [2940 m]; 1980; N Rockies. This is an acronym from the names of the members of the first ascent party—Roger **Lau**rilla, Conrad Gmo**ser** and Samuel Good**hue**.

LAUSSEDAT: Mount [3059 m]; 1911; Freshfield. This summit is named after Aimé Laussedat. *See also* Colonel.

LAW: Mount [2990 m]; **Creek**; S Purcell. On the ridge between Law and Gopher creeks.

LAWRENCE: Peak [3090 m]; 1927; Chaba. Ostheimer applied this name after making the peak's first ascent. He had in mind Thomas Edward Lawrence (1888–1935) "of Arabia," the Welsh-born hero of desert warfare in the Great War. Unfortunately, most of Ostheimer's submissions to the Board on Geographic Nameswere mislaid and not acted upon until almost 60 years later, if at all.

LAWSON: Mount [2795 m]; 1922; Kananaskis. The son of a Cambridge-educated musician, Major Walter Edward Lawson was a topographer with the GSC; he was killed in France during the Great War.

LEAH: Peak [2801 m]; 1912; Maligne. This summit is very near Samson Peak and was named by Mary Schäffer after the missionary-given name of Samson Beaver's wife. Leah was the Old Testament daughter of Job, the senior wife of Jacob and mother of several sons, including Judah.

LEANCHOIL: Locality [1113 m]; 1884; Van Horne. This place, a whistle stop near the sharp bend of the Kicking Horse River, derived its name from Barbara Stuart's ancestral home near Inverness. She was the mother of Sir Donald Smith, Lord Strathcona, who worked his way up to become the dominant figure of the HBC and also of the CPR in its difficult early days. Whymper urged the railway management to develop this area, citing its waterfalls and hoodoos, as well as the beauties of the Ice River Valley.

LEANING TOWERS: Group; 1932; S Purcells. This name was applied by McCoubrey and is purely descriptive inasmuch as all the granitic peaks of this group are of "writing desk" configuration. The major jointing planes in the igneous rock of which they are composed have resulted in precipitous south faces and relatively gentle approaches on the north. The group was earlier referred to as the Fry Pinnacles, as these summits rise above the headwaters of that creek.

LEDA: Mount [2701 m]; 1902; Sir Donald. This name was given by Wheeler in association with the adjacent twin peaks, Castor and Pollux. Leda was their mother in the mythology of ancient Greece. Zeus, their father, approached Leda in the form of a swan. *See also* Jupiter.

LEES: Mount [2972 m]; 1930; S Purcells. Thorington named this one after James Arthur Lees (b. 1852), the other author of *BC 1887*, who, also with Clutterbuck, had previously written *Three in Norway*, a similar travel account.

LEFROY: Mount [3423 m]; 1858; Bow Ranges. Hector named this after Gen. Sir John Henry Lefroy (1817–1890), who was principally noteworthy for his studies of terrestrial magnetism. Lefroy performed such measurements throughout the British empire, including a series at Fort Edmonton in 1844. His other scientific observations might qualify Lefroy as the founder of Canadian meteorology. Hector applied this name to a peak above Vermillion Pass, but the name was relocated due to misinterpretation of Hector's narrative by subsequent visitors.

LEITRIM: Peak [2911m]; 1971; Starbird. This county name from Northern Ireland was brought to these mountains by Professor West.

LEMAN: Mount [2665 m], **Lake** [1938 m]; 1918; Royal. Belgian Lt. Gen. Gerard Mathieu (Comte de) Leman (1851–1920) was the brilliant defender of Liege during the Great War. His defensive actions were a major contribution to the ultimate outcome of the first Battle of the Marne.

LEMPRIERE: Mountain [3208 m], **Town** [744 m]; 1863; Monashee. Lt. Arthur Reid Lempriere was an English military engineer who helped lay out wagon roads in the interior of British Columbia between 1858 and 1863. He was a contemporary, in this work, of Walter

Moberly. Back home in England, Lempriere retired in 1882 with the rank of major-general.

LENS: Mountain [3150m]; 1918; W Rockies. This city in northeast France, whose origins date to Roman times, was in the centre of the Canadian Sector in the Great War.

LEROY: Mount [2970m]; 1919; British. Osmond Edgar LeRoy headed the British Columbia division of the GSC. He was killed at Passchendaele in the Great War, during the costly offensive Gen. Haig mounted in order to draw enemy attention from the many mutinous elements of the French Army. This otherwise fruitless offensive was one of the major causes for the immense number of poppies that later grew in Flanders' fields. *See* Mangin.

LESTER PEARSON: Mount [3063m]; 1973; Premier. This summit, at the southeast of the Premier Range, honours Lester Bowles Pearson (1897–1972), Nobel Peace Prize winner of 1957 and prime minister of Canada, 1963–68. The summit had been called "Zillmer"in 1962.

LEVAL: Mount [2760m], **Creek**; 1924; Royal. Gaston de Leval, legal counsellor to the American Legation in Brussels, diplomat and authority on international law, showed a serious and chivalrous concern for the welfare of Edith Cavell, who was court-martialled and executed for having helped Allied soldiers escape from occupied Belgium. Leval is equally well known for his authoritative writings on jurisprudence.

LEVERS: Mount [2940m], **Pass** [2545m]; 1970; Monashee. Trooper James M. Levers of North Canoe was killed in action during the Second World War. Wallerstein, who ought to know a dome when he saw one, had previously suggested the name "Castle Dome" for this summit, but he was overruled.

LICK: Creek, Peak [2880m]; 1921; Fryatt. The derivation of this name is similar to that of many other "Licks" throughout North America—game animals congregated here because there were alkaline minerals in the soil necessary for their healthy digestive functioning.

LIEUTENANTS: The [3216m]; 1960; Commander. These peaks, both First and Second, lie at the southwest border of the Lake of the Hanging Glaciers. They were named by Professor West for their subordinate position relative to Mount Commander. *See also* Sergeant.

LIGHTHOUSE: Tower [2960m]; 1964; Icefields. This spectacular pylon on the east ridge of Mount Saskatchewan is visible for miles, particularly as one drives north along the Icefields Parkway. In some later writings it was referred to as "Cleopatra's Needle"' after the well-known Egyptian obelisk presently in New York City.

Leaning Towers Group. GLEN BOLES DRAWING

LILLIPUT: Mountain [2908 m]; 1917; Waputik. The ABC applied this name because the jumble of rocks along the mountain's skyline resembled a horde of the little people from Jonathan Swift's *Gulliver's Travels*.

LILY: Glacier, Col [2454 m]; 1889; Sir Donald. Green named the dwindling patch of ice for the young daughter of Reverend Henry Swanzy, his cousin and companion in exploring the Selkirk glaciers.

LIMESTONE: Mountain [2180 m]; 1975; Opal. It's true—this mountain, while hardly deserving of a name in its own right, being merely a bump on the northwest shoulder of The Wedge, is composed wholly of limestone. Likewise the **Peak** [2878 m] on 82N/1 in the Ottertail Range.

LINEHAM: Peak [2730 m], **Lake** [2134 m], **Creek**; 1916; Boundary. John Lineham (1857–1913), a native of England, worked his way west with the CPR and took up timber rights in the Highwood River area. He was quite successful and got into other development projects as well as territorial politics. This summit, however, lies considerably to the south of his principal area of activity.

LION: Mountain [3150 m]; 1958; Cline. This name and the equally exalted **Lioness** were fittingly bestowed by Eric Hopkins on the east and west summits, respectively, of Mount Resolute. Lion was also the name of Admiral Beatty's flagship, a British battle cruiser based in Harwich that was in the thick of the battle of Jutland—and survived, though somewhat the worse for wear.

LISTENING: Mountain [3150 m]; 1919; Chaba. Named by the ABC for the pointed resemblance of a portion of the summit skyline to a pair of wolf's ears on the alert.

152

LITTLE: Mount [3140m]; 1896; Bow Ranges. George Thomas Little (1857–1915) was librarian of Bowdoin College in Maine and an active member of the AMC and later the AAC. The summit was "Nom" or #2 on Allen's map of the Ten Peaks.

LIVINGSTONE: Mount [3094m]; 1858; Icefields. David Livingstone (1813–1873) was a noted explorer and missionary of east and central Africa. The name was originally applied considerably south of this region by Lt. Blakiston of the Palliser Expedition. It was set in its present location by Thorington in 1927. Happily, Mount Stanley is quite close beside.

LLOYD GEORGE: Mount [2925 m], **Group**; 1946; N Rockies. David Lloyd George (1863–1945), first earl of Dwyfor, entered the British parliament in 1890, becoming Chancellor of the Exchequer in 1908. He was responsible for many social-rights improvements and was a confirmed Liberal, an understandable result of his impoverished youth in Wales. As prime minister from 1916 to 1922, he saw the Great War to a successful conclusion and lived long enough to see his old political rival, Winston Churchill, bring the British Empire safely through its sequel. There are a number of summits in this group and some adjacent ranges (Great Snowy and Great Rocky) whose names are not included in this text—they lie beyond the classic realm of early North American alpinism. However, some of the names in that area are well worth attention, having been placed on the land by an unusually erudite set of alpinists, ranging from the sublime Everester, Francis Sydney Smythe (1900–1949) to Dr. Robert West.

LLYSYFRAN: Peak [3141 m]; 1911; Maligne. This is from an old Vaux family name and was given by Mary Schäffer, though she failed to provide details on how the Vauxes came by their Welsh antecedents. In any case, the name is a derivative of the famous and widespread Lewis family.

LOCKWOOD: Peak [2880m]; 1966; Royal. Henry F. Lockwood, of Radium, was killed in action during the Second World War.

LOKI: Mount [2771m], **Creek**; 1902; Valhalla. First appearing on a map of the GSC, Loki is the Norse god of fire, strife and humour. The Joker Lakes are not far distant to the west, but they owe their name to a poker game among miners.

LONGSTAFF: Mount [3180m], **Glaciers**; 1911; Whitehorn. Wheeler suggested this name in honour of Thomas George Longstaff (1875–1964), physiologist, medical doctor and alpinist of distinction. He made 20 visits to the Alps, six to the Himalayas, five to the Arctic, two to Canada and one to the Caucasus, but his best-known activity was in connection with early British attempts on Everest. His younger sister Katherine was an alpinist as well. His brother, Frederick Victor (1879–1961), was a Victoria-based architect, naval historian and chronicler of the famous Glacier House. *See also* Wedgewood.

LOOKOUT: Pass [2530 m]; Ramparts. **Mountain** [2508 m]; 1890; Sir Donald. This is a self-evident name. In the second application, it was coined by Perley for a point above the lower Illecillewaet Glacier that was a popular day walk from Glacier House.

LOOMIS: Mount [2822 m]; 1928; High Rock. Maj. Gen. Sir Frederick Oscar Warren Loomis (1870–1937) of Sherbrooke, Quebec, joined the army as a private in 1886 and rose to command the Third Canadian Division in the Great War. He received the KCB in 1919.

LOOP: Brook; 1885; Sir Donald. This creek, of little mountaineering but great railroading interest, was named by the CPR construction staff because of the convoluted curve described by their track as it gained altitude from the west in order to attain the height of land at Rogers Pass. The "loop" into Loop Creek gained them an additional 120 feet, thus allowing the original grade to the pass to stay at an acceptable 2.5 percent. Most of the sturdy masonry piers for one of the stream crossings remain as challenges to rock climbers.

LORETTE: Mount [2487 m]; 1922; Kananaskis. This was a battle site in northeast France where Canadian troops distinguished themselves during the Great War.

LOTOSKY: Mount [2970 m]; 1961; Freshfield. Trooper William W. Lotosky, of Golden, was killed in action on July 4, 1945.

LOUDON: Mount [3220 m], **Creek**; 1956; Murchison. William James Loudon (1860–1951), author and educator, was professor of mechanics at the University of Toronto. On the side, he wrote a treatise on smallmouth bass and a biography of Joseph Burr Tyrell (1858–1957), *A Canadian Geologist*, in 1930; in addition to eight volumes on studies of his students' lives. His father was also a distinguished educator and a founding fellow of the Royal Society of Canada.

LOUGHEED: Mount [3105 m]; 1928; Kananaskis. Sir James Lougheed (1854–1925) became Queen's Counsel for the North-West Territories in 1885 and thereafter served in various capacities in the federal government as well as occasionally in private business (general counsel for the CPR, etc). His grandson, Peter, became premier of Alberta in 1971. The provincial park is named for the latter. The summit was "Wind Mountain" to Bourgeau in 1858.

LOUIS: Mount [2682 m]; 1916; Sawback. Louis Beaufort Stewart (1861–1937), DLS 1882 (DTS 1887), following in the footsteps of his

Mt. Lucifer. GLEN BOLES PHOTO

father, and the layout team for Banff National Park; he then became professor of surveying and geodesy at the University of Toronto. This summit of vertically standing Devonian limestone is one of the classic rock climbs in the Canadian Rockies. Stewart was also a companion of Coleman on the latter's exploratory forays of 1892 and 1903.

LOUISE: Lake [1731 m], **Town** [1545 m]; 1886. Named by the CPR for Louise Caroline Alberta (1848–1939), the fourth daughter of Queen Victoria. She became the wife of the Marquis of Lorne, who served as Governor General of Canada from 1878 to 1883. In 1882 the lake was named Emerald by Tom Wilson, who had been shown the body of water by Native guide Edwin Hunter. According to Stoney tribal councillor Felix Poucette, in an alternate version we rather like, a Stoney woman was standing near the lake when Tom Wilson approached her and asked what the lake's name was. Mistakenly thinking he was asking for her name, she told him "Louise." In fact, the locals had called it the Lake of the Little Fishes. The CPR had a chalet at the northern end of the lake from 1890, subject to interruption by fire in 1892 and 1924, and the formal divestiture of its hotel properties in 2000. The town and station stop had initially been called "Laggan" by the CPR. Since the rebuilding in 1925, the Chateau Lake Louise has evolved into one of the premier resorts in North America.

LOUIS LEE: Creek; 1865; Windy. Moberly named this tributary of the Goldstream after another of the men who came north with Downie and Carnes to prospect the Northern Selkirks in 1865. They had all left by the end of 1866, and the first Big Bend Gold Rush was at an end.

LOUIS ST. LAURENT: Mount [2390 m]; 1927; Premier. Louis Stephen St. Laurent (1882–1973) was a lawyer and professor of law at Laval University. He became active in Liberal politics and succeeded William Lyon Mackenzie King (1874–1950) as prime minister for the years 1948 to 1959.

LOW: Mount [3090 m]; 1920; Freshfield. Albert Peter Low (1861–1942) was an Arctic explorer and geologist who became director of the GSC and deputy minister of mines.

LOWELL: Mount [3150 m]; 1924; Fryatt. This mountain was named by Ostheimer and other Harvard Mountaineering Club members to honour the president of Harvard University, Abbott Lawrence Lowell (1856–1943), a mountaineer of some consequence and brother of the astronomer Percival, and the poetess Amy.

LUCIFER: Mount [3060 m]; 1956; N Rockies. **Peak** [2758 m]; 1976; Valhalla. This is another of the Kootenay Mountaineering Club's

Lyell Icefield. GLEN BOLES PHOTO

hellish names, but here applied to a nice-looking mountain. *See also* Devils Couch.

LUNETTE: Peak [3398 m], **Creek, Lake**; 1913; Assiniboine. The ABC gave this name, perhaps because someone looked at it through a French telescope. This had been Outram's "Lost Peak" when he climbed it in the fog, unaware of its existence, while attempting the first ascent of Mount Assiniboine—from the south. The next day, the preacher kept more to the left and did it right.

LUNN: Mount [2910 m]; 1966; N Rockies. Lt. Gerald A. Lunn, of the RCAF and Quesnel, was killed in action during the Second World War on April 17, 1944.

LYALL: Mount [2952 m]; 1928; High Rock. David Lyall (1817–1895) of Auchinblae, Scotland, was a naval surgeon (on HMS *Plumper*) and naturalist. He had been on the Belcher Arctic Expedition of 1852–54 and then served on the IBSC. On the Belcher trip, he collected 1,375 species of plants, many of which were named after fellow expedition members. On this same trip he studied and described the beautiful alpine larch (*Larix lyalli*) of the high western timberlands of North America, a landmark tree in the southern Canadian Rockies and Purcells.

LYAUTEY: Mount [3082 m], **Glacier**; 1918; French. Gen. Louis Herbert Gonzalve Lyautey (1854–1934) was minister of war for France in the final years of the Great War and later a highly regarded administrator of then French-held Morocco.

LYCHNIS: Mountain [3155 m]; 1912; Clearwater. Named after a large family of alpine flowers of which the campions are the rarest and most showy.

LYELL: Mount, Creek, Icefield, Group; 1858; N. Rockies. Hector named this major peak of the Continental Divide for one of the important patrons of the Palliser Expedition, Sir Charles Lyell (1795–1875). A lawyer by training, Lyell developed great interest in natural history and geology, becoming noteworthy in both fields. In 1972 the five distinct points of this prominent summit received the given names of the five Swiss guides who settled in Golden in 1912 and thereby started a notable chapter in the history of alpinism. See *The Guiding Spirit*; also Walter.

LYNX: Mountain [3180 m], **Creek**; 1908; Robson. L.Q. Coleman found the skeleton of one of these short-tailed mountain cats on the glacier below this summit.

Hell trembled at the hideous name,
And sighed from all her caves...
—JOHN MILTON (1608–1674), *PARADISE LOST*

MCARTHUR: Mount [3015 m], **Lake** [2249 m], **Pass** [2210 m]; 1886; Waputik. Named by Klotz for James Joseph McArthur (1856–1925), DLS, of Aylmer, Quebec, who performed much of the topographic survey work in connection with the 49th Parallel marking through the Rockies in 1887. He later served with the Alaska Boundary Commission and was responsible for much of the topographic work in the Railway Belt surveys of 1887–93. He ended his days of public service with distinction as the Canadian member of the International Boundary Commission after 1916. The name was once applied to the point now called Mount MacPherson.

MCBEAN: Mount; 1902; Purity. This double peak was named by Wheeler for the proprietors of the Tomatin distillery in Scotland at that time. There is no record of Wheeler's experience with their product (which is a good one), but the first ascent was made by a Scotsman. *See also* Findhorn.

MACBETH: Mount [3033 m], **Group**; 1960; SW Purcells. Its proximity to Duncan Lake inspired Professor West to label the group as a whole after one of Shakespeare's most famous plays. This group might be the Mount Aurora identified by Longstaff and Wheeler from near Bugaboo Pass in 1910.

MACCARTHY: Mount [3062 m], **Glacier**; 1954; Bugaboo. Professor Robinson gave this name after Albert Henry MacCarthy (1876–1955), a graduate of the U.S. Naval Academy who went into private business but came back to service during the Great War as a captain in the United States Navy. He is far better known, however, for having organized and co-led the 1925 expedition that made the first ascent of Mount Logan, Canada's highest mountain and the second highest in North America. He climbed often in the Purcell Range and bought a ranch (Karmax) near Windermere in 1921 from Charles Ellis. MacCarthy climbed often with Conrad Kain. *See also* Pert.

MCCONNELL: Mount [3140 m], **Creek**; 1913; Clearwater. Richard George McConnell (1857–1942), geologist and explorer, was a pillar of the GSC. An assistant to Dawson in 1882, he later became deputy minister of the department of mines. The mountain was named the same year that he was elected to the Royal Society of Canada. This gentleman is not to be confused with N.E. McConnell, who worked for the Topographical Survey in the Columbia Mountains in the 1930s and left a number of other names on the landscape.

MCCOUBREY: Mount [3216 m]; 1926; Farnham. Alexander Addison McCoubrey (1885–1942) was a location engineer for the CPR and primarily responsible for the layout of the Kootenay Central Railway along the upper Columbia River (started in 1911 and completed in 1914). Thereafter, he made a number of first ascents in the Purcell Range and was an important member of the ACC. The mountain was called Peacock on Stone's map of 1915, because the glacier below it glittered in the afternoon sun as seen from Mount Peter.

MCCUAIG: Mount [2884 m]; 1958; French. Maj. Gen. George Eric McCuaig (1885–1957) commanded a division in the Great War and was a stockbroker between conflicts. Previously this had been Fennell Mountain.

MACDONALD: Mount [2883 m]; 1897; Sir Donald. This is the imposing south wall of Rogers Pass, a landmark to a century of transcontinental travellers. Sir John Alexander Macdonald (1815–1891), "Old Tomorrow" of Canadian politics, was the beloved father figure of his dawning nation, despite his known failings (well publicized by the opposition). With one short absence, he held the prime ministership from the founding of the Dominion of Canada until his death—an event that some Canadian newspapers announced with headlines reading only: "HE IS DEAD." The summit was originally known to CPR crews as Mount Carroll, but was renamed by order-in-council. The CPR's two tunnels beneath Rogers Pass were bored almost directly under this mountain.

MCDONALD: Mount [3151 m], **Creek;** 1935; Cline. Angus McDonald was one of the 12 sons of Archibald McDonald (1790–1853) and Jane Klyne [Cline]. He became active in the Western and Oregon departments of the HBC.

MCDONNELL: Peak [3270m]; 1921; Ramparts. This was the maiden name of Mrs. Simon Fraser and was applied here by the ABC. It should be noted, though, that there were two Canadian generals of this name involved in the heavy fighting around Zillibeke. A.H. commanded the Fifth Brigade and Archibald Cameron the Seventh.

MCDOUGALL: Mount [2726m]; 1884; Fisher. Reverend George Millward McDougall (1821–1876) worked among the Stoney people. When he froze to death in a blizzard, his sons, David and John, carried on the work until the latter's death in 1917. *See also* Morley.

MACDUFF: Mount [2990m]; 1960; W Purcells. This was a part of Professor West's Shakespearean outburst. Shakespeare gives credit to Macduff, thane of Fife, for the overthrow and death of the usurper, Macbeth, in 1057. In fact, it was the deed of Malcolm III, Cean More. *See also* Banquo and Macbeth.

MCGILL: Mount [2671 m]; 1907; Hermit. Joseph Hickson made the first ascent of this peak with Edward Feuz Jr., then in his sixth season of work in Canada. Hickson named it after the famous university where he was employed. James McGill (1744–1813), merchant and philanthropist of Montreal, though born in Glasgow, left most of his wealth to establish what is now Canada's oldest and one of its most prestigious institutions of higher learning.

MCGILLIVRAY: Mount [2445 m]; Front. **Ridge** [2716 m]; 1812; Whirlpool. The name seems to have been applied to the ridge by Gabriel Franchère. Both features are named for members of a family prominent in the affairs of the NWC. William Henry (1764–1825) was the eldest of three brothers and the one for whom Fort William was named. Duncan (1770–1808) and Simon (1783–1840) were equally active in the fur trade, making many journeys of great difficulty throughout the mountain and arctic country.

MCGREGOR: River, Pass [1535 m]; 1916; N Rockies. James Herrick

McGregor (1869–1915) was the first president of the B.C. Surveyors' Association. He was killed at Ypres.

MCGUIRE: Mount [3030 m]; 1971; Churchill. Fenton John Alexander "Mickey" McGuire (1911–1973) joined the National Park Service in 1937 and served as chief warden of Jasper National Park, 1957–71.

MCHARDY: Mount [2791 m]; 1974; S Selkirks. Climbed and named by the Kootenay Mountaineering Club for one of its own.

MCHARG: Mount [2892 m]; 1918; French. Lt. Col. William Hart-McHarg, who had served in the Boer War, was a Rossland lawyer in civilian times. He became executive officer of the First British Columbia Regiment and was killed during the Great War. This is the west twin summit of Mount Worthington.

MACHRAY: Mount [2749 m]; 1923; Robson. This name, on the mountain standing south across from The Colonel, was given by the Board on Geographic Names to honour Robert Machray (1831–1904), Anglican archbishop of Rupert's Land from 1865 to his death.

MACKENZIE: Mount [2461 m]; 1887; W Selkirks. This relatively minor summit southeast of Revelstoke was named by the CPR in honour of Alexander Mackenzie (1822–1892). He served as prime minister of Canada, 1873–78, during which time serious construction on the CPR was begun in the east and along the Fraser Canyon in the west. *See* Onderdonk. The northeast buttress of this summit was originally called Tilley after another Father of Confederation.

MACKENZIE KING: Mount [3264 m]; 1962; Premier. William Lyon MacKenzie King (1874–1950) was the grandson (and proud of it) of one of the great rebels of Canadian history, William Lyon Mackenzie (1795–1861). When the grandfather's poorly organized rebellion of 1837 fizzled, he fled to the United States, where he found that American democratic institutions were no less human than the imperial ones of Canada. The grandfather's Liberal political image, however, had a lasting effect on the grandson; having rejected a knighthood in 1946, he served longer as prime minister than any other person in Canadian history (1921–1948), guiding his nation through its worst of times. The summit had been called Mount Hostility by Zillmer.

MCLANDERS: Mountain [2758 m]; 1969; W Purcells. Wagner named this after William McLanders, a squatter and sometime miner of the Duncan Lake area.

MCLAREN: Mount [2825 m]; 1962; High Rock. Senator Peter McLaren (1833–1919) was a prominent landowner hereabouts, back in the days before Alberta became a province.

MCLENNAN: River, Glacier; 1872; Cariboo. Roderick R. McLennan

(1842–1907) of Winnipeg assisted Marcus Smith in the fieldwork connected with early CPR surveys for the Yellowhead Pass route. A few years later he was a contractor for some of the CPR's most difficult construction, in the muskeg area north of Lake Superior.

MCLEOD: Mountain [2880m], **Creek**; 1969; W Purcells. This was another of Dr. Wagner's names; he had in mind one Red McLeod, a likeable horse "borrower" for whom Ta Ta Creek was allegedly also named.

MCMURDO: Creek, Location [790m]; 1888; N Purcells. Archibald McMurdo (d. 1894) was a miner from Golden who prospected the upper tributaries of the Spillimacheen River with sufficient success that the entire area was known as the McMurdo district in 1888. After he died of kidney failure, Carbonate Landing on the Columbia was renamed in his honour.

MCNAUGHTON: Mount [2905m], **Lake**; 1924; Robson. Archibald McNaughton (1843–1900) was the youngest of the Overlanders. He became the HBC's manager in the Cariboo and served as postmaster of Quesnel. His name was applied to the mountain. But that of Andrew George Latta McNaughton (1887–1966) briefly superseded that of Kinbasket on the lake. The latter rose to the rank of brigadier-general in the Great War and commanded the First Canadian Army in the Second World War. Between times, and after the second conflict, he served his nation extensively as a diplomat. After the Mica Dam was completed in 1973, his name was given to the impoundment behind it, but by 1980 a surge of popular support had restored the name of Kinbasket, a Canadian statesman of an earlier era.

MACNICOL: Mountain [2789m]; 1969; W Purcells. This name was suggested by Wagner after James MacNicoll, homesteader of Johnson's Landing, trapper and sometime mountain guide.

MCNICOLL: Mountain [2594m]; 1908; Hermit. The CPR named this isolated summit in honour one of its own. David McNicoll (1852–1916) joined the CPR in 1883 and became its general manager in 1900. He was elected a director and vice-president in 1907. *See also* Vice-president.

MACOUN: Mount [3033m]; 1889; Dawson. Initially dubbed North Sentinel by Topham, for its position guarding the opening to Glacier Circle, this summit was renamed by Green to honour naturalist John Macoun (1832–1920). Macoun was born in Ireland and spent considerable time studying the flora of what are now the prairie provinces. His widely published reports on the agricultural possibilities of this wide area were helpful to the colonizing efforts of the CPR. He and his son, James, had visited Glacier House a year before Green. *See* Macoun's book *Manitoba and the Great Northwest* (Guelph, 1882).

MCPHAIL: Mount [2883 m]; 1924; High Rock. N.R. McPhail of the surveyor general's staff was killed in action in 1917 during the Great War.

MACPHERSON: Mount [2405 m]; 1890; Gold. This minor point southwest of Revelstoke was named for Sir David Lewis Macpherson (1818–1896), a father of confederation who served as minister of the interior, 1883–85, during the heyday of CPR construction through the mountains of British Columbia.

MCQUARRIE: Mountain [2688m]; 1918; Kokanee. Robert Mungo McQuarrie (1867–1918) was the first president of the Kootenay Mountaineering Club, a now defunct group that did much in the early 20th century to popularize recreational climbing in this already worked-over mining area.

MACCARIB: Mountain [2658 m], **Creek, Pass** [2180 m]; 1916; Jasper. This is a widespread Native word for caribou, applied here by Bridgland, who was constantly meeting small herds of them in his mountain travels.

MAGNIFIER: Mountain [2791 m]; 1995; Lardeau. Between Tenderfoot and Spyglass. We don't know the origin of this name.

MAGOG: Lake [2143 m], **Mount** [3095 m]; 1930; 82J/13; Assiniboine; RS. **Spire** [2608 m]; 1948; 82N/13; Adamant; CC. This is an oft-used name for one of a pair of "giants." The term comes from the names of two survivors of a mythical super-race mentioned in Ezekiel and Revelations. The name also appears in various English legends. *See also* Gog.

MAHOOD: Mount [2911 m]; 1871; Jasper. New Brunswick-born James Adam Mahood (d. 1901) was employed under Sandford Fleming as a surveyor for the CPR explorations in the Yellowhead Pass route. During the winter of 1871 he crossed from Tête Jaune Cache to Isaac Lake.

MAIERHORN: [3216 m]; 1974; Cline. Franz Maier, a Swiss guide of a considerably younger generation than the famous Feuz brothers, was employed for the summer by CMH and was intent on leaving his mark in Canada. To help in so doing, Putnam suggested he make a first ascent. "Of what?" asked the guide. "Of that one, there," said Putnam, pointing to the east of their campsite. "What is its name?" asked the guide; and Putnam had to make one up quickly.

MAINMAST: Peak [2863 m]; 1972; Battle. This is the highest of the four points making up the Schooner Ridge. It lies between Foremast and

Mt. Mackenzie King. GLEN BOLES PHOTO

Mizzenmast and was named by Kauffman who led its first ascent, accompanied by David Michael, Arnold Wexler and John Markel.

MAJESTIC: Mountain [3086 m]; 1916; Jasper. The name was suggested by Bridgland because he was impressed with the summit.

MALACHITE: Spire [3002 m], **Creek, Pass** [2235 m]; 1947; N Purcells. Malachite is a green copper carbonate and a common trace ore of the metal. It is found extensively in portions of the Purcell Range. *See also* Azurite.

MALIGNE: River, Lake [1671 m], **Pass** [2235 m], **Mountain** [3913 m]; 1846. Father De Smet named the river "nasty" for reasons unspecified, and the name spread to adjacent features. H.A.F. MacLeod discovered the lake and aptly named it Sorefoot (anyone unwise enough to walk extensively or take horses over the gritty surface of the limestone predominating around its shores will understand why). Mary Schäffer's Native friends called it *Chaba Inme*, which translates to "Beaver Lake."

MALLARD: Peak [2844 m]; 1920; Whirlpool. The ABC noted a ducklike rock near the summit and so derived the name.

MALLOCH: Mount [3099 m]; 1920; Clearwater. George Malloch (d. 1914) was a Canadian geologist and Arctic explorer. He had mapped the area surrounding this summit.

MALLORY: Mount [3270 m]; 1923; Icefield. George Herbert Leigh

164

Mallory (1886–1924), mathematician and Cambridge don, distinguished himself on the 1922 Assault Expedition but lost his life two years later in a summit attempt on Mount Everest in company with Andrew Irvine. His frozen and broken body was found down on the North Face some 70 years later by a Chinese team. The name was applied here by Thorington.

MALLOY: Creek, Mount [3002 m], **Pass** [2690 m]; 1957; N Purcells. Charles Malloy, a Nelson miner and prospector, worked the Silver King claim in 1889 and then disappeared from the local mining fraternity roster.

MALTON: Range; 1963; Monashee. This was the name of a village, actually one of the traditional "rotten boroughs" of English politics, that was the home of Lord Milton. Both Milton's father and uncle had been members of Parliament from Malton. Albreda Station, on the one-time Canadian Northern, was just below these mountains at the head of Albreda River.

MANGANESE: Mountain [2920 m]; 1924; Ottertail. This mountain lies in the only mineralized zone of the Canadian Rocky Mountains, an area that runs northwestward from here through the Goodsirs to just beyond Field, where active mining of base metals took place as recently as 1947.

MANGIN: Mount [3058 m]; 1918; French. Gen. Charles Merle Emmanuel Mangin (1866–1925) was one of the most significant figures in the costly defence of Verdun. He succeeded Petain after the latter had been placed in command of all French forces following the catastrophic Nivelle offensive of April and May 1917. The bloodshed at Verdun was enormous, largely unnecessary and partially responsible for the mutiny that ensued. Mangin was thereafter known among the *poilus* as le Boucher—"the Butcher."

MANX: Peak [3044 m]; 1916; Jasper. Bridgland is alleged to have thought that the shape of the mountain resembled the coat of arms of the island of Manx.

MARBLE: Mountain [3180 m]; 1970; Maligne. This name crept onto the maps because of the quality of the local limestone, marble being merely a version of the usual calcium carbonate.

MARCONI: Mount [3105 m]; 1920; Italian. Marchese Guglielmo Marconi (1876–1937) is widely regarded as the inventor of radio. This is not quite true, but his name is rightly associated with the first practical uses of the radio spectrum. A native of Bologna, his first experiments were done over a 2 km range, communicating with his uncle on the family farm outside of town. Marconi's greatest contribution to the use of radio was recognizing the value of reflective elements in antenna design, both for reception and transmission. He left Italy in his 20s and lived thereafter mostly in England, where his work assumed great importance in the communications needs of the Royal Navy, keeping it consistently ahead of the competition. In the Great War, for instance, the Admiralty knew at once of every order given and position taken by a German capital ship.

MARGARET: Lake [1792m]; 1898; Waputik. Named by C.S. Thompson for a daughter of Reverend Harry Pierce Nichols. *See also* Katherine.

MARION: Lake [1722 m]; 1889; Sir Donald. This was the name of the young daughter of Reverend Green and was applied by the doting, if absent, father. Small and mosquito-ridden, the lake is on the lower north slope of Mount Abbott. **Mount** [2966 m]; 1961; 82K/6; S Selkirks; CS. Marion had been the name of Capt. Armstrong's small, shallow-draft vessel that he used in the late season when water was low. In 1909 it was taken apart and shipped over Rogers Pass to Revelstoke, where it was reassembled for use on the Arrow Lakes. The vessel had been partially bankrolled by the Cochrane family, of early Alberta ranching fame, who had business interests near Windermere.

MARLBOROUGH: Mount [2973 m]; 1917; French. This was the name of Admiral Burney's flagship during the Battle of Jutland. It was the victim of a torpedo and fell out of action but was able to return to base and be refitted for service. However, it was less able to withstand the forces of peace, becoming a victim of the 5–5–3 Washington Naval Limitation agreement; it was scrapped in 1930. The name came into the British lexicon from the titled name of John Churchill, the first duke of Marlborough (1650–1722), who, as the famous "Iron Duke," defeated the French forces in the Wars of the Spanish Succession at the outset of the 18th century.

MARMOLATA: Mountain [3033 m]; 1930; Bugaboo. Cromwell gave this name because the mountain resembled the highest of the Italian Dolomites, not from any accident with marmalade. Once called "Center Peak" from its position between the branches of the Bugaboo Glacier, it stands south across the main stream from Snowpatch. Its easterly forepeak is called Hound's Tooth.

MARMOT: Mountain [2597 m], **Pass** [2245 m]; Murchison. This is a common name in alpine areas, generally deriving from the presence of these "whistlers" doing their thing. *See also* Arctomys, Bobac, Groundhog and Siffleur.

MARPOLE: Mount [2997 m]; 1901; Waputik. Whymper suggested this name to honour Richard Marpole (1850–1920) of Vancouver, who was born in Wales. A 20-year veteran of the CPR, he became general executive assistant of the Pacific Division. On the earliest Dominion maps this point was Mount McMullen, after John Mercier McMullen (1820–1907), a journalist whose third edition of *A History of Canada* appeared in 1892.

MARSHAL: The [3190m]; 1913; Assiniboine. Lying to the northwest of Sturdee, this summit was named by the ABC for its leading position to the west of the Assiniboine group.

MARTEN: Mountain [2747m], **Creek**; 1953; S Selkirks. This weasel-like animal, sometimes a nuisance in mountain cabins, is about the size of a domestic housecat and thrives on a similar diet. The woods of British Columbia are full of them.

MARTHA: Mount [3170m]; 1967; Clearwater. This was the name of the lady friend of Bradford Fuller Swan, a member of the first ascent party.

MARTIN: Creek, Lake [1871m]; 1916; Clearwater. Henri Martin (1879–1959) was the Swiss consul in Montreal during the pre-Great War years when the Swiss guides imported by the CPR encountered a few employment adjustment problems. He was of material assistance to the guides who travelled widely in these mountains, and they were grateful.

MARTINI: Peak [2830m]; 1995; Battle. An early ascent party enjoyed a pre-mixed martini in celebration of the ascent. *See also* Thomas.

MARTINS: Peak [3027m], **Creek**; 1912; Ottertail. Thomas Mower Martin (1838–1934) was a landscape artist of distinction. Born in London, he founded the Royal Canadian Society of Landscape Artists. He visited frequently in these mountains, often as the guest of the CPR. See his book with poet William Wilfred Campbell (1861–1918), *Canada* (London, 1907); 77 of Martin's works are reproduced therein.

MARVEL: Peak [2660m], **Creek, Lake** [1789m], **Pass** [2125m]; 1917; Assiniboine. This name followed the ABC's pattern of applying superlative names in this area. It was also the name of a destroyer of the 12th Flotilla that was involved in the Battle of Jutland. *See also* Wonder.

MARY VAUX: Mount [3201m]; 1908; Maligne. Mary Vaux Walcott (1870–1940) came from a prominent Philadelphia family that was, among its other distinctions, collectively responsible for the first serious and sustained glaciological studies in the mountains of Canada. She was an original member of the ACC and was the first woman to serve on the U.S. Board of Indian Commissioners. Both of her brothers served as treasurer of the AAC, and her husband was director of the United States Geological Survey and subsequently of the Smithsonian Institution. He was also for many years the American member of the International Boundary Commission. The name was applied by Mary Schäffer. *See also* Vaux.

MASON: Mountain [2880m]; 1969; SW Purcells. This was named by Wagner for "Sandy" Mason, a native of Scotland who worked at the Mount Lavina fire-lookout tower for 22 years and was of considerable help to climbers, advising them on means of access to the peaks to the east.

MASSEY: Mount [2940m]; 1927; Chaba. Standing across the Athabasca valley from Mount Alberta, Ostheimer suggested this name to honour Charles Vincent Massey (1887–1967), educator, military officer and industrialist (Massey-Harris). He was the first Canadian minister to the United States, 1926–30, and was Canadian High Commissioner in London, 1935–46. He served as Governor General of Canada, 1952–59, the first Canadian-born person to do so.

MASTODON: Mountain [2940m], **Glacier**; 1924; Ramparts. The ABC applied this name because someone was imagining ancient elephants rampaging around the area. This summit is near Elephas.

MATHER: Mount [2966m]; 1960; Freshfield. Corporal William Mather, of Donald, was killed in action on April 22, 1945. His name was applied here as part of a program instituted in the 1960s to honour those who died in the Second World War by naming features of the landscape near their homes after them.

MAUDE: Mount [3042m], **Brook**; 1918; British. Maj. Gen. Sir Frederick Stanley Maude (1864–1917) was, among other things, private secretary to the Governor General of Canada, 1901–4. During the Great War he was responsible for the campaign that took the city of Baghdad.

MAYE: Mount [3246m]; 1928; Starbird. This was the given name of Mrs. Thomas Starbird and was originally applied to the Lake of the Hanging Glaciers. Upon McCoubrey's instigation, the name was transferred to the high point east of the lake after the ACC held its 1928 summer camp in this area.

MAZINAW: Mountain [3006m]; 1970; Battle. This is the lower northeast summit of Mount Nautilus and was named by Iroquois Walter Robinson for the lake in Bon Echo Provincial Park, some 130 km southwest of Ottawa, which was a favourite practise area for the party making the first ascent of this peak.

MEDA: Mount [2904 m]; 1921; N Front. Origin unknown; named by the GSC.

MEDEA: Mount [2719 m]; 1975; Windy. This one is near Argonaut and was named by Putnam for the enchantresss of Greek mythology who, among her other activities, helped Jason get the Golden Fleece away from her father, Aeëtes, king of Colchis.

MEDEN AGAN: Mountain [3295 m]; 1971; Farnham. Wagner named this after "the cryptic message recorded at the Oracle of Delphi and meaning 'nothing too much.'" (Misspelled on map sheet 82K/10.)

MEDICINE: Lake [1436 m], **River**; 1859; Maligne. This name was known to the Earl of Southesk and is a translation from the Cree, indicating ceremonial or religious aspects of tribal visits to the area.

MEDICINE TENT: River; 1875; Maligne. This name (somewhat akin to the previous entry) was first applied by the earl of Southesk after being informed that some of his guides' people used to set up a tent in this valley for certain religious observations.

MELVILLE: Glacier, Group; 1964; Battle. Herman Melville (1819–1891), after leaving his New York City home for a life at sea, wrote numerous stories, of which *Typee, Omoo, Redburn, White Jacket, Moby Dick* and *Billy Budd* have found their way onto the landscape of the Battle Range, along with some of the subordinate characters in these stories. The trend of nomenclature Anger and Silverstein initiated in this area has had considerable extension.

MEPHISTOPHELES: Mount [2728 m]; 1976; Valhalla. This name was suggested by Pat Ridge of the Kootenay Mountaineering Club as fitting the theme of sorcery and hellish names that had been established in this area. The original was a devil who won the soul of Doktor Johann Faustus, according to 16th-century German legend.

MERCER: Mount [2970 m], **Creek**; 1918; Sundance. Maj. Gen. M.S. Mercer, CB, commanding the Third Division of the Canadian Expeditionary Force, was killed in action at Zillibeke on Flanders' Fields in 1916.

MERIONETH: Peak [2667 m]; 1969; Starbird. The name of a county in Wales was applied here by West because the other names in this immediate area all have Welsh origins.

MERLIN: Lake [2234 m], **Valley, Castle** [2840 m]; 1911; Slate. Named for the picturesque towers overlooking the lake, which prompted one early observer to imagine them part of a magician's domain.

MERMAID: Mountain [2765 m]; 1971; Windy. Noting the nautical and mythological theme of other names farther north in the Windy

Range, Kauffman and Putnam, organizers of the first climbing party to enter the Remillard Group, applied this name to the peak at the northern end of the Yardarm Ridge for the skyline's seeming resemblance to the uplifted tail of a mermaid.

MESSINES: Mountain [3100 m]; 1920; Lyell. This town in Flanders is near Ypres and was the scene of severe fighting by Canadian units in the final years of the Great War.

METAWAMPE: Mount [3090 m]; 1967; Cline. This is an Agawam aboriginal name that was brought from the Berkshire hills of Massachusetts to western Canada by a group of AMC climbers.

MICA: Creek, Dam; 1901; Windy. **Creek, Mountain** [2850 m]; 1924; Cariboo. This is a name with an obvious derivation, applied in the first case by Golden prospector Percival "Kid" Price, who found in a chasm sheets of mica that measured as much as 23 by 15 inches. In the second instance the name was applied by Carpé after noting that the creek seemed to be flowing with fragments of this platy mineral. Nevertheless, it is now known as Tête Creek.

MICHAEL: Peak [2696 m]; 1901; Waputik. Whymper suggested this name in honour of his friend, Harvard chemistry professor Arthur Michael (1853–1942), a prominent member of the AMC.

MICHEL: Peak [3077 m]; 1901; Dawson. This was applied by Wheeler in honour of Friedrich Michel of Meiringen, who was briefly employed as a guide at Glacier House. He became so homesick after only a few weeks on the job in 1901 that he was discharged. The peak is the lowest and most westerly of the various summits of Mount Dawson, and Michel never got near it. *See also* Feuz.

MIDGARD: Peak [2789 m]; 1961; Valhalla. This is the Norse mythological name for the Earth, formed by the sons of Bor from the inert body of Ymir.

MIDGE: Peak [2911 m]; 1937; S Purcells. Thorington named this peak after the shallow-draft launch that Baillie-Grohman brought overland to Bonners Ferry, Idaho, and thence into the Kootenay district of B.C. The boat was admitted duty-free into Canada as an agricultural implement, necessary, said Baillie-Grohman, for pulling a plow across his flooded bottomlands. *Midge* was one of the two boats that actually made the trip through his canal. The name of the boat may have come not from the insect but from that of the miller's son, a companion of Robin Hood. *See also* Canal.

MIDWAY: Peak [2917 m]; 1918; Waputik. This summit was determined by the Interprovincial Boundary surveyors to be just about halfway between Stairway Peak and Mount Synge. **Peak** [2946 m];

Mermaid Mountain from Windy Creek. ROGER LAURILLA PHOTO

1974; Remillard. Partway along the ridge west of the OK Glacier, this peak lies across Windy Creek from Mount Onderdonk and was named by Thomas Dabrowski and his friends.

MIETTE: River, Roche [2316 m], **Pass** [1965 m]; 1866; Jasper. Hector says (and Henry Moberly agrees) that this was the name of a NWC employee known as Bonhomme Miette, who made the first ascent of the rock and sat on the top of the cliff smoking his pipe. Miette is also the French word for "crumb"or "morsel."

MIKE: Mount [3300 m]; 1964; S Rockies. Pte. 2 Sebastian Mike, of Cranbrook, was killed in action during the Second World War.

MILTON: Mount [3185 m]; 1863; Monashee. William Wentworth Fitz-william, Viscount Milton (1839–1877), was an epileptic and eldest son of the Sixth Earl Fitzwilliam, who travelled with his physician and amanuensis, Dr. Cheadle, across these mountains in 1863. When moving down the Albreda River they saw "a magnificent mountain, covered with glaciers," to which Cheadle applied the name of his friend and employer.

MINARET: Spire, Col [2800 m]; 1911; Sir Sandford. Palmer gave this name to the crumbling, 40 m pylon of insecure rock that stands in the col west of Mount Sir Sandford. It has defied all who have pondered a safe way to make its ascent. The best suggestion to date was advanced by Judge David Michael, who advised a "basket-weave" approach by several multimembered roped parties climbing simultaneously.

MINNEWANKA: Lake [1475 m]; 1916; Front. The name appears to be a translation from the Cree, meaning "lake of the water spirit." It had earlier been called Devil's Lake or Cannibal Lake in Stoney and Long Lake in Cree. George Simpson named it Peechee Lake after his guide.

MINOTAUR: Peak [2780 m]; 1929; Ramparts. This name was applied by Cyril Wates after the legendary Cretan monster, half-man, half-bull, confined in the labyrinth by King Minos and ultimately slain by Theseus. This was also the name of a ship involved in the Battle of Jutland.

MINSTER: Mountain [3120 m]; 1892; Cline. Professor Coleman applied this name to the line of high ground opposite (south of) his Cloister Mountains because of the "imposing walls of cathedral-shaped mountains."

MINTON: Mount [3050 m]; 1964; Italian. Lt. Harold D. Minton, of the RCAF and Fernie, was killed in action during the Second World War.

MISKO: Mountain [2902 m], **Creek, Pass** [2455 m]; 1904; Bow Ranges.

This summit, south of Mount Biddle, bears the Cree word for red, applied here by the Topographical Survey.

MIST: Creek, Mountain [3140m]; 1884; Highwood. This is a generic name—often used by German-speaking alpinists during periods of poor visibility and other difficulties. It was applied here by Dawson. *See also* Brouillard.

MISTAYA: Mountain [3095 m], **Lake** [1667 m], **River**; 1901; Waputik. This is the Stoney word for "much wind," not, as some have reported, for grizzly bear.

MISTY: Mountain, Glacier; 1896; Chaba. In this instance the name was used by Jean Habel on his second exploratory trip into the Rocky Mountains. Coleman, coming along a few years later, found his "Misty Mountain" at the head of Chisel Creek, where it is presently known as Brouillard Mountain. The precise point named by Habel is not clear.

MITCHELL: Range, River; 1859; Mitchell. **Mount** [3040m]; 1970; Churchill. Capt. William Roland Mitchell (1829–1925), a British traveller and sportsman, attached himself to the Palliser Expedition in 1858–59. He was accompanied by Brisco. *See also* Smythe.

MITRE: Creek; 1890; Dawson. This name was originally applied by Topham to the Bishops Group, but after the official change of nomenclature on this massif was retained only on the creek draining westward into the Incomappleux. **Peak** [2889m], **Pass** [2575m]; 1893; Bow Ranges. Allen showed this name on his first map of the Lake Louise area.

MIZZENMAST: Peak [2789m]; 1972; Battle. Applied by the first ascent party, including Putnam and Matthews, as part of the pattern with Schooner Pass. This is the second-highest summit of the massif and third from its bow.

MOAT: Lake, Pass [1935 m]; 1920; Ramparts. This name was applied by the ABC to the long lake on their north as part of the pattern connected with the Ramparts.

MOBERLY: Pass [1780m], **Location** [789m]; 1871; Sir Sandford. Walter Moberly (1832–1915), the oldest of three brothers, was a pioneer surveyor of the interior of British Columbia. He crossed this pass from his cabin on the Columbia in midwinter on snowshoes. When he reached the mining settlement of French Creek on the Goldstream he was understandably weary. Finding an old friend with a warm stove, Moberly "discussed" a few glasses of rum and water before sleeping soundly on the floor. See his book *The Rocks and Rivers of British Columbia* (London, 1885). The middle brother, Henry John (1835–1931), was 40 years in the employ of the HBC and also wrote a book,

When Fur Was King (New York, 1929). The youngest was Frank, also a surveyor, who had been employed in some of the tentative work for the CPR in the Peace River district in the 1870s. There was a Moberly Peak [8750 ft] not far from this location on the 1892 map of Drewry and McArthur, but with the passage of time it has become officially unnamed. It lies some 10 km east of the CPR whistle stop downstream from Golden, near where Walter had his cabin in 1870.

MOBY DICK: Mount [3154 m], **Glacier**; 1962; Battle. Anger noted that "the partly white face" and other features of this sharp and prominent summit made it appropriate to call it after Melville's great white whale.

MOFFAT: Mount [3090 m]; 1930; Maligne. This summit near Maligne Lake was named in honour of Thomas Black Moffat (1870–1938), who was elected president of the ACC in 1928.

MOLAR: Mountain [3022 m], **Creek, Tower** [2901 m]; 1858; Murchison. Doctor Hector felt that the tower resembled a large tooth.

MOLARS: The [2940 m]; 1972; S Purcells. This name pertains to a group of summits lying between the Wisdom Tooth and Eagle Crest, in the Leaning Towers.

MOLLISON: Mount [2952 m]; 1898; Ottertail. Joseph Henry Scattergood (1877–1953) gave this name in honour of the four Mollison sisters who managed by turns the mountain hotels of the CPR during their heyday as eating stops. Annie was the best known and was primarily associated with the Mount Stephen House at Field. Jean was at Glacier House and then at Wapta Lodge. Scattergood was a businessman and philanthropist of Philadelphia, treasurer of both Haverford and Byrn Mawr colleges and a founding member of the AAC.

MOLOCH: Mount [3094 m], **Creek, Pass** [2240 m], **Group**; 1914; W Rockies. Professor Hickson felt that this summit's forbidding aspect, darkly dominating the western Selkirks, deserved a forbidding name. On his second attempt, he was the first to climb it, in company with guides Edward Jr. and Ernest Feuz. Moloch was a generally unsavoury deity, worshipped and feared in various guises among tribal groups of the eastern Mediterranean.

MOLSON: Mount [2498 m], **Creek**; 1978; W Rockies. Though not a notable high point as mountains go, this summit did rate a precise triangulation and the name certainly is famous among Canadians. It all began with John (1764–1836), who emigrated from Lincolnshire in 1782 and set up his brewery in Montreal (now the oldest in North America, though somewhat assimilated by the heirs of Adolph Coors)

Mt. Moby Dick. ROGER LAURILLA PHOTO

where he also became a pioneer in steam navigation and banking. In 1888 Algernon St. Maur employed a hunter guide named Molson who had great familiarity with the upper Columbia region.

MONARCH: Mount [2777 m]; Jasper. **The** [2904m]; Ball. Both applications came from the misconception that the summit was dominant over its neighbours. When peaks are seen from nearby valleys, the visual foreshortening often leads to false estimates of relative altitude. The Monarch had been called Mount Massive by Outram, though it lacked the 10,000-foot altitude he ascribed to it. There was also a Monarch Mine at Field, operating intermittently from 1894 until the late 1940s.

MONASHEE: Mount [3246 m], **Range**. This name is from the Gaelic for "mountain of peace" and is alleged to have been applied by Donald McIntyre, who prospected the area and opened the Monashee Mines, which were actually in the Gold Range, south of where this name is more narrowly applied. McIntyre apparently looked over to the west one evening and was so taken with the peaceful view that he bestowed this name.

MONCHY: Mountain [3210 m]; 1920; Lyell. Wheeler suggested this name for the French village retaken by Canadian troops after heavy fighting in August 1918.

MONICA: Mount [3059 m]; 1911; Farnham. Harnden named this fine peak for his mother, who was born Monica King.

MONKHEAD: [3211 m]; 1950; Maligne. This name was applied by the ACC and for the cowl-like look attributed to the summit. *See also* Paul.

MONKMAN: Pass [1030 m]; 1922; N. Rockies. Alexander Monkman (1870–1923), a native of Manitoba, drifted with mining booms and finally settled near Edmonton. Establishing a trading post at Grand Prairie, he and railway location engineer Murray Hill set out to find the easiest method of getting to and from his emporium.

MONRO: Mount [3092 m]; 1918; British. Maj. Gen. Sir Charles Carmichael Monro (1860–1929), after service on the Northwest Frontier of India and the Boer War, commanded the First Canadian Division in the British Expeditionary Force of 1914.

MONS: Peak [3083 m], **Icefield, Creek**; 1916; Lyell. This is the name of a town in Belgium that was retaken by Canadian forces just prior to the armistice in 1918. It had also been the site of a sharp, but losing, battle in August 1914.

MONTE CRISTO: Mountain [2954 m]; 1922; Robson. This mountain was quietly named for Curly Phillips' dog.

MONTEZUMAS FINGER: [3130 m]; 1973; Gothics. This spectacular pinnacle off Pioneer Peak was christened by Jones after a trip to Latin America.

MONUMENT: Peak [3094 m]; 1910; Farnham. The GSC found this peak imposing. The geologists were involved in determining the bedrock structure of an area that had attracted considerable interest from wandering prospectors.

MOONCASTLE: Lake; 1980; Odin. This name was suggested by the Kootenay Mountaineering Club for the beautiful tarn immediately south of Frigg Tower.

MOONRAKER: Peak [2850 m]; 1907; Dogtooth. This name for the highest point of the Dogtooth Group was applied by the Topographical Survey at the request of the Dominion Parks Commission. Apparently, Jim Lees asked the proprietor of Golden's Queen's Hotel about it in the summer of 1887. The hotelier's response: "You can call it what you darn like; every outfit that comes along gives it a new name."

MOOSE: River, Pass [2000 m], **Lake** [1032 m]; Jasper. This is a common name applied across North America, generally because someone saw a moose in the vicinity. This creature, similar to the elk of Europe, was known as *l'orignal* to the French-Canadian coureurs du bois.

MOOSEBONE: Pass [2606 m]; 1974; Monashee. This name does not refer to the discovery of skeletal remains of *Alces americana* near the height of land; Putnam merely found it a convenient designation for the divide between Moose and Bone creeks.

MORAINE: Lake [1887 m]; 1899; Bow Ranges. Wilcox named the lake for the picturesque pile of glacial debris that forms the dam holding back this body of water. Collectively, the peaks to the south have become one of the most photographed sights in Canada. Allen had earlier called the lake "Heejee."

MORDEN LONG: Mount [3040 m]; 1966; Premier. Morden Heaton Long (1886–1965) was professor of history at the University of Alberta, notable for his writings on the lives of the explorers of the Canadian West. He was also the first chairman of the Geographical Board of the province of Alberta.

MORIGEAU: Creek, Mount [3155 m]; 1884; S Purcells. Dawson applied this name for François Baptiste Morigeau of St. Martin, Quebec, who had been in residence near this stream since 1819 and whose son's first wife, Colette, was a daughter of Chief Kinbasket. Among their descendants were a hunting guide to St. Maur in 1888 and several who took part in the mining boom after 1890.

MORLEY: Village [1244 m]; 1884; E Rockies. This location, east of the mountains, was named by the CPR for Methodist clergyman William Morley Punshon (1824–1881), who served the mission here for five years from 1868. The location had previously been known as the McDougall Ranch, after its first pastor.

MORRISON: Mount [2760 m]; 1918; British. Maj. Gen. Sir Edward Whipple Bancroft Morrison (1867–1925) was a journalist who joined the Canadian militia to partake of the Boer War, and stayed in. He commanded the Canadian Artillery Corps in the Great War. **Mount** [2880 m]; 1972; Icefields. This name was suggested by the ACC to commemorate member Roland Morrison (1941–1972), who had been killed by a falling serac in the Duplicate Icefield.

MORRO: Peak [2912 m]; 1964; S Rockies. This name also appears in the Jasper area, in both cases owing to the summits' castellated appearance, similar to the most famous such structure in the western hemisphere, completed in 1774.

MOSQUITO: Creek; Murchison. A lot of people who have been in the mountains have applied this name—plus a number of unprintable but appropriate adjectives—to the cloud at hand. In this case it stuck, along with nearby No-see-um Creek.

MOUNTAIN: Creek; 1883; Sorceror. This is the major tributary of the Beaver River, crossed by the CPR as it makes its climb up the valley side toward Rogers Pass. Helper engines were stationed nearby at

Beavermouth, since this was where the mountain began again. This creek separates the peaks largely accessible from Glacier from those that are more remote. *See also* Nordic.

MOWAT: Mount [2843 m]; 1912; Jasper. This summit was named by the Topographic Survey for Sir Oliver Mowat (1820–1903), a father of confederation and champion of provincial rights, who was both premier and attorney general of Ontario before moving on to become lieutenant-governor.

MUIR: Mount [2758 m]; 1924; High Rock. In 1867 Alexander Muir (1830–1906) wrote *The Maple Leaf Forever*, thereby assuring himself a place in Canadian memory.

MULVEY: Creek, Lakes [2180 m], **Meadows**; 1962; Valhalla. Thomas Mulvey was a down-and-out but quite popular member of the local mining fraternity, who worked mostly from a base at Lardeau.

MUMM: Peak [2962 m]; 1910; Robson. Collie named this for his friend Arnold Louis Mumm (1859–1927), a lawyer and publisher by trade, although connected with the champagne family. Mumm was much better known as a prominent member of the AC who climbed everywhere. He died and was buried at sea while returning to England from Asia.

MUMMERY: Mount [3328 m], **Glacier, Creek**; 1898; Freshfield. Collie applied this name to honour Albert Frederick Mummery (1855–1896), one of the finest alpinists of his day. His name is recalled when describing the style of climbing a crack wide enough to insert one arm and leg, which is then ascended by alternately jamming each. He lost his life near the high Diama Pass while attempting a circuit of Nanga Parbat in the Himalayas.

MUMMY: Lake [2240 m]; 1922; Bow Ranges. This name is part of the Egyptian nomenclature pattern of the vicinity. *See also* Haiduk.

MUNIN: Mount [2730 m]; 1999; Odin. Steven Horvath named this for the companion raven to Hugin, on the Norse god Odin's other shoulder.

MURAL: Glacier; 1928; Robson. This name is a substitute for "wall," referring to a glacier that hangs high on the wall of a mountain, generally as a remnant of a larger mass of ice, diminished by climatic warming.

MURCHISON: Mount [3333 m], **Towers, Creek**; 1858; Murchison. Sir Roderick Impey Murchison (1792–1871) was a prominent English geologist who identified the Silurian system and recommended Hector for the post of geologist to the Palliser Expedition. He was president of the Royal Geographical Society and a notable figure of

British science. The local First Nations people believed that this massive peak, although well east of the divide, was the highest of the Rockies.

MURRAY: Mount[3023 m]; 1918; British. Gen. Sir James Murray (1721–1994) commanded the left wing of Wolfe's forces during the crucial battle on the Plains of Abraham. He was thereafter British military commander and then governor of Canada, known for his conciliatory dealings with the defeated French-speaking Native people.

MUSHROOM: Peak [3210 m]; 1947; Icefields. Named for the shape of a large cornice dominating the crest of this peak when it was first ascended.

MYSTIC: Mountain [2659 m]; 1929; Sorceror. This name was offered by George G. Aitken, of the GSC and, after 1912, chief geographer of British Columbia. He considered the mountain "remote from human comprehension," being south of Sorceror, west of Iconoclast and east of Moloch.

I know not how it has been with former conquerors during their lives, but I believe there never was a human being who united against himself such a mass of execration and abhorrence as this man has done. There is indeed, on the other hand, an admiration of him equally enthusiastic, as for every great conqueror there always must be; but I have never yet seen the person by whom he was regarded with affection.

—John Quincy Adams, diary of November 4, 1812

NADIR: Notch [2124 m]; 1971; Windy. This was the low point reached by Putnam and Boss, both in terms of terrain and their morale, as they sought to cross the final ridge separating them from Fairy Meadow and their objective camp in upper Windy Creek.

NAISET: Peak [2820 m]; 1913; Assiniboine. The ABC applied this name from the Stoney word for "sunset."

NAKIMU: Caves; 1904; Hermit. This word is believed to be from the Cree for "spirit sounds" and was applied by prospector Charles Henry

Deutschman (1875–1962), in keeping with the noise made by the subterranean flow of Cougar Creek through the caves near Glacier that he developed into a tourist attraction.

NANETTE: Mountain [2910m]; 1971; Starbird. This name appears to have belonged to a friend of sometime guide Arnor Larson.

NANGA PARBAT: Mountain [3240m]; 1898; Freshfield. This name was transposed by Collie from present-day Pakistan, where the world's ninth-highest peak, Nanga Parbat, had become the last resting place of his friend Mummery.

NAPOLEON: Spur [2361m]; 1901; Hermit. This is a prominent gendarme on the south ridge of Mount Cheops and was so designated by Wheeler because to him it resembled the "Little Corporal" in effectively blocking the way up this strikingly pyramidal peak.

NARAO: Peak [2974m]; 1916; Bow Ranges. The ABC reported this name as being translated from the Stoney phrase for "hit in the stomach."

NASSWALD: Peak [3043 m], **Lakes** [2285 m]; 1913; Assiniboine. This is the name of the town in the Karnische Alpen of Austria that was the birthplace of Conrad Kain. The famous guide was then assisting Wheeler's survey party to climb an adjacent summit.

NAUTILUS: Mountain [3130m]; 1959; Battle. Hendricks had called the prominent peak rising southwest of the confluence of Duncan River and Houston Creek after Jules Verne's Capt. Nemo, from his 1870 book *Twenty Thousand Leagues under the Sea*. In keeping with Hendricks' terminology, Anger and Silverstein named the highest peak in this group after the mysterious captain's vessel.

NEAVE: Mountain [2820m]; 1972; 82K/2; S Purcells. This name does not commemorate the brothers Neave, Roger (1906–1991) and Ferris (d. 1976), who were among the first alpinists to enter the Leaning Towers Group; instead it relates to one Harry Neave, a landowner along the lower part of the creek who got there even earlier.

NEEDLE: Peak [2970m]; 1919; Whirlpool. The ABC applied this name because the peak is sharply pointed—why else?

NEEDLES: Gendarmes; 1920; 82N/5; Bow Ranges. These are a series of gendarmes along the east ridge of Mount Whyte that were traversed by the Swiss guides resident at Lake Louise when taking clients up that routine ascent. The name is fiercer than the climbing.

NELSON: Mountain [3294m], **Creek**; 1807; Farnham. When David Thompson, the great fur-trade explorer of the NWC, was moving through the upper Columbia valley, he received word of the great

Needle Peak. GLEN BOLES DRAWING

naval battle off Spain's Cape Trafalgar, which had occurred almost three years earlier. He proceeded to pay homage toponymically to its victor, Horatio, Lord Nelson (1758–1805), who was killed during the battle. On the next map published by Aaron Arrowsmith, the entire area later called the Purcell Range was designated as "Nelson's Mountains." Subsequently, this mountain's name was mixed up with Hammond. There is another **Nelson** [3165m] on map sheet 83C/6.

NEMO: Mount[2901 m], **Group, Glacier**; 1947; Battle. This word, which means "no man" in Latin, was given by Hendricks to the most striking yet-unnamed peak in the western view from Silent Pass. It has a nautical flavour, being the name Jules Verne applied to the hero of his most famous work. A dozen years later, Anger and Silverstein carried the name onto the large adjacent glacier. *See also* Nautilus.

NEPTUAK: Mountain [3237m]; 1894; Bow Ranges. This is #9 of the Ten Peaks designated by Allen and one of the few that retains his original Stoney-derived name.

NEPTUNE: Peak [3201 m]; 1939; Windy. This name seems to have been applied by surveyor Norman McConnell and was certainly in place when the first ascents were made in the Windy Range. It derives from the Italian god of water, who gradually came to be identified with the Greek god Poseidon.

NEREUS: Peak [2910 m]; 1989; Windy. Members of the Kootenay Mountaineering Club noted that this snow dome at the southwest edge of the Escarpment Icefield was in proximity to other marine characters from Greek mythology. Nereus was the mythical son of Pontus and Gaia, who fathered 50 daughters, and is is sometimes referred to as "The Old Man of the Sea." The *Nereid* was one of the ships destroyed in the Halifax disaster, December 6, 1917.

NESTOR: Mount [2975 m]; Assiniboine. **Peak** [2970 m]; British. This was the name of a destroyer (890 tons) sunk at the Battle of Jutland. It also belongs to the mythological king of Pylos, recorded in the *Iliad* as being of extreme old age and great sagacity, and *nestor* means brother-in-law in Cree.

NETTIE L: Mountain [2474 m]; 1892; Badshot. E.D. Crockett located this prospect, which became one of the most productive mines in the Trout Lake district. Palmer named this lesser summit (which he also climbed) after the mine, some 2,000 feet above what was then the town of Ferguson and four miles by road, on the mountain's lower southwest slopes. No one has yet described the lady who started it all.

NEY: Mount [3060 m]; 1964; French. Roger Neave applied this name in honour of Marshall Michel Ney (1769–1815), one of Napoleon's most trusted subordinates. But it was the critical absence of Ney's forces, unsuccessfully seeking to prevent the arrival of Gen. Blücher's Prussians, that led to the defeat at Waterloo and Napoleon's famous, but easily understandable, remark: "Merde!" Ney was subsequently executed for treason.

NIBLOCK: Mount [2976 m]; 1894; Lake Louise. Of Irish ancestry, John Niblock (1849–1914) was superintendent of the western division of the CPR for several years at the turn of the century. The present name shows up on Allen's second map instead of Pope's Peak, which was in itself a replacement.

NICHOLAS: Mount [2822 m]; 1960; S Rockies. Toby Nicholas, of Cranbrook, was killed in action during the Second World War.

NIFLHEIM: Mountain [2870 m]; 1970; Gold. The name means "fog home," but in Norse mythology it refers to the dark, cold lowest level of the underworld, presided over by Hela. This summit lies just west of Mount Thor.

NIGEL: Peak [3211 m], **Creek, Pass** [2105 m]; 1898; Maligne. Nigel Vavasour was a guide and hunter who accompanied Stutfield and

Collie in their travels around the headwaters of the Sunwapta and nearby rivers in 1897.

NILAH: Peak [2970m]; 1914; N Rockies. This is from the Cree word for "hand," describing this lesser appendage of Kitchi, the Great One, as Mount Sir Alexander was first known. Nearby are other lesser summits, Kisano (Cree for "old man") and Awasis (Cree for "child").

NILES: Mount [2972m], **Pass** [2536m]; 1898; Murchison. C.S. Thompson gave this name to honour one of the early climbers in these mountains, William Harmon Niles (1838–1910), a professor of geology at MIT who also served as president of the AMC.

NIVELLE: Mount [3256m], **Glacier, Creek**; 1918; French. Robert Georges Nivelle (1856–1924) preceded Pétain as commander of the sector at Verdun and went on to command the French armies of the north. He was relieved of his post after the catastrophic failure of his 1917 spring offensive led to mutinies among the *poilus*.

NIVERVILLE: Mount [2960m], **Glacier, Meadow**; 1914; Freshfield. Joseph Boucher, Chevalier de Niverville (1715–1804), soldier and explorer of New France, sent a party up the Saskatchewan River in 1751 to build a trading post. Though soon destroyed, his Fort La Jonquière seems to have been near the forks of the Saskatchewan—a long way from these Rocky Mountains.

NOBILITY: Group, Glacier; 1953; Adamant. The names in this group that lies north of the Adamant pluton are collectively those of various alleged baronets, hardly nobility. Their names were once made official, but upon further reflection and discovery by officialdom of some additional information, the official status was withdrawn. But the group name remains in use. *See also* Baronet and Sir William.

NOEL: Peak [3150m]; 1927; Chaba. Named by Ostheimer for Noel Odell, the noted British geologist who was then visiting professor at Harvard and an alpinist of great fame. This designation languished in the files for two generations, until after Odell's death, before being officially shelved.

NOIRE: Roche [2925 m]; 1916; Jasper. Bridgland suggested this name because the crest of the summit is composed of the black Ordovician sediments found throughout the Rocky Mountains, the subject of comment by early voyageurs.

NORDIC: Mountain [2937m]; 1902; Sorceror. This line of lesser peaks was beyond and to the north of Mountain Creek, hence Wheeler's label. Earlier names for this mountain had been "Truth" and "Vandal." This name is also found on a ridge [3011 m] in the Clearwater area on map sheet 82N/5.

Nordic Mountain. ROGER LAURILLA PHOTO

NORMAN WOOD: Creek; 1937; Windy. N.E. McConnell applied this name after Norman Clark Wood, BCLS 1914, who had been killed in action, September 2, 1918, while helping to repulse Hindenburg's final offensive of the Great War.

NORQUAY: Mount [2522 m]; 1904; Bow Ranges. A native of the province, John Norquay (1841–1889) was premier of Manitoba for 10 years from 1878. He visited the nascent Banff National Park and climbed this summit the year before his death. The premier's name was originally spelled Norquet, and he was particularly proud of his Métis ancestry.

NORTH: Peak [2664 m]; 1939; Bugaboo. This may have been merely another of the compass-point names applied in the Vowell Group by Georgia Engelhard at the time alpinists first visited the area, but she was accompanied by the Californian medical doctor Francis North (1904–1984). *See also* East Peak.

NORTHEAST: Mountain [3024 m]; 1937; Windy. N.E. McConnell applied this name to the point at the northeast terminus of his triangulation net.

NORTHOVER: Mount [3003 m]; 1917; British. Lt. A.W. Northover was a posthumously decorated member of the Canadian Expeditionary Force in the Great War.

NORTHPOST: Spire [2911 m]; 1930; Bugaboo. Thorington applied this name as part of his pattern with Eastpost Spire.

NORTH STAR: Peak [3124 m], **Creek, Glacier**; 1952; Starbird. This was the name of one of the less effective sternwheelers plying the upper Columbia River until 1914. Having been "smuggled" across the border from the United States and through the remnants of Baillie-Grohman's canal, it was impounded for 10 years at Golden and saw little actual use on the river. The boat was owned by Armstrong, but the name was put here by Robinson, whose good sense of local history was well applied in his travels through these mountains.

NORTON: Mount [3060 m]; 1927; Icefield. Ostheimer applied this name in honour of Edward Felix Norton (1884–1954), a British military officer who had been attached to Canadian units during the Great War. He was later the deputy leader of the 1922 Everest Expedition and then led the 1924 epic on which Odell distinguished himself and Mallory and Irvine were lost.

NOWITKA: Mountain [2911 m]; 1937; S Purcells. This was another of the Columbia ramshackle craft immortalized on the summits of the Purcells by Thorington. It was owned by the Columbia River Lumber Company of Golden and used mostly to take logs down the river to be milled.

NOYES: Mount [3084 m]; 1898; Murchison. Charles Lathrop Noyes (1851–1923), born of American missionary parents resident in India, travelled with Stutfield and Collie in the Rocky Mountains. He was councillor of exploration for the AMC and a New England clergyman.

NUB: Peak [2755 m]; 1924; Assiniboine. Applied to the bump on the end of the long ridge extending east, then south, from the summit of Nestor Peak.

NUMA: Mountain [2550 m], **Pass** [2350 m], **Creek**; 1916; Vermilion. This name is allegedly Cree for thunder, which seems to fit, since the mountain was at one time called Roaring Mountain.

*I agree with you entirely in condemning the mania of
giving names to objects of any kind after persons still living.
Death alone can seal the title of any man to this honour,
by putting it out of his power to forfeit it.*

—Thomas Jefferson to Benjamin Rush, 1800

OASIS: Lake [1975 m], **Creek**; 1959; Battle. The lake lies at the mouth
of an otherwise desolate hanging valley near the head of Houston
Creek. In midsummer wildflowers surround its shores and softwoods
grow above its northern bank. Silverstein named it one snowy August
day when the skies cleared just as his party reached its hospitable surroundings.

OATES: Mount [3120 m]; 1913; Whirlpool. Capt. Lawrence Edward
Grace Oates (1880–1912) was a member of Scott's party, which came
second in the race to the South Pole. As the discouraged group re-
treated, famished and freezing, Oates walked out into the blizzard
to his certain and immediate death, so as to offer better hope of sur-
vival to the others. This heroic, though unsuccessful, act was well described in Scott's journal. The name was applied here by British alpinist Geoffrey Eliot Howard (1877–1956), on his third trip into these
mountains.

O'BEIRNE: Mount [2637 m]; 1922; Jasper. The ABC applied this name
to one of its boundary points. Fifty-eight years old and Cambridge
educated, Eugene Francis O'Beirne was a scholarly drifter and ne'er-
do-well who attached himself to Milton and Cheadle, adding greatly
to the difficulties of their journey, as is well recounted in their book.
Having been expelled from a seminary at age 21, O'Beirne spent much
of his later life in a career of anti-Catholic speech-making. He was last
reported in Queensland, Australia.

OBSERVATION: Peak [3174 m], **Glacier**; 1898; Murchison. Noyes
described this summit as offering by far the best viewpoint that he
and his companions had found in the Rockies. This was later verified
by the ABC, which occupied the summit most usefully for its triangulation work.

OBSTACLE: Peak [2769 m]; 1947; Battle. Applied by Kauffman
because this summit was, the party hoped, the final barrier in their
lengthy effort to find a successful approach to the highest peak of the
Battle Range. *See also* Proteus.

Mt. Odaray. GLEN BOLES DRAWING

OBSTRUCTION: Mountain [3205 m]; Cline. It's difficult to determine precisely what this mountain obstructs that makes it different from all the other piles of rock on this ridge along the south side of the upper Brazeau River.

OCHER: Peak [3094 m]; 1916; SW Purcells. Beds of reddish shale are found on the side of this summit.

OCTOPUS: Mountain [2932 m]; 1913; Assiniboine. This was named by Robert Daniel McCaw (1884–1941), BCLS 1912, but despite lengthy effort we haven't been able to grasp a reason why.

ODARAY: Mountain [3159 m], **Pass** [2518 m]; 1887; Bow Ranges. This name appears to have been given by McArthur, but Habel explained it as being the Stoney word for "very brushy" or "windfall."

ODELL: Mount [3150 m]; 1927; Icefields. Ostheimer applied this name to honour Noel Ewart Odell (1890–1987), even then acknowledged as one of the great figures of mountaineering history. Unfortunately, the name languished in forgotten official files for decades. Odell, one of the most famous and vigorous figures of alpinism, was well known to members of the Harvard Mountaineering Club, to whom he had taught ice climbing one winter on the gullies in New Hampshire's Mount Washington (one of these came to bear his name as well).

ODIN: Mountain [2872 m]; 1928; Gold. **Glacier**; 1908; Purity. This is the Norse god of art, war, culture and the dead. Palmer applied the name to the glacier, and the Topographical Survey named the mountain.

ODLUM: Mount [2716 m]; 1917; Italian. Brig. Gen. Victor Wentworth

Mount Odin. ROGER LAURILLA PHOTO

Odlum (1880–1971) was a journalist with the Toronto *Daily Star* who later commanded the Second Canadian Division in the Great War. Afterward he became High Commissioner to Australia and served as the first Canadian ambassador to China. His father, Edward, was a businessman and scholar of Vancouver.

ODYSSEUS: Peak [2790 m]; 1974; Westfall. Named for its proximity to Scylla by Kruszyna.

OESA: Lake [2262 m]; 1894; Bow Ranges. Allen said this was the Stoney word for ice. The lake has been known to freeze over, especially in the winter.

OG: Mountain [2874 m], **Pass** [2300 m], **Lake** [2050 m]; 1966; Assiniboine. This name comes from that of the king of Basan, who was alleged to be 23,033 cubits tall (something like 9 km) and reputed to drink water from the clouds. He also lived for 3,000 years and was done in by Moses. Our authority is an intriguing little volume by the English clergyman and schoolmaster Ebenezer Cobham Brewer (1810–1897), entitled *A Handbook of Biblical References.*

OGDEN: Mount [2695 m]; 1916; Bow Ranges. Isaac Gouverneur Ogden (1844–1915) was the auditor and vice-president of the CPR after 1883. His younger brother, Herbert Gouverneur Ogden (1846–1906), worked many years for the United States Coast and Geodetic Survey and was primarily responsible for the precise levelling of the North American datum on which is based the current delineation of the 49th parallel boundary.

OGRE: Peak [2838 m]; 1916; Van Horne. There was an apparently fearful-looking rock on the summit ridge when the ABC crew went by.

O'HARA: Lake [2018 m]; 1899; Bow Ranges. Colonel Robert O'Hara (1835–1926), a native of Galway and an artillery officer retired from the British Army, was a frequent visitor to the lake. In time he built a cabin there and made it his summer home. His son James (1865–1928) continued the military tradition, but stayed mostly on the auld sod.

OK: Glacier; 1971; Windy. This name came about as a result of a note by Putnam, who marked on a preliminary map sheet of the federal government 50,000 series the letters OK to indicate that the glacier to which it pertained did, in fact, cover the terrain indicated. Upon returning the corrected sheet to Ottawa, the marginal note unintentionally became the official name.

OKE: Mount [2920 m]; 1896; Bow Ranges. Allen applied this name after one William J. Oke, a prospector whom he ran into on the hillside.

OLDHORN: Mountain [3000 m]; Jasper. There are many such things to be found among these mountains, shed annually by elk, deer and moose.

OLIVE: Mount [3130 m]; 1899; Waputik. Harold Bailey Dixon (1852–1930), British alpinist and chemist, named this summit after his wife, not from any Biblical connotation.

OLIVER: Mount [2536 m]; 1902; Sir Donald. Edward Oliver Wheeler (1890–1962) was the son of the founder of the ACC and joined his father in many mountain adventures, including the survey of this peak, which bears his name. He later participated in the 1921 reconnaissance of Mount Everest and, as Brig. Gen. Sir E.O. Wheeler, in 1938 became head of the famous Indian Survey (a successor to George Everest). He returned to Canada to work with his father for one season on the ABC project. The west summit of this eminence is called Slick Mountain. **Mount** [2983 m]; 1928; Front. Frank Oliver (1853–1933), founder of the *Edmonton Bulletin*, represented the area in the House of Commons from 1896 to 1917. He was Minister of the Interior from 1905 to 1911 and for five years after 1923 was on the Board of Railway Commissioners.

OLYMPUS: Mount [3100 m]; 1926; Maligne. This name comes from that of the highest massif of Greece [2917 m], home in mythology to most of the gods of antiquity. In the *Odyssey,* it never has stormy weather and "there the blessed gods take their pleasure every day." How the mountain accumulates as much snow as it does is then a mystery.

OMEGA: Peak [3060 m]; 1918; Icefields. The last letter of the Greek alphabet. This summit was the end of the line for that season's work by the ABC. It was also called Boundary Peak.

OMOO: Peak [2674 m]; 1972; Battle. The name of Melville's second novel (published in 1847 and given here by Kauffman, refers to the Tahitian native whose name meant "a person who wanders." Denizens of Battle Abbey challenged America's aging high-angle guru, James Peter McCarthy, to climb the prominent pillar of very sound rock at the northeast edge of this peak. He was stumped, but his name remains on the pillar.

ONDERDONK: Mount [2675 m]; 1971; Windy. Putnam and Laurilla applied this name after Andrew Onderdonk (1849–1905), of an old Dutch family in New York. A building and project engineer of considerable note, he held the construction contract for the difficult Fraser Canyon section of the CPR, which was the first part of the great enterprise to be built (starting in 1880) and had been awarded him during the Mackenzie administration. Onderdonk had a part in many construction projects in the western hemisphere and died of complications from the bends while supervising work on the East River subway tunnel in New York City.

O'NEILL: Peak [2813 m]; 1963; S Rockies. Warrant Officer David O'Neill, of the RCAF and Fernie, was killed in action during the Second World War.

ONSLOW: Mount [2790 m]; 1921; British. Richard William Alan (1876–1945), the fifth Earl Onslow, was a British diplomat and member of the British war mission in Paris during the Great War. This was also the name of a destroyer, heavily but safely involved in the action at Jutland.

OPABIN: Creek, Mountain [3097 m], **Pass** [2605 m]; 1916; Cline. This is the Stoney word for rocky and was originally applied to the creek.

OPAL: Range, Ridge [2597 m]; 1884; S Rockies. Dawson found some quartz crystals in this vicinity, coated with opal.

OPPY: Mountain [3330 m]; 1918; Lyell. This is the name of a French village southeast of Lens, around which Canadian units were heavily involved during the Great War.

O'ROURKE: Mount [2883 m]; 1920; (slightly mislocated on map sheet 82J/2) Crowsnest. Pte. 2 Michael Joseph O'Rourke (1878–1958) was a stretcher bearer in the Canadian Expeditionary Force in the Great War. He was awarded the Victoria Cross for his conspicuous heroism in the discharge of his duties under fire in 1917.

ORPHEUS: Peak [2714 m]; 1977; Argonaut. Brian Berry and his friends named this for the musician of Greek legend.

OSGOOD: Mount [3063 m]; 1969; Clearwater. This name was suggested by Putnam to honour William Osgood Field (1904–1994), geographer and alpinist of distinction who received the International Glaciological Society's Seligman Crystal in 1983. Field was honoured by alpine and geographical societies around the world for his studies of glacial recession and associated phenomena; he also made the first ascent of the Columbia Icefield's South Twin in 1924.

OSIRIS: Peak [2880 m]; 1973; Commander. This is the northernmost of the Egyptian Peaks and was named by Wagner for the sun god of ancient Egypt. *See also* Amon Ra.

OSPREY: Peak [2910 m]; 1954; Bugaboo. West's party saw one of these fish-eating eagles as they were attempting the ascent of this peak.

OTTERTAIL: River, Pass [2018 m], **Range**; 1884. Dawson averred that this was the translation of the Native name for the river. The name spread upstream from Leanchoil.

OTTO: Creek, Pass [2106 m]; 1904; Van Horne. Otto Klotz went up this creek in 1886 to take an astronomic sighting for the Railway Belt survey. Few others have found a sensible reason to follow. The name here is not to be confused with various other "Otto" features found near Jasper National Park. Those were named for the three Otto brothers, Jack, Bruce and Closson, packers and outfitters who worked primarily out of Jasper.

OUBLIETTE: Peak [3090 m]; 1931; Ramparts. This is another name dealing with various aspects of castles and fortresses in the vicinity of the Ramparts, but this one was given by Wates, not the ABC.

OUTLAW: Peak [2850 m]; 1974; Kananaskis. Diligent ACC official Don Forrest, mistakenly thinking that neighbouring Banded Peak was actually "Bandit," decided this was an appropriate name.

OUTPOST: Peak [2880 m]; 1921; Ramparts. This name was applied by the ABC as fitting with the local theme. **Peak** [1670 m]; 1950; Gothics. Putnam and his friends named this northeasternmost outlier of the Adamant/Gothics pluton.

OUTRAM: Mount [3240 m]; 1921; Lyell. Applied by the ABC to honour Sir James Outram (1864–1925), whose grandfather of the same name had been important in the subjugation of India, and who served as vicar of St. Peter's Church in Ipswich, England, until 1900, when he immigrated to Victoria. He made a number of first ascents in Canada, including that of Mount Assiniboine. After 1902 he tended to restrain himself to pack-train travel. See his book *In the Heart of the Canadian Rockies* (London, 1905). Outram's son became a bit of a gentleman prospector in British Columbia.

OUTRIGGER: Peak [2825 m]; 1970; Battle. Following the Melville theme, Kruszyna put this handle on the rocky peak just south of Typee and west of the lesser point that Kauffman named after Omoo.

OVENTOP: Ridge [2987 m]; 1952; Monashee. It was a terribly warm day when Arnold Wexler and Hendricks' other friends made this ascent. By the time they had crossed it, they were hot, thirsty and dehydrated.

OVINGTON: Mount [2940 m]; 1966; N Rockies. Pte. 2 Roy E. Ovington of Alenza Lake, B.C., was killed in action on August 28, 1944.

OWEN: Mount [3087 m]; 1886; Bow Ranges. McArthur told the late Lillian Gest, of Philadelphia, that he applied this name after a member of his survey team, Frank Owen.

Mt. Oubliette. GLEN BOLES PHOTO

OYSTER: Peak [2777 m]; 1884; Slate. Dawson named this summit for the curious fossil shells he found in the vicinity.

OZ: Mount [2862 m]; 1961; Purity. This was the nickname of Dr. George Sexsmith, a member of the GSC field party under the distinguished John Oliver Wheeler, which camped nearby in the course of its labours.

Adam gave names to all cattle, and to the fowl
of the air, and to every beast of the field.
—GENESIS 2:20

PACKENHAM: Mount [3000 m]; 1922; Opal. Rear Admiral William Christopher Pakenham (1861–1933) commanded the Second Battle Cruiser squadron during the Battle of Jutland. After the war he was assigned to command of the North American station and retired in 1926. Note that the spelling of his name became altered when it hit the high country.

PALISADE: Mountain [2696 m], **Pass** [2524 m]; 1910; Sir Sandford. Given by Palmer to the ridge forming the north border of the Sir Sandford Glacier, it was one of the outer "defences" of the highest peak of the Selkirk Range. Palmer used its easterly crest (above the ACC's Ben Ferris Hut) extensively as a survey station.

PALLISER: Pass [2088 m], **Range, River**; 1916; British. John Palliser (1807–1887) was of Irish birth. He had travelled extensively in the western prairies of the United States in the 1840s and was selected in 1857 to lead an official three-year, British-funded, exploratory party to determine the nature of the Imperial domains in the Canadian West. The results of this scientific and exploratory work influenced the future development of the Canadian nation. There was a CPR location by this name in the Kicking Horse valley from 1899 to 1940. *See also* Fairholme.

PALMER: Mount [3019 m], **Creek**; 1914; Sir Sandford. Howard Palmer (1883–1944), a lawyer and manufacturer of New London, Connecticut, was a leading figure in the AAC, serving it for many years in various official capacities. He spent several summers in the Canadian Alps but is best known for his tireless attempts to ascend the highest peak of the interior British Columbia ranges—Mount Sir Sandford. His *Mountaineering and Exploration in the Selkirks* (New York, 1914) ranks high among the classics of North American alpine literature. The peak now bearing his name was called Taurus on his first map of the region. Palmer also collaborated with Thorington on the first edition of *The Climbers' Guide to the Rocky Mountains of Canada* (1921).

PALU: Mountain [2938 m]; 1922; Robson. Wheeler, who had visited the Alps, suggested this name for the summit's supposed resemblance to Piz Palu [3905 m] of the Bernina Alps, in the Grisons southeast of St. Moritz.

PAMBRUN: Mount [3063 m]; 1937; S Purcells. Pierre Chrysologue Pambrun (1792–1840), a native of Quebec, was employed by the HBC after 1815 and reached the rank of chief trader at the Walla Walla post in the Oregon Territory.

PANCAKE: Peak [2941 m], **Pass** [2270 m]; 1952; Monashee. Not only did Hendricks's party have pancakes for breakfast, but the late Arnold Wexler averred its members were camped in a flat meadow with two flat snowfields above them. Then they went for the Oventop.

PANGMAN: Peak [3170 m], **Glacier**; 1920; Freshfield. Peter Pangman (1744–1819), of German ancestry but New England birth, was employed by the NWC after 1787. Assigned to the Saskatchewan River, he is noted for having carved his name on a tree near Rocky Mountain House. The tree survived and his visit was thus verified two generations afterwards.

PANORAMA: Ridge [2824 m]; 1959; Bow Ranges. The derivation of this name is self-evident, but we are unsure who applied it first. In any case, the ski area near Radium is on map sheet 82K/8.

PANTHER: River, Mountain [2942 m]; 1884; Front. Dawson supplied the name as being as close a translation as he could make of the Stoney name "river where the mountain lion was killed."

PARA: Pass [2675 m]; 1926; Ramparts. Lying as it does between mountains labelled Parapet and Paragon, how could this high col be called anything else? Named by Wates, whose own name remains on a mountain cabin within sight of this pass.

PARADISE: Valley; 1894; Bow Ranges. Allen named this because it looked so attractive from above when he first saw it. He also compared its beauty very favourably with the neighbouring valley of the Ten Peaks, which he had already decided to name "Desolation." The **Parridice Mine**, however, was prospected in 1900, at an elevation of 7,800 feet above sea level near Mount Farnham, which was about as close as many miners thought possible to heaven.

PARADOX: Mountain [2990m]; 1973; Farnham. This was a derivation from "Parridice," placed here by Curt Wagner. This summit had been one of The Pyramids to Harnden in 1911.

PARAGON: Peak [3030m]; 1921; Ramparts. Named by the ABC as a part of its work in this area, though this particular summit was not included in the fortification motif used so heavily nearby.

PARAMOUNT: Mountain [3033m]; 1973; Farnham. This was the higher of Harnden's Pyramids in 1911 and has a similar derivation to Paradox.

PARAPET: Mountain [3030m]; 1924; Waputik. This was named for its association near Barbette. **Peak** [3090m]; 1921; Ramparts. Wates followed the theme for this area already established by the ABC.

PARK: Mountain [2975m]; 1890; Bow Ranges. The vegetation in the vicinity of this peak is "parkland" (lightly wooded grassland).

PARNASSUS: Mount [2910m]; 1936; Fryatt. This name went along with Olympus and Xerxes here in the Rockies, but referred originally to the 2457m mountain of central Greece that was sacred to Apollo and the Muses. There is also a flower, common in these mountains, called "Grass of Parnassus."

PARSON: Locality [790m]; 1912. Previously known as Hog Ranch, for then obvious reasons, this locality on the upper Columbia was renamed after Henry George Parson (1865–1936), a resident of Golden who was active in the mining business and a member of provincial parliament after 1906. **Peak** [2872m]; 1949; Bonney. This point—on the west ridge of Mount Bonney—was later named for the two clergymen who made its ascent, reverends Green and Swanzy.

PATIENCE: Mountain [2730m]; 1966; Albert. Professor West continued his pattern of virtuous nomenclature.

PATTERSON: Mount [3197m]; 1917; Waputik. Wheeler suggested this name after John Duncan Patterson (1864–1940), a founding member of the ACC who was elected its third president in 1914.

PAUGUK: Pass [2545m]; 1929; Ramparts. Cyril Wates showed his erudition in this one. After an early start, his party barely escaped serious injury from a rockfall as they ascended the icy slopes. He paused only long enough to remind his associates that "the eyes of Pauguk glare upon me in the darkness; I can feel his icy fingers clasping mine amid the darkness," a reference to the mythical flying skeleton of Native legend.

PAUL: Mount [2805m]; 1911; Maligne. Mary Schäffer named this summit for her young nephew, Paul Wistar Sharples. Though only nine years of age, the lad was part of the first ascent party. The summit has been called "Thumb" in some early accounts, and "Monkhead" in others.

PAWN: The [3100m]; 1978; Icefields. Kruszyna considered this the least of the pieces surrounding the upper reaches of his Chessboard Glacier.

PEARCE: Mount [2848m]; 1901; Sorceror. William Pearce (1848–1930) of Winnipeg, DLS 1880, was an original member of the board of examiners for Dominion Land Surveyors and later chief of the Alberta Indian surveys.

PEARY: Mount [3120m]; 1923; Chaba. Schwab named this summit for Robert Edwin Peary (1856–1920), who had been trained as a civil engineer at the United States Naval Academy. Peary became interested in the Arctic and took many leaves of absence as well as officially assigned tours of duty trying to attain the North Pole, an event that finally occurred in the spring of 1909, bringing him great—if possibly undeserved—honour and years of controversy with Dr. Frederick Cook.

PECK: Mount [2921m]; 1924; S Rockies. H.M. Peck, an assistant on the staff of the GSC, was killed in action during the Great War.

PEECHEE: Mount [2935m]; 1884; Fairholme. Dawson named this summit after the Metis guide who accompanied Sir George Simpson on his famous trip across the continent in 1841. Simpson had previously put the name on what is now Lake Minnewanka, but since it had not really stuck there, Dawson moved it to the hill overlooking the lake.

PENGELLY: Mount [2594m]; 1914; Crowsnest. This is not a significant summit, but it was an ABC triangulation point occupied by Wheeler's assistant, Alan Campbell, who, having married into the family, had good reason to think highly of this name. The Pengelly family was from Cornwall and had put their mining heritage to good use in the Slocan area.

PENNY: Mountain [3000m]; 1960; Premier. This was originally called Holway's Peak, for he made its first ascent. When Carpé and Chamberlin arrived there in 1924, they found that the only record left by the first ascent party was a coin. The coin was still there in 1949 when the Hendricks party arrived and renamed the summit Holway's Penny. The present name came when a further repagination occurred with more premiers' names being added.

PEQUOD: Mountain [2979m], **Pass** [2450m], **Glacier**; 1959; Battle. Anger named the peak west of the head of what is now called the south fork of Butters Creek after Moby Dick, the great white whale of Melville's novel, because its summit appeared to be like a giant whale's tail, splotched with white from snow. Other nearby peaks were then named for others of those involved in pursuit of the whale—Ishmael and Ahab.

PERLEY: Rock [2410 m]; 1888; Sir Donald. Harry Allison Perley (1849–1933) was manager of the famous Glacier House for 10 years after its opening in October 1887. He had been in the hotel business prior to his employment with the CPR and returned to hotel ownership after leaving Glacier, doing much to encourage mountain tourism in the interim. His "rock" was a bald nunatak on the east edge of the upper Illecillewaet Glacier, just at the skyline when seen from Glacier station. It became a popular hiking destination for hotel guests.

PERREN: Mount [3051 m]; 1968; Bow Ranges. Walter Perren (1914–1967) was a guide of distinction who arrived in Canada from his native Zermatt, Switzerland, in 1950. In time he became chief warden and founded the National Parks Rescue School, where he was mountaineering instructor for all park wardens and the RCMP. Previously, this summit was Allen's "Sapta"—#5 of the Ten Peaks.

PERT: Peak [2665 m]; 1937; S Purcells. This was another of the craft on the upper Columbia, launched in 1890 and immortalized on a Purcell peak by Thorington. *Pert*'s skipper was Andrew Morrison Taylor (1875–1945), who went on from Golden to Alaska in 1915 and into mountaineering fame for his part in the epic 1925 Mount Logan expedition. *See also* MacCarthy.

PESKETT: Mount [3121 m]; 1968; Murchison. Reverend Louis Peskett, a youth-camp group leader, was killed by a falling rock near Mount Cline in 1966. The peak is prominent in the view from the lower reaches of Cline River.

PÉTAIN: Mount [3183 m], **Glacier, Creek**; 1922; French. Henri Philippe Pétain (1856–1953), Marshal of France, hero of the 1916 Battle of Verdun and reviled for his role in the Vichy government during the Second World War, remains an enigma to his countrymen. He became dear to the lowly *poilus* because of his insistence on softening up the enemy with intensive artillery bombardment prior to launching an infantry attack—thereby saving many lives—in marked contrast to the bloody, almost murderous, human-wave tactics used by his associates up to that time. After making good his promise at Verdun ("*Ils ne passeront pas*"), he was appointed commander in chief of the French armies and later minister of war and ambassador to Spain. Pétain's subsequent collaboration with the Germans after the disastrous spring of 1940 severely clouded his reputation as a hero of France.

PETER: Mountain [3338 m], **Pass**; 1924; Farnham. This was "Mount St. Peter" to Stone in 1915, but in reality was named after Peter Kerr, a member of the 1914 climbing party into this area, who died in France in 1917 of battle wounds sustained in the Great War.

PETERS: Mount [2850 m], **Creek**; 1928; Front. At Bridgland's suggestion this name was applied to honour Frederick Hathaway Peters (1883–1982) of Quebec City, DLS 1910, who was surveyor general of Canada from 1924 to 1948 and whose father had been premier of P.E.I.

PETRIE: Mount [2880 m]; 1968; N Rockies. Wallerstein named this summit after Robert Methven Petrie (1906–1966), a prominent astronomer in service to Canada. A native of St. Andrews, Scotland, Petrie was president of the Royal Astronomical Society of Canada and served as vice-president of the American Astronomical Society, the International Astronomical Union and the American Association for the Advancement of Science. He was best known for his studies of binary stars.

PETTIPIECE: Lake [1600 m], **Pass** [1688 m]; 1938; Monashee. Robert Pomatier Pettipiece was a local newspaperman who published the first Revelstoke city directory in 1899.

PEVERIL: Peak [2686 m]; 1932; Jasper. This was the "Portal Peak" ascended by Bradley Gilman and others in 1926. It stands across the Portal Valley from Lectern Peak. The current name derives from Sir Walter Scott's 1923 novel *Peveril of the Peak. See also* Blackhorn.

PEW: The [2920] m; 1975; S Purcells. This summit is lower than, and located so as to appear in front of, the Pulpit.

PEYTO: Lake [1860 m], **Peak** [2970 m], **Glacier**; 1896; Waputik. Ebenezer William (Bill) Peyto (1868-1943) came to the Canadian west with the CPR and stayed to become a well-known guide, packer and park warden. His name was applied to the landscape by Wilcox, who considered him one of the best. The glacier is one of five Canadian mountain glaciers that have been intensively measured and studied since 1960. *See also* Ram.

PHACELIA: Pass [2300 m]; 1933; Bugaboo. This is the botanist's Latin name for the showy purple scorpion weed found above timberline in many parts of these mountains, conferred by Dr. Thorington.

PHANTOM: Crag [2329 m]; 1958; Front. Lying to the north of Devil's Gap and overlooking Ghost River, east of Lake Minnewanka, this had been called "Devil's Fang Mountain" in 1928.

PHARAOH: Creek; 1911; S Purcells. This was named by Earl Grey during the course of his trip through the Purcells, just after he had passed below Harnden's Pyramids. **Peaks** [2711 m], **Creek, Lake** [2118 m]; 1922; Ball. This title of the ancient Egyptian rulers was applied by the Topographical Survey as part of the pattern with nearby features. *See also* Scarab.

PHILLIPS: Mount [3249 m]; 1910; Whitehorn. Collie gave this name after Donald "Curly" Phillips (1884–1938), who had been his guide and packer. Phillips later became the leading authority on the mountains near Jasper. His packtrips went far beyond the northwest horizon for weeks at a time, reaching through the intervening passes to the distant Mount Sir Alexander. Phillips died in an avalanche in the Victoria Cross range, west of Jasper. When Holway, Gilmour and Palmer climbed this summit in 1916, they assumed it was unnamed and called it Mount Dorland after Holway's maternal grandfather. The mountain has also been referred to as "Resolution." **Peak** [2920 m], **Pass** [1570 m]; 1916; S Rockies. The great wildlife conservationist William Hornaday suggested this name after his friend and co-author, John MacFarlane Phillips (1861–1953), businessman, conservationist and game commissioner for the state of Pennsylvania. However, according to White, this name derives from Michael Phillips, who came to B.C. in 1863 and was clerk of the HBC post at nearby Wild Horse Creek in 1865. In 1875, he was the first white man to cross Crowsnest Pass. There is also Benjamin D. Phillips, who was a pioneer sheep rancher in northwest Montana; his animals strayed throughout the area and were frequently found well into Alberta.

PHOGG: Peak [2693 m]; 1960; Carnes. Ferris and Putnam were hampered by poor visibility when their party made this ascent.

PIERCE: Mount [2848 m]; 1916; High Rock. The ABC applied this name in honour of Benjamin Clifford Pierce, a member of the surveyor general's staff who was killed in 1917 during the Great War.

PIERRWAY: Mountain [2790 m]; 1960; Cariboo. Grenadier Alfred Pierrway of Quesnel was killed in action on July 12, 1942, during the Second World War.

PIGEON: Mountain [2394 m]; 1858; Front. Hector saw a flock of wild pigeons that appeared to be nesting below this mountain. **Spire** [3124 m]; 1916; Bugaboo. This summit, which appears to have been named by MacCarthy, has subsidiary points called Pigeon Toe and Pigeon Feathers.

PIKA: Peak [3023 m]; 1928; Slate. The pika (*Ochotona princeps*), or little chief hare, is sometimes also called "cony" or "snafflehound." With their rounded mouse-like ears and absence of tail, they are readily distinguished from alpine squirrels and packrats. They emit a distinctive squeak and collect hay to line their underground nests and provide winter forage. They are found all through the Canadian Alps and can become charming and harmless companions to the very patient.

PILKINGTON: Mount [3285 m]; 1898; Freshfield. Charles Pilkington (1850–1919), an alpinist of distinction, was elected president of the AC in 1886. He and his brother, Lawrence, made the first ascent of the Inaccessible Pinnacle on the Cuillin of Skye in August 1880. *See also* Freshfield.

PILOT: Mountain [2935 m]; 1884; Ball. Dawson named this one for the same reasons the name is often applied elsewhere—the summit was visible for a long way down the valley as the party approached.

PINNACLE: Mountain [3067 m]; 1898; Bow Ranges. Wilcox chose this descriptive name. It is a highly generic name and is also found on a pass at 2050 m on sheet 82F/15.

PINTO: Lake [1755 m]; 1893; Cline. As he was returning from his trip to Mount Brown, Coleman lost track of a pinto horse a day or two before reaching the shores of this scenic lake, where the horse finally turned up on its own.

PIONEER: Peak [3245 m], **Pass** [2910 m]; 1910; Adamant. This name was given by Palmer because his party was the first to visit the Gothics Glacier and this was their initial ascent. **Mountains**; 1969; SW Purcells. Wagner named all the peaks in this group at the western edge of the Purcell Range for his friends, the early pioneering settlers in the Argenta area, east of Kootenay Lake.

PIPESTONE: Mountain [2970 m], **Creek, Pass** [2449 m]; 1860; Clearwater. This name was given by Hector because his Native associates were said to be in the habit of carving pipes from the easily worked sedimentary rocks found in this valley. Dawson called it "Argillite."

PLASKETT: Mount [2910 m]; 1968; N Rockies. Dr. Wallerstein applied this name after John Stanley Plaskett (1865–1941), who had been chief astronomer and the first director of the Dominion Observatory in Victoria. For his studies in galactic rotation he received the Gold Medal of the Royal Astronomical Society and was similarly honoured by astronomical societies around the world.

PLUTO: Peak [2831 m]; 1950; Windy. Fabergé named this peak after the Greek god of the underworld. Perhaps he also had in mind the canine companion of Walt Disney's famous mouse. It is also the name of the ninth planet of the solar system, predicted to exist by astronomer Percival Lowell and finally sighted in 1930, 14 years after his death. However, the point Fabergé actually had in mind was some 5 km south of where the name now rests.

POBOKTAN: Pass [2270 m], **Mountain** [3323 m], **Creek**; 1892; Maligne. This is the Stoney word for owl and was applied by Coleman because he'd seen a number of the birds in the forest below the pass.

POCATERRA: Creek; 1922; Opal. George William Pocaterra (1882–1972) was a native of Italy who arrived in the New World in 1903, via Bern, Switzerland, and became a pioneer rancher in the Alberta foothills. He operated a dude ranch known as Buffalo Head and was an influential figure in the area, with many business interests. He was the first to explore Elk Pass. *See also* Elpoca.

POLAND: Mount [2840 m]; 1966; Freshfield. Pte. 2 Herbert John Poland of Golden was declared missing in action on August 9, 1944, near the close of the Second World War.

POLARIS: Mount [3046 m]; 2004; Battle. This was the name of a ship, famous in Arctic exploration, but Laurilla applied the name to the sharply pointed crest due west of his campsite at the head of the Duncan Glacier.

POLIGNE: Creek; 1960; Maligne. This is the combination name applied to the stream draining south to Poboktan Creek from Maligne Pass.

POLLINGER: Mount [2816 m]; 1902; Waputik. Joseph Pollinger (1873–1943) came from an old guiding family of St. Niklaus in the Valais. He visited Canada with Whymper in 1901.

POLLUX: Peak [2786 m]; 1896; Sir Donald. Professor Fay named this lesser summit by association with its adjacent twin point, Castor, and their mythological mother, Leda. *See also* Jupiter.

POLTERGEIST: Peak [2970 m]; 1970; Palliser. The first ascent party of Swaddle and Michael Hewitt Benn noted the considerable number of avalanches slithering down the neighbouring ghost-like peaks in the warmth of early summer. *See also* Apparition.

POMMEL: Mountain [2750 m]; 1914; N Rockies. Phillips looked down at his saddle and then named this summit for the familiar looking shape of its crest.

POOL: Mount [2868 m], **Creek**; 1895; Badshot. This name migrated up the hillside from a set of mining claims on the Silvercup ridge.

POPES: Peak [3126 m]; 1887; Lake Louise. Initially called Boundary Peak because it was a point on the Rocky Mountain National Park Boundary, it was renamed to honour John Henry Pope (1824–1889), an active participant in Canadian government and politics from age 33. By 1885 he had become minister of railways and canals in the Macdonald administration. *See also* Niblock.

Mt. Polaris, Duncan, Beaver in the Battle Range.
ROGER LAURILLA PHOTO

PORCUPINE: Creek, Lake [1899 m]; 1956; Murchison. This lake shows up on the Collie map of 1898, but with no name. However, this name was used by Jimmy Simpson long before it became official. Some of us have been in this valley more than once, but fortunately have never run across any of the prickly critters.

PORPOISE: Peak [2841 m]; 1950; Windy. Unofficially named for many years, this point lies north of Dolphin.

PORTAL: Peak [2790 m]; 1916; Waputik. This was named by C.S. Thompson because the peak seemed to him to be a part of the gateway from Bow Lake into the Waputik Range.

POSEIDON: Peak [2814 m]; 1951; Windy. This name was applied by a Harvard Mountaineering Club party in keeping with the other mythological marine names in the vicinity. After engineering the demise of the Titans, Zeus allotted Poseidon dominion over the seas and fashioned his trident.

POST: Peak [3009 m]; 1956; Gothics. Minor in appearance, this point has a name that reflects its afterthought status relative to the nearby Gargoyle.

POSTERN: Mountain [2963 m]; 1910; Ramparts. This is the back door of a fortified castle, so named by the ABC in association with the rest of this group.

POTTS: Mount [3002 m]; 1973; Opal. During the centennial year of the RCMP, Boles named this summit for Jerry Potts (1840–1896), a celebrated scout and interpreter for Canada's national police force after 1874. Among his actions was the decision on where to locate Fort Macleod. Some of his descendants, Bill and Wattie, were packers and characters of the Banff area in the early 20th century. Bill finished his days as chief warden of the Banff Park, while Wattie demonstrated an insurmountable fondness for John Barleycorn.

PRAIRIE: Lookout [3121 m]; 1969; British. That's exactly what happens here: one looks out over the prairies of southern Alberta.

PREMIER: Range; 1927; Cariboo. This, the central and highest portion of the Cariboo Mountains, was reserved by the predecessors to the Canadian Permanent Committee on Geographic Names for the names of past, present and presumably future political leaders of Canada. Starting in 1927 the names in this area were shifted to lesser features or eliminated entirely, causing confusion to the mountaineering community.

PRESIDENT: The [3138 m], **Range, Pass** [2972 m]; 1907; Waputik. The ACC wished to honour the CPR leaders who had been so instrumental in assisting the organization with its first annual camp, so it named the highest peaks of a nearby group after these gentlemen. However, it was soon discovered that their names (Shaughnessy and McNicoll) were already applied elsewhere, so their titles were substituted. The summit had previously been called "Emerald" in concordance with the lake to the south.

PRESTLEY: Mount [2728 m], **Lake**; 1964; S Rockies. Pte. 2 Michael T. Prestley of Nelson was killed in action during the Second World War.

PRINCE ALBERT: Mount [3209 m]; 1913; Royal. This summit and five others were named by the ABC for the various children of King George V and Queen Mary (of Teck). Collectively, with the parents' names, these closely adjacent summits are known as the **Royal Group. PRINCE EDWARD: Mount** [3200 m]; **PRINCE GEORGE: Mount** [2880 m]; **PRINCE HENRY: Mount** [3227 m]; **PRINCE JOHN: Mount** [3236 m]; **PRINCESS MARY: Mount** [3084 m]. **PRINCESS MARGARET: Mountain** [2502 m]; 1958; Fairholme. Just inside Banff National Park, this point was named for the sister of Britain's Queen Elizabeth II at the time the lady visited western Canada. Because of its proximity to Canmore, we note also an earlier Princess Margaret (d. 1093), the sister of Edgar Atheling, the last Saxon king of England, who became the queen of Malcolm III (MacDuncan) Cean More. Subsequently canonized for the influence her piety brought to the

Church in Scotland, three of this remarkable woman's sons also ruled the land—Donald Bane, Duncan II and Edmund. Her feast day is November 16, but only in Scotland.

PRIOR: Peak [3270 m]; 1924; Freshfield. Edward Gawler Prior (1853–1920) was a mining engineer, merchant and politician who was appointed lieutenant-governor of British Columbia in 1919.

PRISTINE: Mountain [3037 m]; 1951; Purity. This was named by members of the Harvard Mountaineering Club from its association just east of Mount Purity.

PROSPECTORS: Valley; 1899; Bow Ranges. Wilcox named this area because he found an abandoned prospector's camp near its entrance. In 1927 the upper part of this valley became the site of ACC's first mountain hut, named in honour of Charles Ernest Fay. It was destroyed in a 2004 forest fire, but rebuilt two years later.

PROTECTION: Mountain [2786 m]; 1911; Sawback. This summit shuts off an attractive view from Baker Creek.

PROTEUS: Mount [3198 m], **Glacier**; 1963; Battle. This is the highest point of the legendary Battle Range. When first noted by Palmer, Holway and Butters in 1908, they called it Big Battle Mountain. As such, it was the climbing objective of Holway and Butters in 1914. Their supplies and time were sufficient only for them to reach the summit of what is now called Mount Butters. A generation later, other alpinists tried for the highest point. After several attempts, Andrew and Betty Kauffman with Norman Brewster reached the elusive summit and submitted the name Butters for official approval. The Board on Geographic Names, however, placed that name on its present, and quite appropriate, summit, reserving another name for the highest point. It was then tentatively called Ishmael after one of the characters from Melville's *Moby Dick*. This idea, however, was a misapplication of Anger's suggested name (1960) for the present Mount Butters. Subsequently, the highest point of the Battle Range received the name Proteus after the prophetic and elusive old man of the sea in Greek mythology. This name was also that of the ship that took A.W. Greely's party to its base in Lady Franklin Bay and was subsequently crushed in the ice while trying to effectuate their relief. In fall 2004 Kauffman's ashes were left on this summit by Putnam, Laurilla and chopper pilot Don McTighe.

PROW: Mountain [2858 m]; 1956; Front. The near end of this summit ends in an overhanging point reminiscent of a ship's prow.

PRUDENCE: Peak [2779 m]; 1966; Albert. Professor West's list of virtues was limited only by the number of high points he was able to visit in one season. *See also* Fortitude.

PTARMIGAN: Peak [3059 m], **Valley, Lake** [2332 m]; 1909; Slate. Hickson named this peak at the time he and his favourite guide, Edward Feuz Jr., made its first ascent. They had sighted an unusually large number of the fearless "fool hens" while approaching the peak.

PTOLEMY: Mount [2813 m], **Pass** [1716 m]; 1914; S Rockies. The ABC, in the person of Dominion representative James Wallace, suggested this name because the peak resembled a recumbent body, sitting with arms folded. It had previously been called "Mummy," but Wallace considered this undignified.

PULPIT: Peak [2728 m]; 1898; Waputik. C.S. Thompson felt this term to be descriptive of the peak. There is also a prong [3002 m], 1975, at the south end of Hall Peak and above The Pew, among the Leaning Towers.

PULSATILLA: Mountain [3035 m], **Pass** [2350 m]; 1916; Sawback. This is the botanical name for one of the earliest spring flowers, the crocus or pasque flower, which is plentiful in the upland meadows of the Canadian Alps.

PURCELL: Range; 1859. Dr. Goodwin Purcell (1817–1876) was the last chieftain of the O'Leary. He taught James Hector in therapeutics and medical jurisdiction and served on the selection committee for the Palliser Expedition. In his honour, Hector gave the name to the larger range of mountains west of the Columbia River southward from the mouth of Beaver River.

PURITY: Mount [3149 m], **Glacier, Pass** [2820 m], **Group**; 1890; Selkirks. This name was given by Harold Topham for the summit's white and regular appearance when seen from the north. It is a prominent and major summit of the central Selkirk Range.

PURPLE: Mountain [2795 m]; Cline. This is an outlier of Resolute Mountain.

PUTNIK: Mount [2940 m]; 1918; British. Gen. Radomir Putnik (1847–1917) commanded the Serbian army during the first years of the Great War.

PYRAMID: Mountain [2763 m], **Lake** [1179 m]; 1916; Jasper. Dr. Cheadle stated that "Priest's Rock [an earlier name] was of curious shape, its apex resembling the top of a pyramid and covered with snow." The peak is visible to the north of Jasper.

PYRIFORM: Mount [2789 m]; Highwood. We have been unable to determine how a mountain gets to be pear-shaped, though we have known a number of mountaineers who have gotten that way.

PYTHIAS: Mount [2724 m]; 1948; Adamant. This name, its commonly

Mt. Purity. GLEN BOLES DRAWING

appearing form being a misspelling from "Phintias," stands on the east side of Friendship Col, Damon being on the west. The col was named by Putnam for the famous friends cited by Cicero as being willing to lay down their lives for each other. Dionysius (405–367 B.C.), tyrant of Syracuse, was so touched by their sincerity that he released them both from the death sentence he had previously imposed.

Good men must die, but death cannot kill their names.
—Bohn's *Handbook of Proverbs*, 1855

QUADRA: Mount [3173 m]; 1910; Bow Ranges. Wheeler noted that this mountain has four distinct pinnacles; the highest three were traversed during Hickson's first ascent. Wilcox had earlier lumped the mountain together with Bident as one massif.

QUADRANT: Mountain [2727 m]; 1948; and **Spire** [2690 m]; Adamant. Colossal Enterprises (and Kauffman) noted there were four separate crests to this lesser granitic peak near the northeast extremity of the Adamant/Gothic pluton. (There is a slightly lower spire to the northeast that was not considered when this name was applied.)

QUANSTROM: Mount [2940 m]; 1967; Cariboos. Flight Officer William Quanstrom was declared missing in action during the Second World War.

QUÉANT: Mountain [3120 m]; 1918; Alexandra. This came from a village in France retaken by Canadian troops at the beginning of the general defeat of German forces in the autumn of 1918.

Mt. Quadra. GLEN BOLES DRAWING

QUEEN: Mountain [3110m]; 1978; Icefields. Among the peaks surrounding Kruszyna's Chessboard Glacier, this was the most difficult, though attractive, summit.

QUEEN ELIZABETH: Mount [2849 m], **Glacier**; 1918; Royal. This name commemorates the consort of Albert, king of the Belgians, a man admired by alpinists around the world. This was also the name of a British battleship severely damaged in the Dardanelles campaign of the Great War.

QUEEN MARY: Mount [3245 m]; 1913; Royal. This was not only the name of the consort of Britain's ruling monarch, but also that of a British battleship that blew up early in the Battle of Jutland. The vessel weighed in at 26,350 tons, had eight 13 ½-inch guns, was capable of 28 knots and had 9 inches of waterline armour; nonetheless, 1,266 men lost their lives when superior German gunnery got to her.

QUEENS: Peak [3350m]; 1978; Alexandra. This is the alpinist's name for the lower north peak of Mount Alexandra, also named for the Danish-born consort of King Edward VII.

QUESNEL: Locality, Lake [725 m]. Jules Maurice Quesnel (1786–1842) of Montreal was a trader at Edmonton for the NWC, 1804–11, during much of which time he was with Simon Fraser on his exploratory voyage down the river bearing that name.

QUIBBLE: Peak [3145 m]; 1969; S. Purcells. Wagner must have had a long discussion about naming this point above Duncan Lake.

QUINCY: Mount [3150m], **Creek**; 1892; Chaba. Lucius Quincy Coleman was a rancher at Morley, Alberta, who accompanied his more famous geologist brother on many exploratory trips into the Rocky Mountains. This was a family name from their mother, who claimed a relationship with the second and sixth presidents of the United States. *See also* Coleman.

QUINN: Range, Creek; SW Rockies. On some early 20th-century maps, the range had been designated as the Herchmer Mountains, after Lawrence William Herchmer (1840–1915), a native of Oxfordshire who had served in India and in 1886 become commissioner of the RCMP. The origin of Quinn is unknown.

QUINTET: Peaks [2775 m]; 1910; Bugaboo. On his one trip into this area, Wheeler noted that there were five of these relatively innocuous peaks, all in a row and all south of Bugaboo Pass.

So long as the wild boar delights in the mountain tops,
The fish in the rivers, and the bees feed on thyme,
So long will the glory of thy name remain.
—Virgil, *Eclogues v*

RADIANT: Peak [2789 m]; 1931; S Purcells. According to Thorington this name was "descriptive of its symmetrical, snowy appearance."

RAE: Mount [3218 m]; 1859; Highwood. Hector named this for John Rae (1813–1893), initially the HBC surgeon at Moose Factory, 1835–43. He then became actively interested in exploration and made several noteworthy Arctic journeys, some in the Franklin Search and later for a telegraph line from Red River to the Pacific. Rae, an Orkneyman, later won the £10,000 prize for discovering the fate of Sir John Franklin.

RAJAH: The [3018 m]; 1921; Jasper. This prominent summit was named by Cautley of the ABC. The summit appeared to preside, in the manner of an Indian potentate, over the Snake Indian Valley. *See also* Ranee.

RAM: River, Glacier; 1812; Clearwater. This name first appears on David Thompson's map. The glacier has been an object of intense measurement and analysis since the mid-1960s as the easternmost of a series of five Canadian mountain glaciers of this latitude, data on whose health and behaviour could be regarded as typical of all glaciers in this latitude. *See also* Peyto and Illecillewaet.

RAMPART: Ridge [2576 m]; 1897; Sir Donald. Harold Bailey Dixon (1852–1930) gave this name to the fine escarpment that towers above the west side of the Asulkan Valley. Dixon was a British authority on the chemistry of gases, largely responsible for the discoveries that led to the development of neon lighting. Collie, however, contended that he, rather than Dixon, was the true discoverer of the process.

RAMPARTS: The; 1920; N Rockies. Though in prior usage, this very descriptive name was officially applied by the ABC to the entire massif lying along the Divide to the west of the Amethyst Lakes. Most of the peaks in this group were named by the ABC for various aspects of a medieval castle and are identified separately in this text. From the east, this massif is particularly impressive. *See also* Vista.

RANEE: The [2939m]; 1929; Jasper. This peak is the consort of the Rajah and stands beside it, on the east side of the upper Snake Indian valley.

RAUSH: River, Glacier; 1924; Premier. This river was originally known as Shuswap River, a name that clearly duplicated the south-flowing stream with headwaters only a few dozen kilometres distant. It was therefore changed to French, written as Riviere au Shuswap, and then contracted.

RAVELIN: Mountain [2725 m]; 1910; Sir Sandford. Palmer used a number of fortification terms as names for the lesser neighbours of Mount Sir Sandford. This word refers to a detached outwork and is applied to the summit immediately adjacent to the main peak on the north; it is largely composed of the distinctive violet-coloured and coarsely crystalline marble that outcrops in this area.

RAZOR'S EDGE: The [2750m]; 1950; Badshot. This name came into print after Dr. and Mrs. Kenneth Karcher visited these mountains. They found the sharp edge of this ridge to be stimulating of thought, if nothing else.

REARGUARD: Mountain [2720m]; 1922; Robson. This name was given by the ABC to the peak toward the back (as they envisaged the north) of the Robson massif. It lies north of Waffl.

RECONDITE: Peak [3356m]; 1927; Clearwater. This summit was climbed on Palmer's last major trip to these mountains. Its name suggested that the peak was hidden away and difficult of access. This is true if one's perspective is aimed at the main chain of these ranges. However, this is still a major summit and was the penultimate to be climbed of those in the Rockies exceeding 3353 m in altitude.

REDAN: Mountain [2894m], **Glacier**; 1910; Sir Sandford. This part of the outer defences of Mount Sir Sandford lies two ridges north of the main peak, thus the appropriateness of using a term for an unfortified entrance, though still near enough for Palmer to include on his map of the area. *See* Haworth for some interesting local paleobotany.

REDBURN: Mountain [3090 m]; 1970; Battle. Kruszyna was still indulging himself in Melvilleana. This peak's name was taken from the title of the author's fourth volume, published in 1849.

REDCLIFF: Peak [2914 m]; 1965; Badshot. It has just what its name implies.

REDEARTH: Pass [2090 m], **Creek**; Ball. This name aptly describes the soil and rock colour near the crest of this pass.

RED LINE: Creek, Peak [3216 m]; 1898; Farnham. The creek derived its name from a mining claim located by Ben Abel. The mine was acquired by Starbird in 1900, then transferred to the McDonald Creek Mines Company in 1902. Professor West extended the name to the peak in 1960, because it stands at the head of the creek.

RED MAN: Mountain [2905 m]; 1917; Blue. The ABC applied this name with reference to the nearby White Man Mountain and Pass.

REDOUBT: Mount [2902 m]; 1906; Slate. This was applied by the Topographical Survey; no explanation was given. **Peak** [3120 m]; 1920; Ramparts. The ABC continued the pattern it had already established in this area.

REDTOP: Mountain [3060 m]; 1916; Commander. MacCarthy and Stone applied this name to one of the two prominent peaks 6 km north of Earl Grey Pass, the other being Mount Earl Grey. In so doing they replaced the name "Needle Peak," applied by Harnden five years earlier, on the theory that there were already too many "needles" and these summit rocks were red. Collectively the two summits were the "Shining Range" to Stone when he had viewed them from Monument Peak.

REEF: Icefield; 1923; Robson. The ABC noted that there was a prominent nunatak, or dividing strip of rock, in the central portion of this glacial mass. Of course, things are different most of a century later: the glacier has largely disappeared.

REMILLARD: Peak [2881 m], **Group**; 1942; Windy. Louis Norbert Remillard began working this area in 1910, in company with Messrs Kitson, Fallmore and Williams. They fell by the wayside, but he continued for 20 years as head of the French Creek Development Company, working placers near the head of the Goldstream. During much of this time, his daughter, Edith May, a registered nurse, was the Big Bend area's only medical resource.

REMUS: Mount [2688 m]; 1940; Fisher. This peak was noted to be some 150 m lower than its twin, as well it should be, according to legend. *See also* Romulus.

Remillard Mountain, north face. ROGER LAURILLA PHOTO

REPLICA: Peak [2794 m]; 1923; Maligne. Palmer gave this name because the peak appeared quite similar in outline to the nearby, but considerably higher, Mount Brazeau. He climbed them both.

RESOLUTE: Mount [3150 m]; 1958; Cline. This is the joint name for Lion and Lioness massif.

RESPLENDENT: Mountain [3425 m], **Valley**; 1910; Robson. Collie, accompanied by Mumm and guide Moritz Inderbinen, gave this name for the aspect of this summit when he saw it in the first rays of the morning sun.

RESTHAVEN: Mountain [3120 m], **Icefield**; 1923; N Rockies. The ABC found this ascent to be long but easy.

REVELSTOKE: City [450 m]; 1885. This was the titled name of Edward Charles Baring (1828–1897), managing partner of the once great British financial house of Baring Brothers. Baring's critical underwriting decision in the final year of construction allowed the CPR to be finished. After completion, the railway almost immediately began operating at a profit, and Baring's faith in assuming $15 million of its securities was amply rewarded. The CPR was equally grateful. The location had been known as Big Eddy in the days of canoe travel on the Columbia, then Second Crossing (of the Columbia) when the railway line was first projected, and later Farwell after Ontario-born Arthur Stanley Farwell (1841–1908), the surveyor who platted much of the area. As was typical in many such situations, Farwell staked out for himself what he assumed would be the prime commercial locations, but the CPR refused to be victimized and located its yard and other premises across the Illecillewaet River from Farwell's original plat.

REVENANT: Mountain [3065 m]; 1963; Palliser. This is part of the spectral pattern of nomenclature that has been followed in the area northwest of Ghost Lakes, in this case offered by Dr. Swaddle. *See also* Apparition.

REVENGE: Mount [2797 m] 1971; N Monashees. There must have been some indigestion after naming the Pancake Glacier.

RHEA: Peak [2939 m]; 1950; Argonaut. Professor Fabergé named this peak after Neptune's mother, the wife in Greek mythology of Cronus, whose oldest daughter, Hera, became the wife of Zeus. While in keeping with other names in this area, it was only belatedly accepted as official.

RHODES: Mount [3063 m]; 1927; Icefield. Thorington named this craggy overhanging crest after the great promoter-explorer-statesman of East Africa, Sir Cecil Rhodes (1853–1902), who made a large fortune in the extraction of diamonds and left most of it to fund a program of scholarships available to gifted university students in Great Britain, her various colonies, the United States and Germany.

RHONDDA: Mount [3055 m]; 1917; Waputik. The ABC named this summit after David Alfred Thomas, Viscount Rhondda (1856–1918), who had become a prominent member of the British War Cabinet. He had previously been involved in a syndicate to develop the Peace River area. *See also* Habel.

RIBBON: Creek, Peak [2880 m]; Kananaskis. The creek is a tiny ribbon as it flows east into the Kananaskis River. Prior to 1952 there was a small coal-mining town in this valley known as Rovach.

RICHARD BENNETT: Mount [3124 m]; 1962; Premier. Richard Bedford Bennett (1870–1947) represented the Calgary area in the federal parliament for many years as a Conservative. In 1930 he became the party leader and served as prime minister until the election of 1935, when his party was roundly rejected by the electorate. This summit was Carpé's "Kiwa Peak" in 1925, and a few years later it was "Goodell" to Zillmer (after "Slim" Goodell, packer for Carpé).

RICHARDS: Peak [3063 m]; 1953; N Purcells. This beautiful summit was named by Robinson after Professor Igor Armstrong Richards (1893–1979), who thoroughly deserved the honour. Richards and his wife Dorothea (née Pilley) (1894–1986) were indefatigable alpinists, a notable team in mountaineering, literature and scholarship. They last climbed in these mountains in 1940. A much lower crest on map sheet 82H/4 is named for Capt. (later Admiral) George Henry Richards (1820–1896) RN, who was the second British commissioner on the IBSC and had command of His Majesty's forces during a confrontation (the "Pig War") with the United States over jurisdiction of one of the San Juan Islands. He was later chief hydrographer of the Royal Navy.

RICHARDSON: Mount [3086 m]; 1859; Slate. Hector named the summit after Sir John Richardson (1787–1865), who was surgeon and naturalist on two of Franklin's earlier Arctic expeditions and on Rae's Franklin Search expedition of 1848–49.

RIDICULOUS: Mount [2540 m]; 1979; Battle. Dr. Donald Hubbard, who explored and climbed his share of peaks in western Canada, felt it was ridiculous to even call this a mountain; but it does offer some fine scrambling and an excellent view of many Battle Range peaks.

RINGROSE: Peak [3281 m]; 1894; Bow Ranges. Allen named this peak after an acquaintance from London, A.E.L. Ringrose, whom he had met while visiting the Rocky Mountain area. Allen described him "as an extensive traveller and of great familiarity with the Rockies."

Mt. Robson. GLEN BOLES DRAWING

ROARING: Ridge, Creek [3125 m]; 1969; Clearwater. When Putnam and Kauffman were camped below this ridge, the wind passing over its crest was extremely noisy.

ROBERTSON: Mount [3194 m]; 1920; British. Sir William Robertson (1860–1933) was a soldier's soldier. He joined the British army as a private at age 17 and rose to become chief of the Imperial General Staff during much of the Great War.

ROBSON: Mount [3954 m], **Pass** [1650 m], **River, Park, Glacier**; 1863; N Rockies. This summit, the quintessential and highest of the Rockies in Canada, was known by its present name to the locals, who so identified it to Lord Milton and Dr. Cheadle. The exact derivation remains obscure. Some trace it to a corruption of Robertson, for Colin Robertson (1783–1842), the NWC official who sent fur traders into this area. Among those traders was Pierre Bostonais, known frequently by his nickname of Tête Jaune, or Yellowhead. Coincidentally, John Robson was the B.C. provincial secretary and minister of mines, 1883–92.

ROCKBOUND: Lake [2206 m]; 1859; Sawback. This body of water, up in the barren area "behind" Castle Mountain, was aptly described by the name Hector gave; cliffs and scree surrounded it on all sides. When he saw it, there was considerably less vegetation in the vicinity than there was a century later when two of these compilers came by.

ROCKRIDGE: Peak [3002 m]; 1930; Bugaboo. Unimaginatively named by Cromwell.

ROCKS: Valley of the; 1913; Assiniboine. The ABC noted the huge boulders that litter the valley, the precise geological derivation of which has been debated ever since.

ROCKY: Mountains; 1752. The name for the entire range first appears in the journal of Legardeue de St. Pierre as "Montagnes de Roche," although the locals had their own names even before that. The Native names translate variously as "shining" or "glittering" mountains. See Thorington's book *The Glittering Mountains of Canada* for a deeper analysis of the derivation. Rocky Mountain House, established in 1799, was for many years the NWC's main base of operations in the Canadian southwest. Though located in the plains, it was so named because of its relationship to the mountains, which are prominent along the western skyline.

ROGERS: Pass [1330 m], **Mount, Peak** [3169 m]; 1883; Hermit. The pass by which the CPR crossed the Selkirks (it later became the Trans-Canada highway) was named by the CPR for its discoverer, who won the company's $5,000 prize for so doing but carried the cheque around for a year until Van Horne threatened to cancel it if Rogers didn't cash it. Seven years later, Carl Sulzer (1865–1934) of Zürich named the three-crested mountain in honour of Major Albert Bowman Rogers (1829–1889), the American railroad locator from Orleans, Massachusetts. Sulzer was a member of the team that made the first ascent of Mount Sir Donald and other peaks in the vicinity in 1890. The British Columbia Legislative Council had played it safe in 1869 when voting on a motion (aimed at Walter Moberly) to offer a reward of "$1,000 to any party who will discover a suitable pass ... through the Selkirk Range of mountains at not a higher elevation than 2,500 feet." The motion, impossible to achieve since *no* pass in the Selkirks meets the elevation criterion, was defeated by a vote of 2 to 8.

ROMULUS: Mount [2832 m]; 1940; Fisher. This is the higher of a pair of summits. The legendary founder of Rome, and his scoffing twin brother, Remus, are often cited in this sort of instance.

RONDE: Roche [2138 m]; 1916; Jasper. The name, literally translated, means "round rock," which is not inappropriate for this relatively minor point.

ROOK: Mountain [3100 m]; 1978; Icefields. Kruszyna applied this name to "a turreted, rocky peak," one of the more formidable "pieces" surrounding the upper regions of his Chessboard Glacier.

ROSITA: Mount [3270 m]; 1965; Lyell. Joan Rosita Torr (1893–1967), an English geographer, writer and lecturer, was better known by her first married name, which she continued to use after divorcing Colonel Ronald Forbes. Coincidentally, this summit is an outlier of the striking peak named for Edward Forbes.

ROSS: Peak [2331 m]; 1885; Sir Donald. James Ross (1848–1913) was superintendent of construction for the CPR in the mountain sections.

His peak is not all that high, but it is prominent on the "military crest" southwest of Loop Creek. After the main work was completed on the CPR, Ross went on to many other railway construction projects, both as contractor and investor.

ROSS COX: Mount [3000 m]; 1920; Whirlpool. Ross Cox (1793–1853) was employed by J.J. Astor's American Fur Company. He had barely learned his way around Astoria when the fort was ceded to the NWC. In 1817 he decided to leave the fur trade and journeyed overland to civilization with the annual brigade, via Athabasca Pass. His book *Adventures on the Columbia River* (New York, 1832) is an excellent primary source document on fur-trade activities.

ROSTRUM: Peak [3300 m]; 1918; W Rockies. This is the highest summit of the Bush massif; it overlooks the upper Bush River.

ROTH: Mount [2606 m]; 1916; S Rockies. This name was first applied by Hornaday after John Ernest Roth (1869–1951), banker, industrialist and sportsman of Pittsburgh, Pennsylvania. Roth was a patron of Ben Rosicki, hunting and camping guide to the Top of the World area.

ROWAND: Mount [2972 m]; 1930; S Purcells. This feature was named by Dr. Thorington for John Rowand (1787–1854), a trader with the NWC who built Fort Edmonton in 1808. After the merger of 1821 he became the chief factor for the HBC in the Saskatchewan District. His son and namesake continued with the HBC in a similar capacity.

ROYAL: Group, Valley; 1913; S Rockies. The ABC named both the group and its principal summits after several members of the English royal family of the day. *See* Prince Albert.

RUDOLPH: Peak [3507 m]; 1972; Lyell. This point, the most northeasterly of the five summits of Mount Lyell, was named to honour Rudolph Aemmer (1883–1973) of Matten (part of modern Interlaken), who lived in Golden from 1912 until his formal retirement in 1950. He then returned to his birthplace. His remains, however, and those of his wife, Clara, were brought back to Golden, where they rest beside their two sons who stayed in Canada but predeceased their parents. *See also* Walter.

RUFUS: Peak [2759 m]; 1922; Ramparts. The Latin word for red, this is a name that goes well with some of the exposed rocks on this lesser summit.

RUNDLE: Mount [2949 m]; 1859. Hector named this striking summit near Banff after Robert Terrill Rundle (1811–1896), a Methodist missionary who travelled among the First Nations of the Rockies and adjacent plains during the 1840s, until ill health forced his retirement to

217

England. The summit is a prominent landmark near Banff, and portions of its northeast face (EEOR) are very popular with high-angle climbers.

RUSSELL: Peak [3065 m]; 1964; S Rockies. Pte. 2 George W. Russell of Cranbrook was killed in action during the Second World War.

RUTHERFORD: Mount [2847 m]; 1954; Jasper. Alexander Cameron Rutherford (1853–1941) headed the first provincial government of Alberta until 1910. He resumed the private practice of law thereafter until he was called in 1928 to become chancellor of the University of Alberta.

What's in a name? That which we call a rose
By any other name would smell as sweet.
—Wm. Shakespeare (1564–1616),
Romeo and Juliet 2.2

SABINE: Mount; 1858; SW Rockies. This point, difficult to identify precisely but certainly not far from the vicinity of Radium, was named by Palliser for Sir Edward Sabine (1788–1883), an arctic explorer of note who took a special interest in terrestrial magnetism. He was president of the Royal Society, 1861–71. *See also* Stanford.

SADDLE: Mountain [2414 m]; 1894; Bow Ranges. This summit is hardly a summit at all, being but a lower southeast shoulder of Fairview; yet the name is historic, having been on the earliest map of the Lake Louise area—that of Allen. The mountain has a gentle saddleback [2330 m] west of its crest. **Peak** [2831 m]; 1916; S Rockies. Named for an abandoned riding saddle that was later found in the vicinity.

SAFFRON: Peak [2920 m]; 1937; S Purcells. Thorington named the peak for the colour of the silt in the creek below, a brilliant yellow derived from erosion of the Kitchener Formation, which outcrops extensively in the area.

ST. ANDREW: Mount [2606 m]; 1929; N Rockies. The ABC commemorated the patron saint of Scotland on this interprovincial boundary point. St. Andrew was an apostle and martyr whose feast is celebrated on November 30.

ST. BRIDE: Mount [3312 m]; 1898; Clearwater. This name, a variant of Saint Bridget (453–523), is that of the patron saint of the Douglas family and was given in association with nearby Mount Douglas. At one time it was called "White Douglas," from the fact that it carried more snow than the other. The saint's feast day is February 1.

ST. CYR: Mount [2627 m]; 1890; Clachnacudainn. Arthur St. Cyr, DLS 1887, of Ste. Anne de la Perade, Quebec, was an assistant to McArthur in mapping part of the Railway Belt in the Selkirks in the late 1880s. He went on to map the Alaska–Canada boundary, 1893–95. The surveyor's name in turn derived from the town wherein is located France's École Spéciale Militaire, which had been founded at Fontainebleau by Napoleon in 1802 and transferred by him to St. Cyr, near Versailles, in 1808. St. Cyril, patriarch of Alexandria (d. 444), is remembered on June 27.

ST. DAVID: Mount [2627 m]; 1929; N Rockies. The ABC team's chosen name honours the patron saint of Wales, so troublesome to the political amalgamation of Great Britain. St. David (Dewi) (d. 588) is remembered on March 1.

ST. GEORGE: Mount [2780 m]; 1929; N Rockies. This is the name of the fourth-century saint who became the patron of England (and slew dragons on the side). His feast day used to be April 23 until he lost status as a result of Vatican II. The peak is on the Continental Divide, here also the interprovincial boundary, and was named by the ABC in a frenzy of commemorating British saints.

ST. JULIEN: Mountain [3090 m]; 1920; Lyell. This name is taken from that of a Belgian village near Ypres where Canadian troops were actively engaged in 1915.

ST. MARY: Mountain [2910 m]; 1931; S Purcells. The Blessed Virgin's name migrated upriver from Father De Smet's mission among the Flathead people of Montana. Thorington applied it to the peak at the head of the Findlay River.

ST. NICHOLAS: Peak [2970 m]; 1916; Waputik. Members of the ABC alleged that some of the rock formations near the summit bore a similarity to the traditional visage of Santa Claus.

ST. PATRICK: Mount [2910 m]; 1929; N Rockies. This peak is about 1 km west of St. George and completely in British Columbia. St. Patrick (385–461) is said to have driven the snakes out of Ireland, and everyone knows his feast day, not merely the Irish.

ST. PIRAN: Mount [2649 m]; 1894; Bow Ranges. Allen appears to have applied this name (without the St.) to a lesser point east of Niblock, in honour of the town near Ligger Bay on the north shore of

Cornwall famous for its "lost church." This was also the birthplace of Willoughby John Astley (1859–1948), the first manager of the Lake Louise Chalet. Astley was clearly more at home on the water than in a hotel; he later ran sternwheelers on the Arrow Lakes for the CPR and did similar service for the British army on the Nile during the Great War. *See also* Annette.

SALIENT: Mountain [2810m]; 1922; Jasper. The ABC noted that this was the sharpest peak around. Immediately following the Great War, there was also strong awareness of the military meaning of the word "salient," for many such things had been held, lost or gained under difficult conditions during those trying years.

SALLY SERENA: Mountain [3030m], **Creek**, **Lakes**; 1911; Starbird. First known simply as Mount Sally, after the wife of Paulding Farnham, Harnden gratuitously embellished the name after the maiden in Spenser's *Faerie Queene*, who went into the fields to gather a garland of wildflowers. Serena was attacked by the Blatant Beast, but saved by the gallant Sir Calidore.

SAM: Mount [2871m]; 1964; S Rockies. Pte. 2 Peter M. Sam of Athalmer was killed in action during the Second World War.

SAMSON: Peak [3081m]; 1912; Maligne. Mary Schäffer named this peak after a Stoney man, Sampson Beaver, who drew the map that showed her how to find Maligne Lake.

SANDILANDS: Peak [2720m]; 1953; N Purcells. Evelyn Montague Sandilands (d. 1921) was of English birth, worked for the Union Pacific, did a little ditch digging for Baillie-Grohman at Canal Flats and, after a spell in the Queen Charlotte Islands, ended his days as mining recorder at Wilmer.

SANDPIPER: Creek, Pass [2635m]; 1930; Maligne. Hendricks gave this name to the creek because he spotted an *Actitis macularia* on the delta where the stream enters Maligne Lake.

SAPPHIRE: Col [2580m]; 1896; Sir Donald. Fay named this col, between Jove and the Dome, for the small, limpid blue lake at its height-of-land.

SARACEN HEAD: [2650m]; 1842; N Front. Not achieving official status until 1928, this point was nevertheless known by this name to Sir John Simpson and other later travellers for the impressive turban-like aspect of this steep crest north of Southesk River.

SARBACH: Mount [3155m]; 1897; Waputik. Peter Sarbach (1844–1930), a famous guide of St. Niklaus in the Valais region of Switzerland, was in Canada with Collie, Dixon and others in 1897. He had also

Mt. Saskatchewan. GLEN BOLES PHOTO

guided Abbot in Switzerland in 1892. Not the first professional mountain guide in Canada—an honour belonging to those from Courmayeur who accompanied the Duke of the Abruzzi on Mount Saint Elias in 1896—he was the first of his trade in the Rockies.

SARRAIL: Mount [3174 m]; 1919; French. Gen. Maurice Paul Emmanuel Sarrail (1856–1929) was a commander during the critical fighting around Verdun, then assigned to the Salonika area. He achieved considerable repute in this latter post and became the French high commissioner to Syria in 1924.

SASKATCHEWAN: River, Mount [3342 m], **Glacier**; Icefields. This is from the Cree word for "swift current" and refers originally to the river, one of whose sources is the glacier that drains the side of the mountain. The name was later conferred on the whole prairie province.

SASSENACH: Mount [2900 m]; 1956; Jasper. This is the Gaelic word for "English" and has often been used as a derogatory term by those who disapproved of English domination of the British Isles. The term was originally used by Highland Scots as a pejorative term for the southerners of the Scottish lowlands.

SATAN: Peak [2637 m]; 1974; Valhalla. This is part of the Kootenay Mountaineering Club theme. *See also* Devil's Couch.

SAUCZUK: Mountain [2820 m]; 1969; SW Purcells. This name pertained to William Sauczuk, homesteader and farmer of Argenta,

221

on Duncan Lake, whence Wagner had made his approach to these peaks.

SAURIAN: Peak [3016 m]; 1913; Resthaven. This name refers to extinct lizards and was applied because of the highly fossiliferous bedrock in this vicinity.

SAWBACK: Range, Creek; 1859; Bow Ranges. Hector named this jagged line of dry limestone slabs north of the Bow River for its seeming resemblance to a saw blade.

SAWTOOTH: Peak [2691 m]; S Purcells. **Mountain** [2930 m]; Maligne. This name is frequently found (including a whole range worth in Idaho and Montana) and describes the appearance of a group of jagged peaks from a distance. This description is certainly valid for the peak in the southern Purcells. **Station** [2727 m] 1915; W Selkirks. Near today's Mount Holway, this was a survey triangulation point.

SCARAB: Lake [2140 m]; 1922; Ball. This comes from the sacred beetle of ancient Egypt and was applied by the Topographical Survey because the lake seemed to have the outline thereof. This initiated the Egyptian pattern of nomenclature in the immediate area. *See also* Haiduk.

SCARLETT O'HARA: Mount [2874 m]; 1972; Starbird. Wagner must have encountered high winds on this lesser summit.

SCARP: Mountain [3000 m]; 1931; Ramparts. Wates applied this name because of the steep, snowy cliff on the north side of this summit where it drops down toward the Fraser Valley.

SCHÄFFER: Mount [2692 m]; 1909; Bow Ranges. Mary Townsend Schäffer (née Sharples) Warren (1861–1939) spent the last 30 years of her life living in and loving the people and scenery of the Frontal Ranges. See her book *Old Indian Trails* (New York, 1911). Her second husband had been her guide and later, with her financial backing, became a prosperous businessman of Banff.

SCHLEE: Mount [2850 m]; 1976; Opal. This was named by Boles and others after making the first ascent. They had in mind their climbing associate, Gerrit Schlee (1934–1975), who had drowned in the Bow River while saving the life of a friend.

SCHOONER: Pass [2424 m], **Ridge**, 1972; Battle. Named by Matthews, a member of the team making the first ascent of Mizzenmast, the second-highest summit of the ridge. The pass, adorned with a distinctive cairn, separates the bow of the schooner from Hubbard's Roost and Omoo, the next mountain mass to the west.

SCHRUND: Peak [2940 m]; 1968; Monashee. Wallerstein reported a huge bergschrund on the north face of this snow-covered summit.

SCOTCH: Peaks [3033 m]; 1955; Starbird. Mike Sherrick gave the bulk of the names in this group. Often considered pejorative, his overall term is now usually limited to whisky. The Irish and Welsh groups are nearby.

SCOTT: Mount [3300 m], **Glacier, Creek**; 1913; Whirlpool. Robert Falcon Scott (1868–1912) was a British naval officer and Antarctic explorer whose insistence on using Shetland ponies and manhauling caused him to come in second to Roald Amundsen and his dog teams in the race for the South Pole. All the members of Scott's sledging party died on the trip back from the pole, but his diary was subsequently recovered and tells a moving tale of extreme suffering and heroism. The name was applied here by Mumm and Howard. *See also* Oates.

SCREED: Mount [3088 m]; 1976; Maligne. The first ascent party had a little fun with this name, probably reflecting the fun they had on the loose rock of this summit. They "screed" down its west side back to camp.

SCRIMGER: Mount [2755 m]; 1918; High Rock. Capt. Francis Alexander Carron Scrimger (1880–1937) was a surgeon with the Canadian Expeditionary Force who distinguished himself in his care for the wounded during the second Battle of Ypres in 1915, for which he received the Victoria Cross.

SCRIP: Range; 1872; Monashee. This is the mid-portion of the greater Monashee Range. Its name seems to have been derived from the use of Dominion-issued scrip for taking up land in this area.

SCYLLA: Mountain [2920 m]; 1946; Battle. This was named by Kauffman and Brewster after the dangerous rock of Homer's *Odyssey*, in reference to the gap between this and their Charybdis through which the party of climbers had to find their way.

SEA LION: Mountain [2914 m]; 1916; Van Horne. Wheeler reported this name to have been derived from its apparent shape as seen from Amiskwi Pass.

SELKIRK: Range; 1821; CC. **Mount** [2938 m]; Mitchell. After the HBC–NWC merger of 1821, this famous range in western Canada was renamed from David Thompson's "Nelson's Mountains" to the titled name of Thomas Douglas (1771–1820). He was the fifth Earl of Selkirk, cousin of John Sholto Douglas, the eighth Marquess of Queensbury, whose boxing rules are used worldwide. In 1803 and 1804, Selkirk sponsored two settlements of Scottish highlanders displaced from their land by sheep farming, in P.E.I. and Upper Canada respectively. After buying a controlling interest in the HBC, Selkirk sponsored the Red River Colony, which led to Metis resentment and ultimately to the first Riel (Northwest) Rebellion. Selkirk's work was nevertheless a notable factor in the development of the nation of Canada. He was a humane man whose efforts were not welcomed by the bulk of fur traders, but is now an honoured figure in the history of Canada.

SELWYN: Mount [3335 m]; 1901; Dawson. Alfred Richard Cecil Selwyn (1824–1902), FRS, was the first director of the GSC. This peak had originally been called "Deville" by Green, in 1888, but was renamed by the Topographical Survey. Selwyn's uncle was the first archbishop of New Zealand.

SENTINEL: Mountain [2600 m]; 1893; Cline. Coleman felt that this peak on the dry side of the range, overlooking the area then known as Kootenay Plains (now generally flooded by the waters of Abraham Lake), was in the position of a sentinel over his campsite. This peak is a north shoulder of Elliott. **Pass** [2611 m]; 1910; Bow Ranges. The Grand Sentinel is the largest of the pinnacles on the Paradise Valley side of this pass. **Peak** [2992 m]; 1946; Adamant. Named by Hendricks, who led the party making the first climbing venture into the Adamant Range and Mount Sir Sandford area since the time of Palmer, for its position overlooking their campsite at Fairy Meadow.

SENTRY: Peak [3267 m]; Ottertail. This peak has been referred to as Little Goodsir. The name is commonly used in place of "Sentinel."

SEPTET: Mountains [3090 m], **Creek**; 1910; Bugaboo. This group of seven lesser peaks, east across the valley from the more famous Bugaboos, is dominated by Mount Ethelbert. Longstaff, Wheeler, Harmon and Kain (an historic mountaineering combination) went through the area and applied this name.

SERAPH: Mountain [2787 m]; 1907; Sorceror. Carson applied this name to the summit some 150 m lower and 3 km southeast of his "Cherub."

SERENDIPITY: Spire [2857 m]; 1971; Remillard. Jones felt that everything about his second trip into this region called for a name of this nature.

SERENITY: Mountain [3223 m], **Creek**; 1920; Whirlpool. This was applied by the ABC because of the peaceful appearance of the mountain as seen from their initial vantage point. *See also* Carnes.

SERGEANT: The [3185 m]; 1960; Commander. Anger applied this name to the southernmost and least of the peaks surrounding the head of the Lake of the Hanging Glaciers. *See also* Commander and Lieutenants.

Sentinel Mountain and Upper Swan Creek.
ROGER LAURILLA PHOTO

SERRATE: Mountain [2910m]; 1969; Starbird. This is a high-class variation on the more prosaic "Sawtooth."

SEXTET: Ridge; 1946; Bugaboo. This handle applies to a group of minor summits off the northeast ridge of Howser Peak, concluding with Frenchman Mountain.

SHACKLETON: Mount [3330m]; 1918; Icefields. Sir Ernest Henry Shackleton (1874–1922) was a notable figure in the exploration of Antarctica and adjacent islands. This name was applied four years before his death on South Georgia Island.

SHAFT #7: Location [2440m]; 1953; Bugaboo. This was the seventh campsite used by the Robinson party as it made its way south from the Carbonate Group in the first complete traverse of the Northern Purcell Range. The location consists of a sheltered cave underneath some boulders, and it became a guidebook reference point thereafter.

SHAMROCK: Lake [2484m]; 1915; Farnham. Stone claims he chose this name from the shape of the lake as he saw it from above. However, this was also the name of a mining claim in Boulder Creek (now Delphine), filed with mining recorder George Goldie in August 1899.

SHANKS: Mount [2844m]; 1927; Ball. Thomas Shanks, DLS, was assistant director general of the Topographical Survey of Canada.

SHANNON: Glacier; 1967; Starbird. West applied this name, taking the name of the longest river in the British Isles for the largest glacier in the area, in keeping with the Irish motif he had already established in this area.

SHARK: Mount [2786m]; 1917; British. This was the name of one of the smaller (935 tons) and older British destroyers (of the Fourth Flotilla) torpedoed and sunk on the evening of May 31, 1916, during the Battle of Jutland. Because of the great confusion among the participating warships, this sinking may have been due to "friendly fire." *See also* Wintour.

SHARKSHEAD: Tower [2911m]; 1933; S Purcells. McCoubrey wasn't telling fish tales when he reported on the fearsome aspect of some of the sheer rock faces in the Leaning Towers Group.

SHARP: Mountain [3049m]; 1901; Ottertail. Scattergood applied this name because it seemed to him descriptive of the outline of this summit as seen from Mount Mollison. **Mount** [2910m]; 1972; Icefield. This name was applied at the request of the ACC in memory of William T. Sharp (1937–1972), a club member killed under a falling serac in the Clemenceau Glacier.

SHATCH: Mountain [2884m]; 1922; French. This is the Stoney word for red and was applied here because of the colour of the summit rocks.

SHAUGHNESSY: Mount [2750 m]; 1900; Hermit. Sir Thomas George Shaughnessy (1853–1923) spent 19 years as the third president of the CPR. He was an American by birth and came to Canada with Van Horne. Under his leadership the mountain hotels and associated amenities were greatly expanded. His name is on the northernmost major summit of those above Rogers Pass and Glacier, while that pertaining to Sir Donald Smith, the CPR's first president, is nearly the southernmost. *See also* President.

SHAW: Peak [2710 m]; 1978; Sir Sandford. Dr. Charles Hugh Shaw, botanist of Philadelphia, was very interested in exploration of the Northern Selkirks and helped organize several early expeditions into these mountains. He drowned in a canoeing accident on Kinbasket Lake in 1910. *See also* Starbird.

SHEOL: Mountain [2779 m]; 1894; Bow Ranges. This name appears on Allen's earlier map and was given for the gloomy appearance of the desolate valley he saw below the mountain. Sheol is the classical Hebrew abode of the dead.

SHIPTON: Mount [3040 m]; 1964; Icefield. Eric Earle Shipton (1907–1977) was an English alpinist of distinction who climbed everywhere in the world but Canada. However, he had admirers among those who did.

SHOESTRING: Glacier; 1948; Adamant. That's about all this glacier was hanging by when it was first crossed by Ferris, Kauffman and Putnam en route to Mount Quadrant from Fairy Meadow.

SHOVEL: Pass [2300 m]; 1911; Maligne. The Otto Brothers, outfitters of Jasper, had to use makeshift shovels to clear snow from some parts of the route across this pass in order to haul a boat over it to Maligne Lake. The discarded shovels remained as landmarks for several years.

SHUSWAP: Group, Lake [347 m]; Gold. This name, subject to a variety of spellings, comes from the name of a Salishan tribe of the interior of British Columbia (now Secwepemc).

SIBBALD: Mount [2963 m]; 1970; N Purcells. John Drinkwater Sibbald (1846–1923) was gold commissioner of the West Kootenay district of British Columbia in 1897. Among other civic activities, he organized the Revelstoke board of trade. His cousin Frank was a rancher near Morley and sometime companion of Professor Coleman.

SIFFLEUR: River, Mountain [3129 m]; 1858; Murchison. Hector put this name in his narrative. The word is from the French for "whistler," as the hoary marmot of the mountains is sometimes and very appropriately called.

SIFTON: Mount [2922 m]; 1901; Hermit. Sir Clifford Sifton (1861–1929) was a Conservative politician who served as minister of the interior for 10 years starting in 1896, and after 1909 was chairman of the Dominion Commission on Conservation of Natural Resources.

SILENT: Pass [2063 m], **Peak** [2710 m], **Lake**; 1937; N Purcells. There is no record on the derivation of this unusual name. It first appears in the mountaineering literature without explanation, but one derivation could be the fact that the stream rushing eastwards from the summit lake soon disappears underground in this limestone country, leaving the delightful timberline scene essentially silent.

SILVERHORN: Mountain [2910 m]; 1899; Murchison. This was Noyes' description of the summit when he first studied it from the summit of Cirque Peak.

SILVERTIP: Mountain [2880 m], **Pass** [2554 m]; 1910; Sir Sandford. Palmer named this minor peak in honour of a grizzly that had been seen near his camp.

SIMILARITY: Mountain [2848 m]; 1953; Badshot. This summit is similar in shape, viewed from some angles, to the adjacent major summit of Mount Templeman, which lies 2 km to the north and some 200 m higher and is composed of equally bad rock.

SIMON: Peak [3322 m], **Creek, Glacier**; 1920; Ramparts. This is another reference to Simon Fraser, applied in this case again by the ABC.

SIMPSON: Pass [2107 m], **Peak** [2874 m], **Ridge, River**; 1859; Mitchell. Hector gave this name to the pass, which had been traversed by the famous and peripatetic governor of the HBC, Sir George Simpson (1792–1860), a dynamic man of uncertain ancestry who managed to merge the NWC and HBC and then lead the fur trade into unprecedented prosperity. **Mount** [3275 m]; 1969; Clearwater. Putnam applied this name to honour James Justin McCarthy Simpson (1877–1972), a notable guide, poacher and raconteur whose abode was at the Num-Ti-Jah Lodge on Bow Lake. Simpson had advised Putnam's group to be sure to take a supply of fish hooks if they were planning to travel via Douglas Lake. How right he was!

SINCLAIR: Mount [2660 m], **Pass** [1630 m]; 1885; W Rockies. James Sinclair (1802–1856) was a free trader of the Red River area who finally joined the HBC in 1853. He made many crossings of the Rockies, at least one using this pass, which opens westward into the lake country of the upper Columbia valley.

SIR ALEXANDER: Mountain [3270 m]; 1914; N Rockies. Cousin of the distinguished professor, Samuel Prescott Fay (1884–1971) was also a very fine alpinist. He led the first party to attempt this summit, which he named for Alexander Mackenzie (1764–1820), who in 1793 became the first person known to cross the full width of the North American continent. Mackenzie's name is also on the wide river by which he reached the Arctic Ocean. A fur trader in the employ of the NWC, Mackenzie was one of the world's most notable explorers. To Mary Lee Jobe (Akeley) in 1914, the mountain was "Kitchi," the Cree word for "mighty."

SIR ANDREW: Mount [2898 m]; 1953; Adamant. This was the "scribe" of the "Baronets."

SIR BENJAMIN: Mount [3002 m]; 1948; Adamant. This was the "senior" of the "Baronets." This name has been periodically and erroneously substituted on an adjacent peak for Palmer's "Wotan."

SIRDAR: Mountain [2810 m]; 1916; Maligne. This is the Indian subcontinent term for a person of high political rank and was suggested for this summit by George Hinton, then passenger traffic manager for the Grand Trunk Pacific. Hinton's own name came to rest on a town midway between Edmonton and Jasper.

SIR DAVID: Mount [2943 m]; 1953; Adamant. This was the "artist" of the "Baronets."

SIR DONALD: Mount [3284 m], **Range, Glacier**; 1887. By order-in-council the name of this prominent peak—among the most spectacular of Canada—was changed from "Syndicate," honouring the group that had assembled the financing necessary to construct the CPR, to a name honouring the principal figure of that group, Donald Alexander Smith (1820–1914), later Lord Strathcona and Mount Royal. Born in Morayshire, he had a long association with the HBC, starting in 1838. A man of great accomplishment, Smith was once described in the English *Dictionary of National Biography* as "a good hater."

SIR DOUGLAS: Mount [3406 m]; 1916; British. This summit was named by the ABC to honour Gen. Sir Douglas Haig (1861–1928), a veteran of campaigns in the Sudan, India and South Africa who commanded the British Expeditionary Force in France after 1915 to the end of the Great War.

SIR ERNEST: Peak [3150 m]; 1927; Icefields. Ostheimer applied this name in honour of the distinguished Arctic explorer, Sir Ernest Shackleton.

SIR GRAHAM: Mount [2904 m]; 1953; Adamant. This was the "scholar" of the "Baronets."

Mt. Sir Donald, NW Arete. ROGER LAURILLA PHOTO

Mt. Sir Douglas. GLEN BOLES PHOTO

SIR HENRY: Mount [2845 m]; 1953; Adamant. This was the "suttler" of the "Baronets."

SIR JAMES: Glacier; 1928; Lyell. This was applied to the glacier in the mistaken belief that the striking summit from which it drains was named for James David Forbes (rather than Edward Forbes), who was, in any case, never knighted.

SIR JOHN ABBOTT: Mount [3398 m]; 1927; Premier. John Joseph Caldwell Abbott (1821–1893) succeeded the great John A. as prime minister of the Dominion of Canada, but served only two years. The summit was originally named Kiwa Peak by Carpé and Chamberlin, the pioneer alpinists of the Cariboos.

SIR JOHN THOMPSON: Mount [3245 m]; 1927; Premier. John Sparrow David Thompson (1844–1894) followed Sir John Abbott as prime minister and died in office. This was Mount David Thompson on Carpé's map of 1925.

SIR JOSEPH: Mount [3030 m]; 1953; Whirlpool. This is a variation on Hooker, applied by Gibson after making the ascent of this summit, which is 3 km west of the more famous Mount Hooker.

SIR MACKENZIE BOWELL: Mount [3275 m]; 1927; Premier. Mackenzie Bowell (1823–1917) followed Sir John Thompson as prime

Mt. Sir John Thompson. GLEN BOLES PHOTO

minister, serving until the collapse of his government in 1896. In 1924 Carpé called this summit Mount Welcome because it was one of the first high points his party saw on its way up Mica (now Tête) Creek.

SIR SANDFORD: Mount [3519 m], **Glacier, Creek, Pass** [2600 m]; 1902. Wheeler named this, the highest peak of the Selkirk Range, after Sandford Fleming (1827–1915), the great Canadian railway executive who had charge of the CPR project from its inception until the close of the Mackenzie administration. Fleming, the prime instigator of Standard Time, was the initial patron of the ACC and its first honourary president.

SIR WILFRID LAURIER: Mount [3516 m]; 1927; 83D/13; Premier; CW. Wilfrid Laurier (1841–1919) was the leader of Canadian liberals (with or without capitalization). A wise and capable politician, he became the first Liberal prime minister since the ill-starred regime of Alexander Mackenzie in the 1870s. Prime minister from 1896 to 1911, he showed a perceptive understanding of the aspirations of both the French and English in his nation. The highest peak of the area, this was Mount Titan to Carpé in 1924.

SIR WILLIAM: Mount [2946 m]; 1953; Adamant. This was the originator of the "Baronet" toponymic hoax.

232

SISSONS: Mount [2946 m]; 1963; Moloch. Putnam named this summit after Charles Bruce Sissons (1879–1965), a classicist of long Canadian lineage who was many years on the faculty of Victoria College. He had worked under Wheeler as an assistant in the mountain surveys in 1900–1902 and served as the first principal of Revelstoke High School. The summit had been occupied by Bridgland as "Holway South Station." See Sissons' memoirs, *Nil Alienum* (Toronto, 1964).

SIX GLACIERS: Plain; 1920; Bow Ranges. From this level area above Lake Louise, with its charming and historic tea house, the eye can take in between five and seven glaciers (depending on what one chooses to count), some in better repair than others. During the heyday of the Swiss guides at Lake Louise, the tea house provided housing as well as summer employment for their wives and adolescent children.

SIX MILE: Pass [2259 m]; 1884; Sorceror. This name originated at a point six miles west along the CPR from Beavermouth station. It migrated up the creek (now Cupola) to the pass. Unfortunately, even the station was renamed—to Rogers—but the pass retains its anachronistic handle, being at least six miles from quite a few places.

SKENE: Mount [3060 m]; 1919; Freshfield. Peter Skene Ogden (1794–1854) joined the NWC in 1811 and became a chief trader after the merger into HBC in 1821. He explored much of the North American west, largely south of the 49th parallel. His cache at the mouth of a side valley northeast of the Great Salt Lake has placed his name prominently on the map of Utah too.

SKIRMISH: Peak [2854 m]; 1987; Westfall. Named by the Kootenay Mountaineering Club, but for reasons they chose to suppress.

SKOKI: Valley, Mountain [2707 m]; 1911; Slate. This is alleged by some to be the Stoney word for "swamp," of which there are several in this valley. Another source—a note left by J.F. Porter on the cabin wall at Skoki—indicates that the name was transplanted from a similarly swampy locality near Chicago.

SKOOKUMCHUCK: River, Mountain [2603 m]; 1931; S Purcells. According to our Kootenay/English dictionary, skookum translates to "strong," and chuck to "water." Thorington pulled the name from the stream up onto the twin-topped mountain.

SLADE: Mount [3218 m]; 1914; Farnham. This name belonged to one of the principals of the Parridice Mine, which was on the south slopes of this massif. In 1911, Harnden had called this summit Boulder Peak.

SLATE: Range; 1916. There is, indeed, a lot of slate (some of it rather crumbly) in this minor range north of the Bow River near Lake Louise village.

SLOCAN: Lake [536m], **Mountains, River;** 1859. Members of the Palliser Expedition noted this lake's name as derived from the Shuswap word for frog. It sounded good and jumped to various places around the area.

SLUMP: Mountain [3090m]; 1968; Cline. This lesser peak, near Mount Coleman, shows a huge cavity in its southwest side, the result of a massive slump of thousands of tons of rock into the valley below. This condition was not reported by Coleman, but was fully noted 70 years later by Howard Stidham of the AMC.

SMALLFRY: Ridge [2777m]; 1948; Moloch. Arnold Wexler, another of the erudite Washingtonian group surrounding Hendricks, named two of the peaks on this minor ridge west of Tangier Summit for Eric Scoredos and Martha Hendricks, children of members of the first ascent party.

SMART: Mount [2863m]; 1901; Sir Donald. The Topographical Survey named this lesser summit after James Allen Smart (1858–1912), deputy minister of the Interior for Indian Affairs, 1897 to 1904.

SMITH: Peak [3097m]; 1960; S Rockies. Able Seaman Thomas Bernard Smith of Natal, B.C., was killed in action during the Second World War.

SMITH-DORRIEN: Mount [3155m], **Creek;** 1919; British. Sir Horace Lockwood Smith-Dorrien (1858–1930) had served in the Zulu War of 1879 and was in command of the British Second Army in the early years of the Great War. He was later in command at the Rock of Gibraltar.

SMOKY: Mountain [3133m]; Clearwater. The river valley was once filled with clouds, hence a derivation similar to Misty or Storm. Farther north, Hector called the river "Smoking" in 1859, presumably from fires in some of the thin coal seams found along its banks. *See also* Swoda.

SMUTS: Mount [2938m], **Creek;** 1918; British. Jan Christiaan Smuts (1870–1950) was the outstanding leader of the Union of South Africa from its inception until his death. A wise and conciliatory statesman, an effective and vigorous general, he became the symbol of all the best in the melange of races he ruled and served. He urged peaceful union of Boers under the British flag, a conciliatory policy toward the defeated Germans after the Great War and was a strong opponent of apartheid a generation later.

SMYTHE: Mount [2772m]; 1960; N Rockies. Origin uncertain. William Smythe (1842–1887) was premier of British Columbia from 1883 until his death, while the distinguished alpinist and prolific author Francis Sydney Smythe (1900–1949), was a member of the first party to visit these very mountains in 1947. The name has also been applied on map sheet 83C/5 to what is officially Mount Mitchell, after J.H. Mitchell, a long-time employee of the National Park Service who laid out the Icefields Parkway. There is another **Mount** [3240 m] in the Churchill Group, SE of Gong Lake.

SNAFFLEHOUND: Spire [2972 m]; 1958; Bugaboo. "Snafflehound" is a term used by some alpinists in preference to the scholarly *Ochotona princeps*, more commonly referred to as the little chief hare, cony or pika. This charming and diminutive high-altitude creature cuts its winter hay in many an alpine meadow and often furnishes breakfast to an awakening bear.

SNAKE INDIAN: River, Falls, Pass [2025 m], **Mountain** [2947 m]; 1812; Robson. This name commemorates a small tribe treacherously murdered by the neighbouring Assiniboines when the latter had invited them to a peacemaking observation—this according to a legend reported by Hector. The name, however, was first applied by David Thompson.

SNARING: River, Mountain [2931 m]; 1858; Jasper. Hector says that the locals who lived along this river obtained their food by snaring rabbits, etc., in pits and with loops.

SNOW: Dome [3518 m±]; 1919; Icefields. Collie labelled this simply "the Dome" in 1899. The ABC survey team found that it was the hydrographic apex of North America whence precipitation drains to each of the three surrounding oceans, but mostly toward the Arctic. The ABC gave the present, slightly revised, name. This summit's precise altitude varies, not with the frequently encountered refinements in surveying technology, but with the quantity and quality of snowfall.

SNOWBIRD: Pass [2425 m]; 1956; Robson. Origin unknown, but various derivations suggest themselves: the common junco, the uncommon junkie, a stranded dinghy, an inept skier or a winter resident of Florida.

SNOWCREST: Mountain [2870 m]; 1948; S Rockies. A cornice by any other name would overhang as much.

SNOWMAN: Pass [2260 m], **Peak, Lake** [2210 m]; 1954; N Purcells. Professor Robinson reports that one of his companions, William Briggs, saw unusual tracks in the soft snow on the approach to this col.

SNOW OCEAN: Glacier; 1974; Badshots. The skiers' name for the wide and gentle snowfield making up the major source of the south fork of Laidlaw Creek.

SNOWPATCH: Spire [3063 m]; 1925; Bugaboo. Named by Kain because of the highly visible snow patch perched on the cliff of its northeast side. That five acres is not a hanging glacier; it just sits there with no crevasses. Despite the proximity of one of the world's most famous names in skiing, no one has tried this slope—yet! If you catch an edge there's precious little runout before the 300 m *gelundesprung.* ·

SODERHOLM: Mount [2850 m]; 1966; Royal. Samuel G. Soderholm was serving with the Royal Air Force in Egypt when reported missing in action during the Second World War.

SOLITAIRE: Mountain [3270 m]; 1918; Freshfield. Named by the ABC, this mountain is isolated by the two branches of the Conway Glacier.

SOMERVELL: Mount [3120 m]; 1927; Icefields. Ostheimer suggested this name after the medical doctor of Mount Everest fame, Theodore Howard Somervell (1890–1975), who distinguished himself equally by his years of service in India. He was a collaborator in the study of high-altitude physiology with the celebrated Lewis Griffith E.E. Pugh (1869–1994) and also served as president of the AC.

SONATA: Mountain [3020 m]; 1908; Sorceror. This is another of the names applied by Carson, for which he offered little explanation. But it goes well with Cherub.

SORCEROR: Mountain [3167 m], **Pass** [2024 m], **Creek**, **Glacier**; 1909. This peak was once appropriately labelled "The Hub of the Big Bend" by Dr. Shaw, who approached (but did not climb) it via Tangier Creek in 1900. It was renamed by the Topographical Survey crew under Carson.

SOUTHESK: Cairn [2552 m], **Mount** [3120 m], **Pass** [2250 m], **River**, **Lake**; 1859; Maligne. James Carnegie (1827–1905), ninth earl of Southesk, normally a denizen of the Grampian Mountains, travelled through the Frontal Ranges of the Rockies during some of the same time the Palliser Expedition was in the field. His book *Saskatchewan and the Rocky Mountains* (Edinburgh, 1875) tells the story of an eventful hunting trip. With wanderlust out of his system, upon his return he married Susan Murray, daughter of the earl of Dunmore. *See also* Balinhard.

SPARROWHAWK: Mount [3121 m]; 1917; 82J/14; Kananaskis. This was the name of an older destroyer (935 tons) of the Fourth Flotilla that participated in the Battle of Jutland. During the course of the foggy nighttime melee, it was rammed by HMS *Broke* and then the *Contest*, companion destroyers, and was finally ordered scuttled the next day, when it appeared obviously unsalvagable and no one was sure when or where the High Seas Fleet might reappear. *See also* Wintour.

Snowpatch Spire. GLEN BOLES DRAWING

SPEAR: Spire [3002 m]; 1958; Bugaboo. Alpinist William Buckingham's first ascent team felt this to be "a nicely alliterative name," justified by "the slender summit block."

SPEARHEAD: Mountain [3216 m]; 1915; Farnham. Stone gave this name because of the sharpness of the summit.

SPEKE: Mount [3045 m]; 1927; Icefields. Thorington applied this name to honour the notable English explorer of East Africa, John Hanning Speke (1827–1864), who had been with Richard Burton to Lake Victoria in 1862. Speke's summit lies north of the twin peaks named for Stanley and Livingstone, as were their respective fields of exploration.

SPHINX: Lake [2301 m]; 1915; Ball. This miniscule lake is part of the Egyptian pattern of nomenclature the Topographic Survey applied in this immediate vicinity. *See also* Haiduk.

SPIKE: Peak [2918 m]; 1916; Van Horne. Looking up Otterhead Creek, it is quite impressive.

SPILLIMACHEEN: River, Range, Glacier, Mountain [2880 m], **Locality** [791 m]; 1883; N Purcells. This name was once applied to the Shuswap River, as "Spallumcheen," but migrated considerably to the east and took root on the large tributary of the Columbia flowing southeastward between the Dogtooth Range and the rest of the Purcells. It first appears in the mining recorder reports of this year and translates to "flat meadow." Reflecting the mining interest in the headwaters of the river, the post office on the upper Columbia was once called Galena.

SPINE: Mountain [2857 m]; 1953; Badshots. This is a ridge with a number of minor lumps.

SPINSTER: Creek, Peak [2582 m]; 1908; N Selkirks. Iconoclast and Sorceror are across Mountain Creek to the west. Dominion surveyor Percy Carson had a station here.

SPLENDID: Mount [2970 m]; S Rockies. Before going off to Mount Everest, Pat Morrow furnished this grand name, but the ascent is easy via the north ridge.

SPLIT: Peak [2929 m]; 1916; Mitchell. Indeed, the peak is split. The east summit is considerably more difficult of ascent than the west.

SPLIT ROCK: Spire [2886 m]; 1964; Bugaboo. Kruszyna applied this apt name.

SPOKANE: Creek, Glacier; 1890; S Selkirks. While this particular glacier lies east of Mount Cooper and has no unusual characteristics, its name is typical of many in this mineralized area of southeastern British Columbia. These names all reflect their donors' interests, but one consistent thread is that most of the prospectors were from south of the 49th parallel. *See also* Begbie.

SPRAY: Lakes [1693 m], **River, Pass** [2090 m], **Range**; Kananaskis. In the days before a massive diversion in 1950, the falls in the lower reaches of this river, where it joined the Bow, created considerable spray.

SPRING RICE: Mount [3275 m]; 1918; Alexandra. Sir Cecil Spring-Rice (1859–1918), third Lord Mounteagle, was a British diplomat who served as ambassador to Persia, then Sweden and finally the United States. There are several subsidiary points and glaciers in this area that bear derivatives of this name.

SQUAB: Peak [2750 m]; Bugaboo. This point lies between Pip and Squeak peaks.

SQUABBLE: Peak [3154 m]; S. Purcells. Appropriately, this lies less than 2 km north of Truce Mountain.

SPYGLASS: Mountain [2850 m], **Creek**; 1903; S Selkirks. This name came from a mining claim that was worked by an offshoot of the Ferguson settlement.

STAIRWAY: Peak [2999m]; 1924; Waputik. The east ridge of this peak, dropping down toward Cirque Lake, shows very definite steps, but they are big ones.

STANFORD: Range; 1865; SW Rockies. This name was lost by future generations, but had been applied to the southerly end of today's Brisco Range. It appears to have been given by Edward Stanford (1827–1904), the London mapmaker who was successor to John Arrowsmith in editing the Palliser Expedition's observations into a publishable map. Stanford's business was worldwide and was carried on by his son and namesake (1856–1917).

STANLEY: Peak [3155 m], **Glacier;** 1901; Ball. Whymper applied this name after Frederick Arthur Stanley (1841–1908), Canada's sixth Governor General, whose name is known to all hockey fans. After his five-year term was over, he returned to England as the 16th earl of Derby. His father, Edward Henry Stanley (1826–1893), the 15th earl, was foreign secretary under Disraeli (1874–78) and a great supporter of the Palliser Expedition. Sir Charles Stanley (1819–1894) was the first Governor General of Canada in 1867, after a few active years of supporting the concept of confederation. **Mount** [3090m]; 1927; Icefields. Thorington applied this name to honour Henry Morton Stanley (1841–1904), born John Rowland. He was a newspaper reporter covering both sides of the American Civil War and then went on his most famous trip—to locate and report on the condition of the British missionary and explorer David Livingstone. This summit is the west twin to Livingstone.

STANLEY BALDWIN: Mount [3249 m]; 1927; Premier. Stanley Baldwin (1867–1947), first Earl of Bewdley, was a Conservative politician who served intermittently as prime minister of Great Britain between 1923 and 1937. This summit was originally named Challenger by Carpé.

STARBIRD: Pass [2439 m], **Glacier, Ridge;** 1912; 82K/10; CS. Thomas Starbird, a native of Massachusetts, lived many years at his Mountain Valley Ranch, a guest house 18 km up the valley of Horsethief Creek from the Columbia River. He discovered the Lake of the Hanging Glaciers and originally named it after his wife, Elsie Maye (née Lewis). He was active in the mining business of the Purcell area after 1898. He died by suicide in 1914, after his wife became "involved with Dr. Shaw." Thereafter, the ranch was abandoned and reclaimed by the forest.

STARK: Mount [3063 m]; 1974; 82K/2; S Purcells; CS. George Starke (1854–1918) bought the Colorado Mine from Stockdale in 1901 and worked several other prospects in the upper reaches of Toby Creek.

In the foreground, Mts. Stanley, Livingston and Rhodes.
The prominent mountain in the upper centre is Tsar Mountain.

GLEN BOLES PHOTO

STARLIGHT: Range; 1923; 83E/7; N Rockies. Thanks to the ABC, this infrequently visited area is crowned by a number of stellar names like Arcturus, Vega and Sirius, some of the brighter points of the heavenly firmament.

STARVATION: Peak [2841 m], **Lake** [2143 m]; 1928; Flathead. This name commemorates the near demise of some men connected with the IBSC who strayed off course, got wintered in without sufficient supplies and were unable to feed themselves. Fortunately they were found.

STELFOX: Mount [2627 m]; 1956; Cline. English-born Henry Stelfox (1877–1974), having served his hitch in South Africa, settled in Alberta at age 29 and became a leading advocate of the Stoney people. His work was so meaningful to the tribe that he was elected an honourary chief of those living in the vicinity of Rocky Mountain House. See his book *Rambling Thoughts of a Wandering Fellow* (1972).

STEPHEN: Mount [3199 m], **Glacier**; 1886; Bow Ranges. George Stephen (1829–1921), a native of Aberdeen, worked his way up to the presidency of Canada's oldest and largest bank, the Bank of Montreal, in 1876. Thereafter he headed the CPR in its formative years. The mountain south of and above the town of Field was named for him and from it he took his peerage title in 1891—Lord Mount Stephen. The glacier was long a source of serious annoyance to the CPR, period-ically dumping vast quantities of debris on the tracks and occasionally even on the trains, until a massive restraining wall and roof were built in 1987. Stephen was a first cousin of Sir Donald Smith—his mother was sister to Sir Donald's father.

STEWART: Mount [3312 m]; 1902; Cline. George Alexander Stewart (1830–1917) and his son surveyed the boundaries of what has since become known as Banff National Park, of which the father was superintendent, 1887–99. This name was applied by Coleman, who was accompanied on two of his journeys by the son. *See also* Louis.

STICKLE: The [3146 m]; 1953; Adamant. This impressive spire was named by W.V. Graham Matthews (1920–2004), then of the Harvard Mountaineering Club, who led its first ascent. The summit manifests a very pointed aspect from all sides.

STILETTO: The [2975 m]; 1964; Italian. Members of the ACC felt this to be the sharpest pinnacle in the French Military Group.

STITT: Creek; 1920; Sir Sandford. Ormond Montgomery Stitt (1884–1918), DLS 1911, was killed in action during the Great War.

STOCKDALE: Mountain [3124 m], **Creek, Group**; 1924; Farnham. Francis Clarence Stockdale (1869–1947) of Cartwright, Ontario, came west en route to the Klondike in 1898, but stopped off in Athelmere. He liked what he saw in the upper Columbia valley and got no farther. The mining urge remained, however, and by 1915 he owned the Iron King.

STOCKMER: Mount [2820 m]; 1909; Adamant. This is a compound of the names of its first ascent party, Benjamin Sayre Com**stock** (1859–1941) and Howard Pal**mer**.

STONE: Mount [3033 m]; 1954; Bugaboo. Robinson named this summit after Winthrop Ellsworth Stone (1862–1921), a chemistry professor and subsequently president of Purdue University. A latecomer to alpinism, he lost his life making the first ascent of Mount Eon in the Rockies. Stone had previously taken part in two trips into the southern Purcell Range.

STORELK: Mount [2880 m]; 1915; High Rock. Even the ABC had trouble with acceptance of its names; this acronymic job did not become official for 21 years.

STORM: Mountain [3091 m], **Creek**; 1884; Highwood. This name was applied by Dawson because of some foul weather around this peak during his attempts to observe its altitude. **Mountain** [3161 m]; 1884; Ball. A generic name, applied here for the same common and obvious reasons.

STORNOWAY: Mount [2886 m]; 1939; N Rockies. This name derives, probably by way of an HBC employee, from a small town on the Isle of Lewis off the west coast of Scotland.

STORUS: Mountain; 1973; Commander. This should have been "Horus," but somehow was misrecorded. It is one of the Egyptian Peaks south of Monica and the name seems to have stuck, even if wrong. Wagner's handwriting may have confused the toponymy department.

STRACHAN: Mount [2704 m]; 1918; High Rock. Lt. Henry Strachan (1889–1917), a twice-decorated hero of the Canadian Army, was killed in action during the Great War.

STRAHAN: Mount [3060 m]; 1920; Freshfield. Sir Aubrey Strahan (1862–1929), KBE, was director of the Geological Survey of Great Britain.

STRANGE: Mount [2887 m]; 1954; Jasper. Maj. Gen. Thomas Bland Strange (1831-1925) had served in the Indian Mutiny and was called from retirement at his ranch to command the Alberta Field Force, which helped put down the second Northwest Rebellion in 1885.

STRIPED: Mountain [2807 m]; 1915; Ottertail. In this predominantly sedimentary area, a lot of mountains have this appearance.

STROM: Mount [3023 m]; 1960; Assiniboine. Once known as Survey Peak and later as Norwegian Peak, this is named for Erling Strom (1898–1985), a native of Oslo who, with the Italian Marquis degli Albizzi (scion of an ancient Florentine family), developed skiing in the Canadian Rockies starting in 1928. After a few years he began to operate a ski lodge at Assiniboine for the CPR. The lodge is now owned by the B.C. provincial park and managed by Sepp and Barbara Renner. Strom was an avid and famous skier largely responsible for popularizing skiing in western Canada.

STRUTT: Peak [2691 m]; 1956; N Purcells. It is tempting to suggest that this peak is named for Colonel Edward Lisle Strutt (1874–1948), a much decorated English military officer who became the military commander of Danzig and was later second-in-command of the 1922 Mount Everest Assault. But candour compels us to state that this name derives from William A. Strutt, who was the mining recorder at nearby Beaton for five years after 1912. His own home survived Beaton's disastrous fire of 1904 because the neighbouring assay office was blown up to create a firebreak.

STUART: Knob [2850 m]; 1888; Sawback. This name was applied by McArthur, but he gave no rationale. Barbara Stuart, mother of Sir Donald Smith, had two brothers, Robert and John, who both played parts in the exploration of western Canada. *See also* Leanchoil.

STUBBS: Mount [2950m]; 1974; S Selkirks. Lewis St. George Stubbs (1878–1949), a socialist MLA of Manitoba, was very popular among unionized miners, of which there were quite a few in the Slocan area.

STURDEE: Mount [3155 m]; 1917; Assiniboine. Sir Frederick Charles Doveton Sturdee (1859–1925) was the victorious commander of the British Squadron at the 1914 Battle of the Falkland Islands. This was the first good news the British Navy could announce in the Great War; Graf von Spee's squadron was soundly defeated and its leader met his death. Sturdee was later in command of a part of the Grand Fleet at Jutland and became Admiral of the Fleet in 1921.

STUTFIELD: Peak [3450m], **Glacier**; 1899; Icefields. Hugh Edward Millington Stutfield (1858–1929) was a companion of Woolley, Spencer and Collie for two seasons and made several first ascents in these mountains. He subsequently collaborated with Collie on a book called *Climbs and Exploration in the Canadian Rockies* (London, 1903).

SUGARLOAF: Mountain [3256m]; 1890; Purity. Topham labelled this prominent summit because of its shape and whitish appearance from the north and east, the directions from which he saw it.

SUGARPLUM: Spire [2850m]; 1954; N Purcells. Because its crest was "frosted white like a cake," Professor Robinson felt this to be a very apt name.

SULLIVAN: Peak [3022 m], **River**; 1859; Lyell. John William Sullivan (1836–1886) was secretary and astronomer to the Palliser Expedition, but took a relatively minor part in the actual work of exploration. He went on to New Zealand with Hector in 1862.

SULPHUR: Mountain [2451 m]; 1916; Bow Ranges. This lesser summit west of Banff takes its name from the odour of the hot springs near its base. The northwesterly point of the mountain has been crowned with a cosmic ray recording station since 1956.

SULTANA: Peak [3185 m]; 1911; Farnham. Harnden named this summit after a mining claim on its lower slopes.

SUNBURST: Peak [2830m], **Valley**; 1953; Assiniboine. This was "Goat's Tower" in 1910 when climbed by Katherine Longstaff.

SUNDANCE: Ridge [2900m], **Pass** [1755 m]; Bow Ranges. Native dances and worship were alleged to have occurred in the vicinity of this mountain pass and beside the creek leading up to it.

SUNDIAL: Mountain [3182 m]; 1919; Chaba. The ABC noted an unusually placed rock on the summit, which looked like the arm of a sundial.

SUNSET: Pass [2065 m]; 1898; Cline. Coleman was merely the first to record that this place routinely offers one of the finest sunset views in Canada.

SUNWAPTA: River, Pass [2030 m], **Peak** [3315 m], **Falls**; 1892; Maligne. Coleman applied the Stoney words for "turbulent water" to the river for obvious reasons; it migrated thence to adjacent features.

SURPRISE: Rapids; 1865; N Selkirks. Moberly noted the name, but did not take credit for it. In the days when canoe travel was commonplace on the Columbia, this horrendous rapid was a place to be avoided. Several fatal accidents were reported here, just a mile below the placid reaches where the Bush and Gold rivers joined the main stream. Except in times of unusual drawdown at Mica Creek Dam, this feature is now safely buried beneath the waters of the expanded Kinbasket Lake.

SURVEY: Peak [2667 m]; 1897; Lyell. This peak lies north of Glacier Lake and near the headwaters forks of the Saskatchewan River. It was climbed by Collie to get a good vantage point for his plane table survey of the nearby mountains.

SWAN: Creek; 1937; Adamant. There were allegedly some swans seen by Norman McConnell's survey party near the mouth of this creek, which entered the Columbia midway between Surprise Rapids and Kinbasket Lake (all now submerged under the expanded Kinbasket Lake). **Lake** [2275 m]; 1973; Maligne. Putnam suggested this name to honour his friend Bradford Fuller Swan (1907–1976), a member of the first party to camp near this lake. A notable member of the AMC and AAC, Swan was also a prominent art and drama critic of New England.

SWANSON: Peak [2780 m]; 1964; S Rockies. Pte. 2 Kurt W. Swanson of Cranbrook was killed in action during the Second World War.

SWANZY: Mount [2891 m]; 1897; Sir Donald. Fay named this summit for the Reverend Henry Swanzy (1841–1910), a cousin of Green, who accompanied him on their noteworthy trip to the Selkirks in 1888 under the auspices of the Royal Geographical Society.

SWIDERSKI: Mount [3133 m]; 1964; Italian. Sgt. Alexander Swiderski of Fernie and the RCAF was killed in action during the Second World War.

SWISS: Peak [3167 m]; 1888; Hermit. Named by Carl Sulzer (1865–1934) of Zürich who made the first ascent of this peak in company with a local porter–guide at Glacier House known to posterity only as Yves.

SWODA: Mountain [3003 m]; 1923; Robson. This was the Stoney name for the Smoky River. The old name was moved up onto one of the headwaters tributaries and thence to the mountain when the main river was renamed by white surveyors.

SYLVAN: Pass [2338 m]; 1901; French. Wilcox gave this nice name, but it's not really appropriate since the pass (west of Mount Joffre) is decidedly above timberline.

SYNCLINE: Mountain [2972 m]; 1953; N Purcells. Since it had been surrounded by clouds, Robinson first tried "Brouillard," but because the skies cleared and that name was taken, he then chose this geological term (referring to a trough, or downfold). This name was also applied to a lesser summit in the Rockies near the headwaters of the Oldman River.

SYNGE: Mount [2972 m]; 1924; Waputik. Irish-born Capt. Millington Henry Synge (1823–1907), engineer, soldier and author, prepared a map in 1852 showing essentially the present route of the CPR main line across the continent. His work was ridiculed and ignored for seemingly more attractive alternatives to the north. But time, as in many similar cases, has proven him right.

SYPHAX: Mount [2880 m]; 1953; N Purcells. This name was mentioned by Joseph Addison (1672–1719), the famous English essayist, as the name of a Numidian soldier-king who deserted Carthage to join Scipio in 203 B.C. but was later killed by Marcus, son of Cato. Professor Robinson, however, who put the name onto this summit, took it from Jules Verne.

As to the adjective, when in doubt strike it out.
—MARK TWAIN, *PUDD'NHEAD WILSON*, 1894

TABERNACLE: Mountain [2538 m], **Creek**; 1909; Adamant. Palmer appears to have named the ridge, but did not explain why. He climbed it for the first time to see if he could deduce a route to Mount Sir Sandford. In 1937, the same point was occupied by McConnell as a triangulation station.

TAKAKKAW: Falls; 1897; Waputik. Van Horne applied this name after inquiring for the local (Stoney) word for "magnificent."

TANGIER: Mine, River, Pass [1743 m]; 1895; Sorceror. Moberly knew this as the north fork of the Illecillewaet, and followed it up to the pass in 1865. The present name was applied first to the mine, which is near the crest of the pass. The more important Waverly Mines were beyond (north of) the summit on the east side of the headwaters of Sorceror Creek. The mines were claimed in 1896 and 1899, then operated briefly by an English firm, Gold Fields of British Columbia, Ltd. Reopened in 1918, they were closed again in 1929. Today's owners, most of a century later, offer no knowledge of how the original name was derived.

TANGLE: Creek, Ridge [3000 m]; 1907; Maligne. Mary Schäffer labelled the creek because of the difficulty her party had while descending it from Wilcox Pass. There is also a **Peak** [2787 m] in the Royal Group on map sheet 82J/12, which got its name for the same kind of reason.

TATEI: Ridge [2798 m]; 1928; Robson. This name pertains to the northeast rim of the Robson Glacier and is reported to be the Stoney word for "wind."

TAURUS: Mountain [2972 m], **Group, Notch** [2392 m]; 1916; Starbird. According to Thorington, Austrian-born Kain named this peak for the constellation.

TEEPEE: Mountain [3118 m]; 1933; Ottertail. Katie Gardiner gave this name for the shape of the summit as it appeared when she and Lillian Gest made its first ascent.

TEMPLE: Mount [3543 m]; 1884; Bow Ranges. Dawson named this impressive summit for Sir Richard Temple (1826–1902), an economist who was leader of the British Association field trip to the Canadian Rockies in that year. Temple was primarily concerned with India, and this was his only visit to Canada. Some of the more adventurous members of his party went beyond the "end of steel" to visit the Selkirk Mountains, farther west.

TEMPLEMAN: Mount [3074 m]; 1924; Badshot. William Templeman (1844–1914) was a senator and minister of inland revenue and mines under Laurier between 1906 and 1911. He was also the owner of the Victoria *Times*. His summit is the striking pyramid that dominates the Badshot Range.

TEN PEAKS: Valley of the; 1894; Bow Ranges. This is the second valley east of Lake Louise, called "Desolation" by Allen and Wilcox, in contrast to the intervening "Paradise" valley. Allen numbered the peaks clockwise from the northeast around and above Moraine Lake, using the Stoney numbers. All but three of them have since

Mt. Temple. GLEN BOLES DRAWING

been renamed. These are now officially and collectively called the Wenkchemna Peaks.

TENDERFOOT: Mountain [2827 m], **Creek, Glacier, Lake** [2124 m]; 1903; Slocan. This was originally the name of a claim that was worked by miners living in Lardeau, at least one of whom was obviously a newcomer to the trade.

TERMIER: Mount [2850 m]; 1924; Freshfield. Pierre Termier (1859–1930) was a professor of mining at St. Etienne, then at Paris, and he headed the Geological Survey of France for many years after the turn of the century.

TERMINAL: Peak [2960 m N—2997 m S]; 1901; Sir Donald. This twin-crested southernmost peak of the Sir Donald Range was originally called Green's Peak in 1889, but was renamed by the Topographical Survey to recognize its position and to avoid confusion with nearby Mount Green, a few kilometres to the west.

TERRACE: Mountain [2940 m]; 1859; Icefields. Hector felt the stratified shape of this mountain justified the name.

TERRA NOVA: Mount [3090 m]; 1953; Whirlpool. ACC members made the first ascent of this summit from their annual camp and applied the Latin term for "new country."

TERRAPIN: Lake [1875 m], **Mountain** [2944 m]; 1924; Assiniboine. This name appears to have first been applied to the lake, for its shape, and then to have found its way slowly up the mountain.

TERRION: Mount [2923 m]; 1964; S Rockies. Corporal James P. Terrion of Michel was killed in action during the Second World War.

TERRY FOX: Mount [2651 m]; 1980; Cariboo. Terrance Stanley Fox

(1958–1981) developed osteogenic sarcoma and suffered a partial amputation of his leg. He set out to run across Canada in an effort to raise money for cancer research. He got more than halfway before his illness overcame him, and his heroism inspired a great outpouring of admiration and support from across the nation.

TÊTE: Glacier, Creek; 1927; Jasper. This name was applied by the Board on Geographic Names from the nickname of Pierre Bostonais "Tête Jaune" (d. 1827), a blond Iroquois employee of the NWC and then the HBC, which established a cache in the early 1820s near what is the present height-of-land of Yellowhead Pass.

TETRAGON: Peak [2910 m]; 1966; N Purcells. Robinson's party felt this summit to be somewhat squarish.

THIMBLE: Peak [3000 m]; 1930; Bugaboo. This is the hydrographic apex of the Bugaboo Group and was first climbed—and named—by Cromwell for its shape.

THOMAS: Mount [2817 m]; 1980; Battle. Laurilla led the ascent of this previously unnamed peak west of Gobi Pass with Putnam, J.A.V. Cade, S.H. Goodhue and D.C. Henley. He then asked if it was proper to name it after his late older brother, Thomas George. The party shared a pre-mixed martini in celebration, from which event the summit has sometimes been called Martini Peak.

THOMPSON: Pass [1985 m], **Mount** [3065 m]; 1898; Lyell. Collie applied this name after Charles Sproull Thompson (1869–1921), a freight agent for the Illinois Central Railroad who climbed extensively in the Canadian Alps. In a vain attempt to join forces with Collie, who was trying an approach up the Bush River from the west, Thompson was the first to follow the Alexandra River to its source at the pass that now bears his name. The two men were close friends; Collie had earlier rescued Thompson from the depths of a crevasse. **Glacier**; 1925; 83D/12; Premier; CW. This is the only landmark (other than his river) bearing the name of the NWC explorer David Thompson (1770–1857), who is widely regarded as the greatest land explorer of English origin. Carpé applied his full name to a peak at the head of the glacier, but in 1925 it was officially deleted in favour of a yet unnamed premier. The glacier is below Trigon Mountain. See the 1962 *Champlain Society* volume by Richard Glover. There is also a lesser **Peak** [2547 m] in the Badshot Group.

THOR: Mountain [2948 m], 1900; Gold. Named for the son of Odin and applied here by some residents of nearby Revelstoke, whence this point is clearly visible to the southwest. **Glacier**; 1908; Purity. This was named by Palmer, along with the neighbouring Odin Glacier, both of which have largely melted away since. **Mount** [2980 m], **Pass** [2750 m]; 1910; Adamant. Named by Howard Palmer, whose party used the steep west approach to the pass en route to Pioneer Peak. The peak itself was subsequently climbed only by Holway. This name goes with those of other Norse gods on the peaks that fringe the south side of the wide Gothics Glacier. The pass is a landmark for alpinists migrating between the Ben Ferris and Bill Putnam huts.

THORINGTON: Mount [3033 m], **Pass** [2590 m]; 1954; Bugaboo. **Tower**; 1967; Churchill. Dr. James Monroe (Roy) Thorington, opthalmologist of Philadelphia, became the greatest scholar of alpinism in North America. Thorington's writings on alpine history are legion, including the lead article in the centennial issue of the *Alpine Journal*. He, with Palmer, initiated the climbers' guidebook series to the Rocky Mountains and he alone initiated the series for the interior ranges of British Columbia (since retitled the Columbia Mountains, but including the Monashee, Gold, Selkirk, Purcell and Premier mountains). Thorington served many years as editor of the *American Alpine Journal* and was elected president of the AAC in 1941. He also wrote *The Purcell Range of British Columbia* (New York, 1946). This summit, at the northwest extremity of the Conrad Group, is infrequently visited, but is very close to the mountain he ensured was named for his friend and frequent guide Conrad Kain.

THOTH: *See* Horus.

THOUSAND FALLS: Valley; 1921; Robson. This impressive valley, upstream from Kinney Lake on the west side of Mount Robson, was named by the ABC because of the numerous and impressive falls that punctuate the stream below Berg Lake. Emperor Falls is the largest, but there are numerous others.

THREE BROTHERS: Mountains [S–3035 m, C–3182 m, N–3118 m]; 1937; Clearwater. Katie Gardiner (1885–1974) named these adjacent peaks because they seemed akin. She was a notable British alpinist, elected president of the Ladies Alpine Club in 1941, and her father was a noted climber as well as an early investor in the CPR. See *The Guiding Spirit*.

THREE SISTERS: The [NE–2694 m, C–2769 m, SW–2936 m]; 1885; Bow Ranges. Dawson applied this name because these three peaks south of Canmore seem to be essentially similar, at least when seen from the Bow Valley. There are three other, less prominent sisters just north of Fernie.

THREE & 1/2: Peak [2902 m]; 1966; Bow Ranges. This is a ridiculously unofficial but quite popular and understandable name for the subsidiary point immediately west of Mount Bowlen, #3 of the Ten Peaks.

THRONE: Mountain [3120m]; 1916; Jasper. Named by the ABC because of its resemblance to a massive chair with arm rests.

THUMB: Spire [2867m]; 1959; Battle. Anger named the primary pinnacle of the Iron Ridge for its prominence relative to the four points to its east.

THUNDERBOLT: Mountain [2870m]; 1964; 83D/6; Monashee; CW. Hubbard, a long-time associate of Hendricks and a distinguished scientist in his own right, averred that this summit was named because he saw it being struck by lightning. There is also a **Peak** [2685 m] near Jasper.

THUNDERSTORM: Tower [2816m]: 1964; Bugaboo. Kruszyna applied this name because of the weather surrounding both himself and the tower at the time he contemplated its ascent.

THUNDERWATER: Lake [2115m]; 1952; Starbird. Due to the warming trend over the past century, this body of water now replaces the Whirlpool Glacier, which has melted completely since it was first observed by Wheeler, Kain, Longstaff and Harmon in 1910.

TIGER: Glacier; 1923; Icefields. Named by Schwab of the 1923 Clemenceau Expedition for the popular cognomen of Georges Clemenceau, "Le Tigre" of French politics, because the glacier drains part of the adjacent summit. This was also the name of a British battle cruiser that was heavily involved in the Battle of Jutland, but survived intact.

TILLEY: Mount [2693 m]; 1924; Gold. Sir Samuel Leonard Tilley (1818–1896), teetotaller of New Brunswick, was a Father of Confederation and minister of finance in the first Macdonald administration. His great-grandfather Samuel had been a loyalist potato farmer on Long Island. This name briefly lighted on a series of prior locations nearby, before settling on the present one.

TILTED: Mountain [2637m]; 1916; Slate. This name reflects the appearance of the strata exposed on the slopes of this mountain.

TIPPERARY: Mount [2960m], **Creek**, **Lake** [1847m]; 1917; Royal. This was Admiral Wintour's flagship, the largest, fastest and most modern of the eight destroyers lost by the Grand Fleet during the midnight phase of the Battle of Jutland. It was spotted by searchlights and then came under fire from several battleships of the High Seas Fleet, leaving it a sinking wreck in a matter of minutes.

TITKANA: Peak [2820m]; 1908; Robson. L.Q. Coleman made the first ascent of this easy summit and called it Ptarmigan Peak, but Adolphus

Moberly suggested they use "his people's" word for the same bird.

TOAD: Peak [3085 m]; 1969; Truce. Wagner offered no reason for this ugly-sounding name.

TOADSTOOL: The [2820 m]; 1953; Adamant. This relatively minor summit, between Gibraltar and Thor in the Gothics Group, was named by Putnam because the mountain crest appears to overhang on all sides. It was first climbed by means of a long, cold, interior crack system that rends the peak into two separate masses of granite.

TOBY: Creek, Mount [3222 m], **Glacier, Group**; 1888; S Purcells. Dr. Levi Toby, physician and prospector, came north from the U.S. military post at Colville, Washington, and settled here in 1864. In 1911 Harnden called the summit Mount Gleason, after the New England preacher who also climbed in the Purcells and wrote about his adventures. In old mining records the creek is often referred to as #1. Gold was panned in this creek in 1886.

TOKUMM: Creek; 1916; Bow Ranges. This is the Stoney word for the common red fox. The name was once applied to the "Prospector's Valley" that had been explored by Wilcox. *See also* Fay.

TOLAND: Tower [2667 m]; 1958; N Purcells. This name was suggested by a Harvard Mountaineering Club group for one of their own. David Sidney Toland (1934–1958) died in a mountaineering accident on Mount Saint Elias.

TOMA: Mount [2755 m]; 1859; Maligne. This was the name of an Iroquois hunter-guide who travelled with the earl of Southesk and had previously been a canoeman for Sir George Simpson of the HBC.

TOMAHAWK: Mountain [2919 m]; 1929; Front. While delineating the more open mountain terrain of the Clearwater drainage, the Topographical Survey people applied several names in partial honour of their Stoney packers. *See also* Wampum.

TOMATIN: Peak [2872 m]; 1902; Purity. This is the southeast peak of Mount McBean and was named for the famous distillery in Banffshire. Wheeler applied the name. *See also* Findhorn.

TOMBSTONE: Mountain [3035 m]; 1884; Opal. Dawson saw rocks standing near the crest that put him in mind of a row of tombstones.

TONQUIN: Creek, Pass [1950 m], **Valley**; 1916; Ramparts. Deville took the name from that of a ship originally owned by John Jacob Astor, which was blown up off Vancouver Island during an elongated fur-trade "misunderstanding" with the locals. By that time Astor had sold the ship to the HBC. The name is a variant spelling of Tonkin, referring to a large part of what is presently called Vietnam.

TONSA: [3057 m]; 1894; Bow Ranges. This is #4 and one of the few of the Ten Peaks to retains its Stoney name as given by Allen.

TOPHAM: Mount [2872 m]; 1902; Dawson. Harold Ward Topham (1857–1915), an English alpinist of distinction, explored the southern Selkirks during the summer of 1890. He had previously done the first Selkirk winter mountaineering in the course of a March visit to the Glacier House. Topham's map and nomenclature have both largely withstood the test of time. His name for this summit, though, was South Sentinel, for its position relative to the entrance to Glacier Circle. Wheeler thought Topham, who went on to attempt Mount St. Elias, deserved better recognition.

TOP OF THE WORLD: Massif; 1915; S Rockies. This name was applied by backcountry guide Anton (Ben) Rosicki (1886–1978) to the high country he frequented between the Van Nostrand and Hughes ranges. *See also* Chrysler.

TORDU: Pic [3216 m]; 1923; 83C/4; Icefields; RN. Schwab applied this name after the more famous peak of the central Alps. The name translates to "twisted peak."

TORII: Mount [3184 m]; 1963; Monashee. This name was applied by a party under the leadership of Hendricks because the jumble of summit rocks seemed to resemble a traditional Japanese ceremonial gateway.

TORNADO: Mountain [3099 m], **Pass** [2150 m]; 1915; High Rock. This was the original "Gould Dome" of Blakiston, but was renamed by Cautley of the ABC because the mountain seemed to be a focal point of thunderstorm activity. "Gould Dome" was then transferred to a lower point somewhat to the south.

TORONTO: Peak [2940 m]; 1975; Icefields. This was called "Ontario" by Habel in 1901, but no one took him seriously. United Empire Loyalists, though, obviously have long memories and resurrected the concept at a later date, though still without official success.

TORY: Mount [2831 m]; 1950; Jasper. Henry Marshall Tory (1864–1947) was the first president of the predecessor institution to the University of British Columbia. He subsequently migrated eastwards to a similar post in Alberta and then on to Carleton University.

TOSS-UP: Peak [2864 m]; 1974; Remillard. There was obviously some discussion about the naming of this point by the first ascent party led by Thomas Dabrowski.

TOTEM: Creek, Tower [3155 m]; Murchison. The tower was named by Putnam in 1973 after his party had made its first ascent. The creek was named considerably earlier, though the origin is unknown. There is a **Peak** [2807 m] of this same name on map sheet 82F/16.

TOWER: Lake [2121 m]; Sawback. This is the lower and smaller of the two lakes "behind" Castle Mountain; it lies closer to the Eisenhower Tower, and the name was clearly derived from its association with that end of the massif. *See also* Rockbound. There is another **Tower** [3117 m] on map sheet 82J/14, as part of the Fortress.

TOWERS: The [2846 m]; 1918; Assiniboine. The ABC felt this simple name was amply descriptive. It is, although it's hardly unique.

TRAFALGAR: Mountain [3033 m]; 1807; Farnham. This name was originally applied by Thompson to a different point, at the time he received belated word of Nelson's great and final victory. Over the course of a series of name changes, made largely in the early 20th century by E.W. Harnden, it was subsequently relocated to the present summit.

TRANQUILITY: Mountain [3152 m]; 1969; Truce. It was a lovely day, and everything was calm and peaceful when Wagner made this ascent.

TRAPPER: Peak [3014 m]; 1892; Waputik. This was a Wilcox appellation given in honour of his packer-guide Bill Peyto, who made a fair living in the winters at this occupation.

TREADMILL: Ridge [2819 m]; 1922; Robson. This ridge is composed of the "two feet up and one foot down" type of sliding scree. Climbing a slope with such footing is tedious and seemingly unending toil, as the ABC decided.

TRIAD: Peak [3030 m]; 1936; Icefields. This point is on the provincial boundary, but was not named by the ABC. There is an element of three-way drainage from this point.

TRIANGLE: Mount [2669 m]; 1909; Sir Sandford. Palmer used this point, at the extreme western edge of the Mount Sir Sandford area, as a secondary triangulation station for his survey of the terrain adjacent to and surrounding his prime objective. His principal points were on the eastern end of the Palisade Ridge and Azimuth Mountain.

TRICORN: Peaks [3155 m]; 1966; N Purcells. The first ascent party noted the summit had three crests, even the fact that the southerly was the highest, but the name was applied subsequently.

TRIDENT: Mountain [3136 m], **Creek**; 1924; Windy. From near Kinbasket Lake this massif seems to have three distinct summits. This was the bellwether name for the area, leading later visitors to a number of mythologically derived names, mostly involving water. There is a striking **Spire** [2810 m] north of the main peak.

TRIGON: Mountain [2950 m]; 1960; 83D/12; Cariboo; CW. Frances Chamberlin Carter, following near the footsteps of her famous father in the Cariboo Mountains, determined that this peak was on the three-way divide of the Canoe, Raush and North Thompson rivers. It was thought previously that the summit called Apex held that position.

TRIKOOTENAY: Peak [2728 m], **Glacier**; 1930; S Purcells. Thorington applied this name because the summit is located at the three-way divide whence drainage is north to the Columbia, southeast to the Kootenay River and west toward Kootenay Lake.

TRIPLE: Peak [2789 m]; 1974; S Selkirks. The Petroske family of Portland, Oregon, climbed its southern point and then named this minor massif.

TROLLTINDER: Mountain [2917 m], **Glacier**; 1897; Waputik. This name was applied by Habel, who explained that it somewhat resembled "a well-known mountain in the Norwegian valley of Rämsdalen." Freely translated from the Norwegian, this becomes "Gnome's Peak." The original, at 5,886 feet, is one of the higher summits of Norway.

TRUCE: Mountain [3246 m], **Glacier, Group**; 1916; SW Purcells. Stone applied this name because the weather, which had been poor when they started the ascent on August 9, cleared as they approached the summit, suggesting a truce with the elements.

TRUDA: Peaks [3050 m]; 1902; Hermit. Gertrude Elizabeth Benham (d. 1938 and buried at sea) was an alpinist of note, yet a solitary person who travelled much and socialized little (she only joined the Ladies Alpine Club when elected an honourary member in 1935). Wheeler applied this name in her honour after she had made a visit to Glacier House and climbed several peaks nearby.

TRUTCH: Mount [3210 m]; 1920; Freshfield. English-born Sir Joseph Trutch (1826–1904) arrived in British Columbia via the California gold rush. He became a civil engineer and later chief commissioner for Lands and Works. After helping negotiate the terms of political union with Canada, he served as lieutenant-governor of the new province, 1871–76.

TSAR: Mountain [3424 m]; 1920; Clemenceau. The ABC applied this name to a striking major peak of the Canadian Rockies. When viewed from the northern Selkirk Range, its isolated black pyramid identifies it immediately. Wheeler wrote, "When I saw it, so strikingly dominating its surroundings in isolated majesty, I named it Czar; but, later, when recording it, the spelling with 'Ts' seemed more appropriate."

TUMBLEDOWN: Mountain [2747 m], **Glacier**; 1956; Moloch. Named

Mount Tsar from Snowy Pass. ROGER LAURILLA PHOTO

by Putnam because there was not much solid rock apparent in the vicinity of this unimpressive and largely snow-covered summit at the head of Downie Creek. Dr. Shaw had travelled through here 50 years earlier but recorded no names.

TUMBLING: Creek, Glacier; 1924; Vermilion. And the ice does, too, right down the east face of Mount Gray.

TUNNEL: Mountain [1690 m]; 1883; Banff. The CPR's original right-of-way plan called for a tunnel under this minor obstacle in the middle of the Bow Valley east of Banff. In the event, due to penny-pinching construction limitations, the line curved north around the mountain, though the name remained.

TUPPER: Mount [2804 m], **Glacier, Creek;** 1895; Hermit. The summit was originally called Mount Hermit because of a striking gendarme on its west ridge. It was renamed by order-in-council after Sir Charles Tupper (1821–1915), a physician by training and a Father of Confederation, who was instrumental in bringing Nova Scotia into the evolving nation of Canada. He served briefly as prime minister in 1896.

TURBINE: Canyon; 1916; British. The ABC noted a deep slot in the local limestone formation that can be stepped across without using any of its five natural bridges. A stream rumbles as it churns through numerous potholes deep within this feature on its way down toward North Kananaskis Pass.

TURBULENT: Mount [2850 m], **Creek**; 1917; Sundance. This was the name of a destroyer of the Tenth Flotilla, which was literally blown out of the water by the German battleship *Westfalen*, near midnight during the Battle of Jutland.

TURNER: Mount [2813 m]; 1920; Blue. Sir Richard Ernest William Turner (1871–1961) was a distinguished British military figure who earned his Victoria Cross in the Boer War. As lieutenant-general he commanded the Second Canadian Division early in the Great War and was elevated to chief of the Canadian general staff.

TURQUOISE: Lake [2155 m]; 1898; Waputik. Baker gave this name, for the usual reason that people apply "blue" names to glacial lakes.

TURRET: Peak [3312 m]; 1911; Adamant. Named by Palmer for the sheer solidity of its appearance from the south. Lying between Adamant and Austerity, it remained untouched for a generation after Palmer's parties climbed its two neighbours and was not climbed in its own right until 1966. **Mountain** [3120 m]; 1926; 83D/9; Ramparts; RN. This is yet another part of the fortification pattern applied by the ABC in this area. **Peak** [2993 m]; 1938; 82K/10; Bugaboo; CS. This name was applied by Cromwell during his visit to this area with Ms. Engelhard and Dr. Francis North.

TURTLE: Mountain [2210 m]; 1880; Crowsnest. Though considerably below our criterion for inclusion and of little interest to alpinists, this summit was named by Louis Garnett because of its shape, and it *does* have notoriety. That fame came about when millions of tons of rock crashed down from its northeast face one night in 1903 and buried most of the coal-mining town of Frank, along with more than 70 of its residents. According to one authority, the catastrophic event "rather spoiled the likeness."

TUSK: Peak [3360 m]; 1920; Icefields. So named by the ABC because it is a "sharp cone of rock."

TUZO: Mount [3245 m]; 1906; Bow Ranges. This is #7 or "Sagowa" on Allen's map of 1894. Its first ascent was made by Henrietta Tuzo (1880–1955), and the summit was thereupon named for this founding member of the ACC. A notable fruit of her marriage in 1907 was geophysicist John Tuzo Wilson (1908–1993), who became the world's leading modern exponent of plate tectonics and for whom a well-deserved memorial can be found at the University of Toronto.

TWILIGHT: Peaks [2714 m]; 1929; Sorceror. Surveyor Ley Harris was working his way westward from Ventego Mountain when daylight ran out on him.

TWIN TOWERS: Peak [2850 m]; 1953; N Purcells. Above Silent Pass, this was the equally descriptive "Notch Peak" until Professor West decided otherwise.

TWINS: Peaks [N–3730 m, S–3580 m], **Tower** [3640 m]; 1898; Icefields. This pair of substantial, similar-looking summits at the north end of the Columbia Icefield was named by Collie, though their ascents came much later.

TWISTED: Rock [2868 m]; 1890; Dawson. Topham named this pile of warped strata on the south ridge of Mount Fox for just what it appeared to be.

TWO JACK: Lake [1506 m]; 1959; Fairholme. Two men named Jack (Stanley and Watters) operated a boat livery on this lake north of Banff.

TYPEE: Mount [2897 m], **Glacier**; 1970; Battle. Kruszyna carried the Melville theme on to the novel of this name, in which the "beauteous Fayaway" cares for the errant seaman. The summit offers a fine view and an excellent ski run down its glacier to the east. Published in 1846, this was Herman Melville's first, but by no means his most famous, novel.

TYRELL: Mount [2755 m], **Creek**; 1884; Clearwater. The brothers Tyrell, Joseph Burr (1858–1957) and James William (1863–1945), were active in surveys and exploration of the Canadian North and West. The elder was chief field assistant in Dawson's 1883 surveys of the Rocky Mountains. There were summits for each, though, a second weighing in at 2819 m on map sheet 82F/15.

TYRWHITT: Mount [2874 m]; 1922; High Rock. Admiral Sir Reginald Yarke Tyrwhitt (1870–1951) was the commander of the Harwich-based force at the start of the Great War and subsequently in charge of various destroyer flotillas in the Royal Navy. His father had commanded HMS *Renown*.

Nihil facit error nominis cum de corpore constat.
(*An error as to name is nothing when there is
certainty as to the person.*)
—Sir William Blackstone (1723–1780),
Commentaries

ULYSSES: Mount [3024 m]; 1964; N Rockies. This area is pretty well out of our range, but we wanted to note that Ulysses' summit is not far from those of his faithful wife, Penelope, and their son, Telemachos. There are a number of other Odyssean names nearby—all instigated by the ubiquitous Professor West.

UNICORN: Mountain [2994 m]; 1946; Adamant. Named by Hendricks' party because of the prominent subsidiary summit to the west of the main mass of the mountain, of which the severe west face has become a challenge to high-angle climbers. *See also* Horn.

UNWIN: Mount [3268 m]; 1908; 83C/11; Maligne; RN. Mary Schäffer named this "fine snow-capped mountain" after her guide, Sidney Unwin, who lost his life in the Great War. He was nephew to the British publisher of much alpine literature, Thomas Fisher Unwin.

UPRIGHT: Mountain [2978 m], **Creek, Pass** [1980 m]; 1911; Jasper. The Geographical Board noted that the sedimentary rocks that make up this mountain are on edge here.

URSUS MAJOR: Mountain [2705 m]; 1901; Hermit. Once known as Mount Roy, it was renamed by Bridgland because of the quantity of bears in the vicinity. For reasons Bridgland neglected to explain, this summit is less lofty than that pertaining to the smaller bear.

URSUS MINOR: Mountain [2749 m]; 1901; Hermit. Once known as Mount Sulzer after Carl Sulzer, the Swiss climber who made the first ascents of Mount Sir Donald and other nearby peaks in 1890, it was renamed by Bridgland in keeping with nearby Ursus Major.

UTO: Peak [2927 m], **Glacier**; 1896; Sir Donald. Professor Fay named this summit for the section of the Swiss Alpine Club to which Carl Sulzer and Emil Huber belonged. They had made the first ascent of this peak, as well as of the neighbouring Mount Sir Donald. In some of the early accounts this is referred to as Eagle Peak, in the mistaken belief it was the same summit as the one to its north.

VALAD: Peak [3250 m]; 1946; Maligne. This peak, overlooking the southeast end of beautiful Maligne Lake, bears the name of the well-travelled Metis guide who escorted Sandford Fleming in 1872 and showed Henry McLeod the way to this lake in 1875.

VALENCIENNES: Mountain [3150 m], **River**; 1918; Lyell. This mountain was named for the city of northeast France that had been the capital of Hainaut in the Middle Ages and became the locus of intense fighting during the Great War.

VALHALLA: Ranges; 1900; S Selkirks. This was the Hall of Odin, the palace whose walls glittered with gold and whence the principal god summoned only those heroes he valued most. This is an appropriate name considering the major exploitation of this area, described well in the GSC bulletin on its mineralogy by Dr. John Reesor. Many of the mountain names in these ranges were applied by parties under the leadership of Howard Ridge, a vigorous member of the original Kootenay Mountaineering Club.

VALKYRIUR: Mountains; 1900; Valhalla. This name recalls the supernatural women of Valhalla who determined the winners and losers in earthly combat and then escorted the heroes into the presence of the gods at Valhalla.

VANBUSKIRK: Mount [2820 m]; 1964; S Rockies. Corporal William E. VanBuskirk of Fernie was killed in action during the Second World War.

VAN HORNE: Range; 1884; **Brook, Glacier**; 1901; Purity. Sir William Cornelius Van Horne (1843–1915) was a railroad executive without peer. A native of the American midwest, he was engaged by Donald Smith on the recommendation of fellow Canadian James Jerome Hill. Van Horne pushed construction of the CPR with enormous vigour. A devout trencherman, his relaxation and poker playing became as legendary as his managerial ability. Upon retiring from the CPR in 1899, he undertook the construction of railroads in Cuba. The name was applied to the range west of the Waputiks by Dawson, and to the glacier and brook by Wheeler. He is the black-bearded, heavy-set man in Canada's most famous railway picture.

VAN NOSTRAND: Range; 1916; W Rockies. Benjamin T. Van Nostrand of Brooklyn was a friend of Hornaday and fellow traveller—even to the extent of delivering a baby mountain goat to the Bronx Zoo for him in 1904. The goat, incidentally, had been captured intact by Edward Feuz Jr.

VARIETY: Mountain [2750 m]; 1960; Sorceror. North of Iconoclast, this point was named because of the variety of rocks that make it up.

VAUX: Mount [3319 m]; 1858; Ottertail. Hector named this peak at the angle of the Kicking Horse River for his friend William Sandys Wright Vaux (1818–1885), for 29 years resident antiquarian at the British Museum. **Glacier**; 1902; Sir Donald. Wheeler applied this name to honour the Vaux family of Philadelphia, amateur glaciologists who undertook regular measurements of the Illecillewaet Glacier starting on July 17, 1887. The brothers, George Jr. (1863–1927) and William Jr. (1872–1909), served sequentially as treasurer of the AAC and in many other civic endeavours. Their sister, Mary (1870–1940), became the second wife of Charles Doolittle Walcott (1850–1927), director of the Smithsonian Institution and for some years the American member of the International Boundary Commission.

VAVASOUR: Mount [2820 m]; 1924; Blue. Lt. Mervin Vavasour (d. 1866), aide-de-camp to the commanding general of Canada, crossed the Rockies with Lt. Warre in 1845 en route to the Oregon Territory.

VENTEGO: Lake [2170m], **Creek, Mountain** [2694 m]; 1907; Sorceror. Carson and Harris, who both worked this area, called this lake after the Esperanto word for "windy."

VERDUN: Glacier; 1927; Icefields. This flows south from Mount Clemenceau, not from a summit with which this name is more properly associated. We are unsure why Ostheimer applied it here.

VERENDRYE: Mount [3086 m]; 1884; Vermilion. Dawson named his summit after Pierre Gaultier de Varennes, Sieur de la Verendrye (1685–1749), the French-Canadian explorer who, with his sons, explored much of the plains of North America, seeking the Western Sea. He certainly got as far as the Black Hills of South Dakota, but probably not much farther.

VERMILION: River, Pass [1651 m], **Range, Lakes**; 1916; S Rockies. This name, applied mostly in the western portion of the Rockies, derives from the ochre beds in iron-rich mineral springs on the south side of the pass. They were used by both the Kootenay and Blackfoot First Nations for ceremonial paint. The pass was first crossed by Hector in 1858. The shallow lakes [1381 m], however, are near Banff.

VERMONT: Creek, Mountain [2862 m], **Group**; 1925; N Purcells. This name started out with the mine located on August 24, 1925, by George

Edwards, a native of Vermont. It was soon consolidated with the Ruth Mine (named for the older daughter of Capt. Armstrong), which had evolved from claims variously entitled Cleopatra, Sheba, Eureka, White Horse, Black Horse and Wild Horse; all filed in 1897.

VERTEBRAE: Mountain [2880 m]; 1916; W Rockies. It's a lumpy and spiny ridge.

VERTEX: Peak [2941 m]; 1917; Jasper. Bridgland must have felt this was the highest point around, and—within a very modest radius—it is.

VERTIGO: Mount [2750 m]; 1960; Sorceror. The garnet-encrusted steep north face may have induced second thoughts at the time of its first ascent.

VESTAL: Mountain [2928 m]; 1955; Purity. This name was applied by members of the Harvard Mountaineering Club in consonance with its position just east of Purity Pass.

VICE-PRESIDENT: The [3066 m]; 1907; Waputik. This name was given by the ACC in grateful honour of David McNicoll of Arbroath, Scotland, who was elected western vice-president of the CPR shortly after the club's first summer camp.

VICTORIA: Mount [3464 m], **Glacier**; 1886; Lake Louise. McArthur named this prominent and popular summit after the granddaughter of King George III and successor to her uncle King William IV, Queen Victoria (1819–1901).

VICTORIA CROSS: Ranges; 1920; Jasper. Many of the summits in these lesser and infrequently visited ranges bear the names of recipients of Britain's highest award for military valour. *See* Zengel. *See also* Cornwell, O'Rourke, Scrimger.

VIDETTE: Peak [2989 m]; 1910; Sir Sandford. Palmer named this summit to the west of Mount Sir Sandford for another aspect of a fortress, thus continuing his pattern of nomenclature in this area.

VIRGIN: The [2886 m]; 1946; Starbird. Professor Eugen Rosenstock-Huessy (1888–1973), in one of his rare appearances in Canada's mountains, labelled this point for its beauty and "for purposes of our own reference."

VIRTUE: Mountain [3025 m]; 1966; Albert. This summit, at the head of Bain Brook, was so christened by West, who had just made its first ascent. *See also* Fortitude.

VISTA: Peak [2795 m], **Pass** [2085 m], **Glacier**; 1917; Jasper. This summit, as its name implies, offered the ABC crews a fine view of the Ramparts to the southwest.

VISTAMOUNT: [2885 m]; 1970; Battle. From this point above the Wrong Glacier, Kruszyna determined that one can enjoy an excellent view of the Nemo Group to the east, the Melville Group to the northwest and the Schooner Ridge to the northeast.

VOWELL: Creek, Glacier, Peak [2990 m], **Group**; 1920; Bugaboo. Once called Warren Creek, this was renamed for Arthur Wellesley Vowell (1841–1912), who after 1886 was variously gold commissioner and magistrate for the East Kootenay and chief constable for the Big Bend. This is a popular area with alpinists, linked topographically and geologically with the Bugaboos proper, to the southeast.

VULTURE: Col [3000 m], **Glacier**; 1917; Waputik. The ABC applied this name from the appearance of a rock on the overhanging ridge of Mount Olive that was shaped like a large bird.

Names are much more persistent than the functions upon which they were originally bestowed.
—T. Woodrow Wilson, 1885.

WADDINGTON: Peak [2630 m]; 1922; Ramparts. Alfred Penderill Waddington (1901–1872) was of British origin but became a leading proponent of British Columbia exploitation. The ABC applied his name on this lesser peak south of Yellowhead Pass many years before it was placed on the highest peak of the Coast Range, an area with which he was more closely associated.

WAFFL: Mount [2890 m]; 1934; Robson. Newman Diefendorf Waffl (1879–1930) was a New Jersey schoolmaster and alpinist who climbed extensively in the Canadian Rockies. After he lost his life in an attempt on Mount Robson, some of his friends applied his name to a nearby peak.

WAGNER: Mountain [2756 m]; 1924; Badshot. This was named for a mine on its lower slopes, opened in 1896, which was so high in elevation [8,000 feet] that its adit was often at the snow line even in midsummer.

WAITABIT: Creek, Lake [2143 m], **Peak** [3090 m]; 1900; Freshfield.

The mouth of this creek marks the lower reach of the tranquil waters of the upper Columbia. Canoe travellers developed the custom of pausing here to ascertain the trim of their craft before venturing into the more turbulent waters immediately downstream.

WALCOTT: Peak [3150m]; 1927; Chaba. This name was suggested by Ostheimer, after the distinguished American scientist Charles Doolittle Walcott, member of the International Boundary Commission. At that time, Walcott was recently deceased. *See also* Mary Vaux.

WALDORF: Towers [2633m]; 1971; Remillard. After Jones and Putnam climbed these crumbling piles of vertical limestone, they decided the original structure bearing this name might be an easier ascent.

WALES: Mount [3120m], **Glacier**; 1927; Chaba. Ostheimer gave this name after William Wales (1734–1798), an English mathematician and astronomer who had visited Hudson Bay in 1769 and been with Capt. James Cook on his second and third voyages.

WALKER: Mount [3303m]; 1897; Freshfield. Horace Walker (1838–1908), a native of Canada, was elected president of the AC in 1890. The name was applied here by Collie, who knew him well.

WALL: Tower [2941m]; 1933; S Purcell. McCoubrey applied this handle to the northernmost of the Leaning Towers, at the head of Fry Creek.

WALLACE: Peak [2940m]; 1952; N Purcells. Professor Robinson offered this name after the notable Canadian surveyor (DLS 1910), historian and geologist James Nevin Wallace (1870–1941), who had been the first Dominion representative on the ABC. *See also* Ptolemy.

WALRUS: Mountain [2780m]; 1965; N Rockies. Dr. Wallerstein may have seen a previously unreported constellation and named this mountain for it. He didn't say.

WALTER: Peak [3400m]; 1972; Lyell. Sydney Raymond Vallance (1890–1979), a long-time functionary of the ACC, suggested that the five distinct summits of Mount Lyell be named, serially from the north, for the five Oberland guides who took up permanent residence in Golden in 1912, opening a new chapter in the history of Canadian alpinism. This fourth summit of Mount Lyell is named for the youngest (and last survivor) of these men. Walter Feuz (1894–1986) never took out an official guide's licence since he was under age when he left the family home in Interlaken, but was trained for the work by his older brothers, Edward Jr. and Ernest. But Walter's businessman son, Sydney, became an honourary member of the Association of Canadian Mountain Guides.

WAMPUM: Peak [2864 m]; 1928; Front. Named by the Topographical Survey in association with Tomahawk Mountain.

WAPITI: Mountain [3033 m]; 1918; Front. This is the Stoney word for the North American elk found in these mountains.

WAPTA: Mountain [2778 m], **Icefield, Lake** [1594 m]; 1886; Waputik. This is the Stoney word for "running water" and is used often as part of a name. It was first applied by Klotz to the Kicking Horse River, where the water is active enough. But Hector's earlier name stuck, and Wapta now applies to no running water at all.

WAPUTIK: Peak [2755 m], **Icefield, Groups**; 1884; Rockies. Dawson applied the name initially to the ranges north of Kicking Horse Pass because it seemed to be a favourite haunt of white mountain goats (*Oreamnos montanus*). The name is the Stoney word for these creatures.

WARDEN ROBINSON: Mount [3000 m]; 1975; 83C/11; Maligne. Guide Willi Pfisterer's party applied this name, but there was no one by such name and title in the park service. It seems to have been meant for James Robertson (d. 1973), who had worked at Waterton Lakes and came to the Banff park in 1959. He was active in mountain rescue work. *See also* Chief Warden.

WARDLE: Mount [2810 m]; 1921; Vermilion. James Morey Wardle (1888–1971) was a highway design engineer who did much work on the Trans-Canada Highway and with the national parks of Canada. He had been acting superintendent of Banff National Park, 1919–21.

WARRE: Mount [2755 m]; 1924; Royal. Lt. (later Gen. Sir) Henry James Warre (1819–1898) was the leader of a small party, including Lt. Vavasour, sent overland in 1845 to determine the feasibility of making a military defence of the Oregon Territory in the face of the many Americans arriving there. He later went on to distinction in the Crimean War and in India. See his book *Sketches in North America and the Oregon Territory* (London, 1848).

WARREN: Mount [3300 m], **Creek**; 1911; Maligne. William Warren (1885–1943) was Mary Schäffer's head packer and guide and, after 1915, her second husband. When he hung up his lariat, he became quite a businessman in Banff, thanks in large part to her financial backing.

WARRIOR: Mountain [2973 m]; 1917; French. This was the name of a British hybrid armoured cruiser of 13,550 tons, which fell out of action at Jutland due to fire. It was taken in tow by the *Engadine* throughout the night, but early in the morning of June 1, 1916, the fires reached its main magazine and the *Warrior* blew up.

WARSAW: Mountain [2696 m]; 1943; Windy. This name was applied at the suggestion of Wells Gray to honour the unquenchable heroism of the Polish people, particularly as demonstrated during the Second World War.

WARSPITE: Mount [2850 m]; 1917; British. This name commemorates one of the most famous of 20th-century British warships. As part of the Fifth Battle Squadron she saw action at Jutland, being struck by many heavy-calibre shells and forced to drop out of the line. Repaired, she rejoined the fleet a few weeks later and stayed on active duty for another 30 years, seeing much service during the Second World War.

WARWICK: Mountain [2906 m]; 1919; Chaba. Named by the ABC in association with Mount King Edward, because it stood opposite to the summit named for the king (Edward IV, we suspect), and because of the mountain's "highly castellated appearance."

WASHBURN: Mount [3039 m]; 1964; S Rockies. Flight Officer Dean J. Washburn of the RCAF and Fernie was killed in action during the Second World War.

WASHMAWAPTA: Glacier; 1916; Ottertail. This glacier's name is translated from the Stoney as "ice river." What could be more appropriate?

WASOOTCH: Tower, Creek [2008 m]; Fisher. This is from the Stoney word *wazi*, meaning unique, and was given with respect to the tower's aspect in this valley.

WASTACH: Pass [2541 m]; 1896; Lake Louise. This name appears on Allen's second map (1896) and was alleged to be the Stoney word for beautiful.

WATCHMAN: Peak [3009 m], **Lake** [1862 m]; 1902; Alexandra. Outram applied this name when he first came up the valley toward Thompson Pass, feeling that this peak watched over him during his journey. The ABC crew shared this sentiment and applied the name to the lake as well, in 1918.

WATERFALL: Peaks [2950 m]; 1939; Maligne. When Lillian Gest climbed these peaks from Poboktan Creek, she passed by two waterfalls on her way up the valley draining northeast from these peaks. The lower fall was some 200 feet and the upper about half that much. The mountain, however, had already been climbed by Weiss.

WATERFOWL: Lakes [1652 m]; 1897; Rockies. On his way north, down the valley from Bow Pass, Collie saw quantities of migrant birds on these wide spots in the Mistaya River. He called them the Duck Lakes.

WATERMELON: Peak [3095 m]; 1966; Murchison. Judge David

Michael, then of Aspen, Colorado, a member of the first ascent party, helped carry a 4 kg watermelon to the summit. The five climbers then proceeded to consume it, despite the inclement weather. Putnam, who had spelled his friend off on the carry, submitted this unique name for approval. Its subsequent failure to gain official status became the subject (and title) of a *Toronto Star* article a few years later.

WATERSHED: Mountain [3150m]; 1931; Icefields. That's where it's at, right on the Continental Divide, west of Mount King Edward.

WATERTON: Lakes [1270m], **Park**; 1858; Boundary. Blakiston, who explored this area thoroughly, named the lakes after Charles Waterton (1782–1865), "English naturalist, taxidermist, traveller and eccentric."

WATSON: Mount [2970m]; 1924; Assiniboine. Sir David Watson (1871–1922) of Quebec was a soldier and journalist who commanded the Fourth Canadian Division during the final years of the Great War.

WAVERLY: Mines [1750m]; 1896; Sorceror. This landmark for bushwhacking alpinists lies to the north of Tangier Summit. The name originally belonged to an English mining engineer who was called in to help develop the properties. Several claims were filed and a road constructed up from Albert Canyon well into the north fork of Downie Creek, today's Sorceror Creek. But the ores were fickle and the boom began to fizzle in 1898.

WEARY: Creek, Gap [2246m]; High Rock. While we made no attempt to perform a personal inspection of the premises (we didn't inspect Fatigue Pass, either), it doesn't take much imagination to figure this one out.

WEDGE: The [2667m]; Opal. This name derives from the shape of the sharp-crested peak.

WEDGEWOOD: Peak [3030m], **Creek**; 1910; Assiniboine. Arthur Felix Wedgewood (1877–1917), a fifth-generation descendant of potter Josiah Wedgwood, was a civil engineer killed in action as an infantry Capt. near Bucquoy, France. His wife, Katherine Longstaff (1880–1976), whom he married in the fall of 1910, was a sister of Dr. Longstaff. She was among the party that made the first ascent of the peak earlier that year, for which reason the peak was initially called by her given name.

WEED: Mount [3080m]; 1903; Murchison. George Marston Weed (1864–1948) was a prominent member of the AMC and participated in a number of first ascents in the Canadian Alps, often in the company of Thompson. The name appears on Collie's map of 1903.

WEISS: Mount [3090m]; 1972; Churchill. This name was applied to honour a pioneer guide and mountain photographer of Jasper, Joseph August Weiss, born in 1896 in Zug, Switzerland, who got around these mountains quite a bit.

WELLS GRAY: Park, Group; 1947; Cariboo. Arthur Wellesley (Wells) Gray (1876–1944) was mayor of New Westminster and, after 1933, minister of lands for British Columbia.

WELSH: Creek, Peaks; 1969; Starbird. This is the central massif of the Starbird Ridge. All its features have been given names of Welsh derivation, mostly by Professor West.

WENKCHEMNA: Peak [3173 m], **Pass** [2600 m], **Glacier**; 1894; Bow Ranges. This is peak #10 on Allen's map of the Lake Louise area. The word is from the Stoney for "10" and has more recently been applied to the group as a whole.

WEST: Peak [3094 m]; 1939; Bugaboo. Georgia Engelhard, travelling in company with Ernest Feuz and Dr. North, was the first to venture into this group of mountains, west of the more famous Bugaboos. Having little better inspiration than a compass, they applied names accordingly.

WESTFALL: River, Group; 1930; Battle. This river drains westward from the Battle Range into the Incomappleux River (Fish Creek).

WHALEBACK: Mountain [2627m]; 1916; Waputik. This less than notable summit was named by members of the ABC for its appearance—bare, dark, smooth, rounded and damp.

WHEELER: Mount [3386 m]; 1904; Purity. Arthur Oliver Wheeler (1860–1945), a native of Kilkenny, Ireland, took up surveying soon after his arrival in Canada in 1876 and received his DLS in 1882 while residing in Winnipeg. His most important surveys were in the vicinity of Glacier in the years from 1900 to 1902, and then from 1913 to 1925 along the interprovincial boundary. The British Columbia representative, he was in charge of the high-country work, while his Alberta counterpart Cautley handled the detail in the passes. Wheeler was also instrumental in founding the ACC in 1906 and served as its principal officer for many years. The name was applied by the Topographical Survey. Wheeler's son, Edward Oliver, became head of the famous Indian Survey; his grandson, John Oliver, became a noted field geologist and studied bedrock for the GSC throughout much of the area his grandfather had surveyed. He was general editor of the nine-volume edition of *Geology of Canada*. See Oliver and A.O. Wheeler's *The Selkirk Range* (Ottawa, 1905).

WHIRLPOOL: River, Pass [1810 m], **Group**; 1850; N Rockies. This is shown on the Palliser map and the name is mentioned by Henry Moberly as indicative of the numerous eddies found in the swirling currents of the river, a tributary of the Athabasca.

WHISTLING: Valley; 1958; Ball. It was the marmots' warnings that brought this name onto their domain.

WHISTLING ROCK: Ridge [2929 m]; 1978; British. Guide Bernie Scheisser's group dislodged some rocks along this spectacular ridge north of Mount Sir Douglas Haig, which went whistling down the west face.

WHITE: Mount [2755 m]; 1884; Front. Dawson named this summit after James White (1863–1928), his principal assistant in 1884. White later became chief geographer in the department of the interior and a member of the Geographical Board of Canada. In these latter capacities he compiled an authoritative *Dictionary of Altitudes in the Dominion of Canada* and a short toponymic monograph.

WHITEAVES: Mount [3150 m]; 1920; Freshfield. James Frederick Whiteaves (1835–1909) was a paleontologist on the staff of the GSC and a tireless researcher. He was a founding member of the Royal Society of Canada.

WHITECAP: Mountain [2864 m]; 1917; Jasper. A summit cornice by any other name would still be made of snow.

WHITECROW: Mountain [2831 m]; 1922; Whirlpool. This was the birdlike god of the Cree, who once hid the buffalo only from their enemies.

WHITEFACE: Tower [2829 m] 1971; Remillard. This name was suggested by nuclear physicist George Irving Bell (1926–2000) for one of the striking limestone edifices that lay east of Jones's 1971 campsite at the head of Windy Creek, which Bell climbed.

WHITE GOAT: Peaks [NE–3150 m, C–3210 m, SW–3080 m]; 1958; Cline. Sometimes called Thunder Peaks for the afternoon showers that rumble by this area frequently in midsummer, these peaks lie north of Cline and northwest of Resolute in the midst of excellent goat country.

WHITEHORN: Mountain [3395 m]; 1911; N Rockies. Wheeler applied this name during his first visit to this area. He saw the summit as it usually is, snow-covered and sharp.

WHITE JACKET: Mountain [3125 m]; 1970; Battle. This further bit of Melvilleana was applied by Kruszyna after the fifth of the author's novels, published in 1850.

WHITE MAN: Mountain [2977 m], **Pass** [2150 m]; 1884; Royal. Dawson determined that this pass was the one on the crest of which Father De Smet erected a cross in 1845. However, the precise derivation of the name is unclear, and it appears that Sinclair was the white man who crossed it earlier, in 1841.

WHITE PYRAMID: [3275 m]; 1901; Waputik. Collie saw this summit at its snow-covered best and named it in contrast to the darker "Chephren" nearby.

WHITEROSE: Mount [3060m]; 1919; Alexandra. The ABC named this summit for the beautiful, snowy icefall that its members observed across Lyell Creek from their campsite.

WHITE SAILS: Mount [2766m]; 2000; Purcells. Named by Hamish Mutch for the white snowy patches seen at the time of his ascent.

WHITE TAIL: Peaks [2970m]; 1953; Vermilion. The late Robin Cyril Hind, a workhorse of the ACC, suggested this name because the peak is at the head of a tributary of the Kootenay River known as White Tail Creek.

WHITEWATER: Creek, Mountain [2772 m]; 1961; S Selkirks. This name came up the slope from a mine near Lardeau opened by J.R. Retallack.

WHYMPER: Mount [2845 m]; 1901; Vermilion. Edward Whymper (1840–1911) is best known for his first ascent of the Matterhorn on July 14, 1865. After the tragic events that marked the descent, he became moody, although he was widely honoured for his part in alpinism. He travelled worldwide and was a great drawing card, such that the CPR engaged him to make several visits to the mountains for publicity purposes. His actual climbing in Canada was limited. The guides who accompanied Whymper, however, made a number of good climbs and some of them left their names on the landscape. See *The Guiding Spirit* and *Adventures of an Alpine Guide* (London, 1932), by Christian Klucker. Whymper's *Travels Amongst the Great Andes of Peru* (1888) contains a discussion of the first extensive observations on altitude sickness.

WHYTE: Mount [2983 m]; 1898, Bow Ranges. Wilcox used this name to honour Sir William Whyte (1843–1914), who was employed by the CPR as superintendent of the Ontario division in 1884. He later became second vice-president of the western division.

WILCOX: Mount [2884m], **Pass** [2425 m]; 1899; Maligne. Collie suggested the pass be named after Walter Dwight Wilcox (1869–1949), who was the first American writer of importance to visit the Canadian Alps. He made several trips to the area and in 1896 crossed this pass, en route to the sources of the Athabasca and Fortress Lake. See his book *The Rockies of Canada* (New York, 1903). After 1905 he was involved in the development of timber resources in Cuba in conjunction with Van Horne's railroads. Wilcox was also secretary of the AAC.

WILDHORSE: Creek; 1865; S Selkirks. This name first appears in

Moberly's report of his 1865 explorations into what was then a developing mining region. The principal mine of the area was named Ymir after the primeval giant of Norse mythology, and the entire area took this name after 1897. Another creek of the same name is found in the southern Rockies near Fernie on 82E/12.

WILKINSON: Mountain [2606 m]; 1969; SW Purcells. This name honours David "Doc" Wilkinson, a versatile man who started as a sailor from Scotland, developed a dental practice in Nelson, trapped in Howser, but earned Wagner's interest by his musical versatility.

WILLERVAL: Mount [3180 m]; 1920; Alexandra. Lying next north of Monchy Mountain, this mountain takes it name from a small village near Lens, which was captured by Canadian forces in the spring of 1917.

WILLET: Mount [2755 m]; 1914; SW Purcells. This name appears to have belonged to one of the early settlers of Argenta, according to Wagner.

WILLIAM BOOTH: Mount [3002 m]; 1965; Clearwater. William Booth (1829–1912) was a Methodist preacher. Concerned with the more practical aspects of charity, he started the East London Revival Society in 1865. By 1878 it had grown into the Salvation Army, of which he became the first "General." This mountain, the only one on the dry limestone ridge east of Abraham Lake to bear an official name, was christened on the centenary of Booth's initial work.

WILLIAMS: Mount [2730 m]; 1918; British. Maj. Gen. Victor Arthur Seymour Williams Jr. (1866–1944), who had been an inspector for the RCMP, became a professional soldier, but was severely wounded and taken prisoner by the Germans near Zillebeke in June 1916. Williams finished his career as commissioner of the Ontario Provincial Police. His father had been killed in action during the 1885 Northwest Rebellion.

WILLINGDON: Mount [3373 m]; 1927; Clearwater. Freeman Freeman-Thomas (1866–1941), first Earl Willingdon, was the 13th Governor General of Canada from 1926 until assigned as Viceroy of India in 1931.

WILMER: Location [904 m]; 1906; Purcells. This was once called Peterborough, a name that resulted in confusion with the much larger location in Ontario. It was renamed to honour Wilmer Charles Wells, member of the provincial parliament from 1899, who had just been defeated for re-election by Parson. *See also* Earl Grey.

WILSON: Range [2485 m]; 1860; Boundary. This less than notable mountain south of Waterton Lakes, straddling the 49th parallel, was named by Palliser after Lt. Charles William Wilson (1836–1905) RE, who had been secretary to the British contingent of the IBSC. Wilson was later involved in the non-rescue of "Chinese" Gordon at Khartoum in 1885 (he died before he could be rescued) and in his final years became director general of the famous ordnance survey of the United Kingdom. **Mount** [3260 m], **Glacier, Ranch**; 1898; Cline. Thomas Edward Wilson (1859–1933) was a well-known packer and guide of the Banff area who worked for a number of famous mountaineering figures. He had previously been with the Mounties and worked with Major Rogers prior to going into business on his own. His horse-breeding activities on the Kootenay Plains were unsuccessful and marred his declining years. This name was applied by Collie as his pack train emerged from the lower Siffleur valley at Kootenay Plains.

WINDERMERE: Lake [798 m], **Locality**; 1916; Purcells. This name was transported from the Lake District in England on the theory that there were great similarities in the terrain.

WINDTOWER: Mountain [2688 m]; 1950; Rundle. Climbers applied this name to the more attractive rock of the sub-peak (tower) northwest of Mount Lougheed.

WINDY: Creek, Group; 1930; N Selkirks. The creek drains into the Columbia from the Northern Selkirks, just upstream from the original Kinbasket Lake. This group interlocks with the Remillard Group and contains many peaks with breezy connotations—e.g. Wildwind Mountain [2931 m].

WINDY CASTLE: Mount [2820 m]; 1947; Maligne. This name is historic, if unofficial; both Odell and Smythe partook in the naming and the first ascent. Their rationale was simple—weather and appearance.

WINNIE THE POOH: Mountain [3063 m]; 1956; Bugaboo. Small wonder this name is unofficial; the "mountain" isn't worth naming, being merely a snow bump somewhat east of and much lower than Mount Conrad.

WINSTON CHURCHILL: Range; 1956; 83C/3; N Rockies. This range south of Jasper was named for the great English statesman while he was serving his second term as prime minister of the United Kingdom. It contains some of the most notable summits of the Canadian Rockies. Winston Leonard Spencer Churchill (1874–1965) did know a bit about mountains, having, in 1951, described to one of these compilers his ascent of the Matterhorn more than half a century earlier.

WINTOUR: Mount [2700 m]; 1922; Opal. Capt. Charles John Wintour (1871–1916) enjoyed a distinguished, if abbreviated, naval career. He had become commander of the Fourth Destroyer Flotilla, which stumbled out of the fog into a line of German battleships near midnight during the Battle of Jutland. The enemy fire was immediate and devastating; Wintour went down with his flagship, *Tipperary*.

WISDOM TOOTH: The [2972 m]; 1972; S Purcells. A dentist would appreciate that this was the last of the Leaning Towers to be climbed.

WITCH: Tower [2643 m]; 1902; Dawson. This point on the northeast ridge of Mount Fox was named by the Topographical Survey for its shape and isolation.

WITHERS: Mount [2895 m]; 1949; Premier. Hendricks named this summit after one A.L. Withers, who had been vacationing near Jasper and went into the Cariboo Mountains in company with Carpé and Chamberlin in 1924. He disappeared from the climbing scene after that venture—apparently he had had enough of the bush.

WIWAXY: Peaks [2703 m]; 1894; Bow Ranges. Allen stated this to be the Stoney word for windy and so designated it on his map.

WODEN: Peak [2704 m], **Creek**; 1917; Valhalla. Odin = Wotan = Woden; all variations in the name of the same entity, the protector of fallen heroes, who live with him in Valhalla. He was also the god of poets and was associated with runes, and he rode an eight-legged horse named Sleipnir.

WOLF: Point [2780 m]; 1948; Adamant. Ferris named this sharp but crumbling east outlier of the Gothics Group for its resemblance to the uplifted muzzle of a howling wolf.

WOLVERINE: Pass [2207 m]; Vermilion. **Mountain**; [2773 m]; Jasper. This name, and a variety of other similar if unofficial applications, all pertain to the presence of this animal. *See also* Carcajou.

WONDER: Peak [2852 m], **Pass** [2425 m]; 1913; Assiniboine. The ABC crew passed out a lot of superlatives during their first season of the Interprovincial Boundary Survey, when they worked in this vicinity.

WOOLLEY: Mount [3405 m], **Shoulder**; 1898; Churchill. Herman Woolley (1846–1920), a publisher by occupation, was a widely travelled British alpinist, a long-time member of the AC and a friend of Collie's, who applied this name to the summit. The shoulder is a toponymic latecomer as it only became an access landmark in the 1970s as a point on the route to the more attractive peaks to the west.

WORTHINGTON: Mount [2838m]; 1956; French. Colonel Donald Worthington of the B.C. Regiment was killed in action in 1944. *See also* McHarg.

WOTAN: Mount [2974 m]; 1910; Adamant. Palmer gave this name to

Wiwaxy Peak. GLEN BOLES DRAWING

a prominent peak on the south edge of the Gothics Glacier. Unfortunately, in later years subsequent parties weren't certain which peak he had in mind, and for some time the literature had this four-pointed peak labelled as Mount Sir Benjamin. Wotan was the king of the gods in the Norse mythological hierarchy. *See also* Woden.

WRONG: Glacier, Peak [2869 m]; 1962; Battle. Flying through fog and clouds, Riley and Silverstein mistook this glacier for the Houston Glacier several kilometres to the north. Their air drop of food was therefore misplaced; as Silverstein subsequently observed, they had "put the groceries in the wrong icebox!" Accordingly, their climbing plans were considerably altered. Little did Silverstein then appreciate the place in Canadian history served by George McKinnon Wrong (1860–1938), long-time secretary of the Champlain Society.

Mt. Xerxes. GLEN BOLES DRAWING

I cannot say the crow is white,
But needs must call a spade a spade.

—HUMPHREY GIFFORD, 1580

XERXES: Mount [2970m]; 1936; Fryatt. This was the name of an energetic king of Persia, whose 21-year reign (ended by his murder in 465 B.C.) saw many developments, including the first attempt to circumnavigate Africa.

Yamnuska. GLEN BOLES DRAWING

Fools' names, like fools' faces,
Are often seen in public places.
—THOMAS FULLER, 1732

YAMNUSKA: Cliff; Front. This is the climbers' name for the south-facing cliff of Mount John Laurie, seen prominently on the right as one approaches the mountains from Calgary. It derives, According to tribal spokesman Felix Poucette, the name derives from the Stoney words *eeam*, meaning "mountain," and *naska*, meaning "flat."

YARDARM: Ridge [2664 m]; 1971; Windy. The first climbing party to visit the Remillard Group included Dr. Eugene F. "Craw" Boss. Their campsite was in a meadow to the east of this ridge. In the early evening, as supper was being prepared, he noted the position of the setting sun, and some liquid cheer was circulated.

YELLOWHEAD: Pass [1145 m]; 1827; Robson. Sometimes this pass appears in the literature as Leather, Cowdung or Jasper Pass. *See also* Tête.

YGGDRASIL: Mountain [2960 m]; 1953; Adamant. The name of the great earth mother goddess of Norse mythology was applied by Matthews to the easternmost of the major Gothics peaks, following the pattern established by Palmer. *See also* Stickle.

YOHO: River, Lake [1824 m], **Pass** [1838 m], **Glacier, Peak** [2760 m],

Park; 1886; Waputik. This is a Cree exclamation of astonishment, applied here by Van Horne because of the impressiveness of Takkakaw Falls.

YOUNGHUSBAND: Peak [3150m], **Glacier**; 1927; **Icefields**. Ostheimer applied this name to honour Lt. Col. Sir Francis Edward Younghusband (1863–1942), a British alpinist well known also as the head of the 1906 military expedition to Lhasa that first opened commercial relations between India and Tibet.

YOUNGS: Peak [2815m]; 1989; Sir Donald. Members of the AMC named this point bounding the west edge of the Illecillewaet Neve after Julia M. Young, manager of the Glacier House after Harry Perley. Toward the end of his life, Ed Feuz Jr. stated that "she was like a second mother to me."

YUKNESS: Mountain [2847m]; 1916; Bow Ranges. This is the Stoney word for "sharpened," as with a knife—quite properly descriptive of this summit.

The glory and the nothing of a name.
—GEORGE GORDON, LORD BYRON, 1816

ZEKES: Peak [2990m]; 1973; British. Bernie Scheisser's dog, Zeke, accompanied the first ascent party. It was a dog route (an easy line to follow).

ZENGEL: Mount [2630m]; 1951; Jasper. Sgt. Raphael Louis Zengel of the Fifth Battalion in the Saskatchewan Regiment, having been previously decorated, was awarded the Victoria Cross for his "most conspicuous bravery and devotion to duty" during the Great War. Lesser peaks nearby were named at the CNR's request for other VC recipients: Pte. 2 John Chipman **KERR**, enlisted at Edmonton in 1914 and took an heroic part in the action at Courcelette on September 16, 1916; Pte. 2 Cecil John **KINROSS**, of the 49th Canadian Infantry Battalion, showed "superb example and courage in action at Meetcheele" on October 30, 1917; Lt. George B. **MCKEEN**, of the 14th Canadian Infantry Battalion, was awarded the VC for one cited action, but "his leadership at all times has been beyond praise"; Pte. 2 John George **PATTISON**, of the 50th Canadian Infantry Battalion, was killed in

Zinc Mountain. GLEN BOLES DRAWING

subsequent action but received the VC for "conspicuous bravery" on Vimy Ridge on April 10, 1917.

ZILLEBEKE: Mountain [3000m]; 1918; Lyell. Wheeler named this mountain after a village and lake east of Ypres, the scene of severe fighting and losses by Canadian troops in 1916. *See also* Mercer and Williams.

ZILLMER: Mount [2911 m], **Creek**; 1963; Cariboo. Raymond Theodore Zillmer (1887–1960) was an ardent conservationist and leader of the Izaak Walton League of America as well as an exploratory alpinist. He made extensive visits to the Monashee and Premier ranges in the years 1939, '45, '46 and '47. In his native Wisconsin, he was responsible for the public acquisition and preservation of the geologically significant Kettle Moraine.

ZINC: Mountain [2990m], **Creek**; 1901; Ottertail. This name was suggested by Whymper after the mineral prospects found on its hillsides, as well as elsewhere in this group.

*I believe intellectual reading, in moderation, to be a rest
for the body after hard labour; it seems to act as a counter irritant,
drawing off fatigue from the muscles to the brain.*

—James Carnegie, Earl of Southesk

INDEX

This lists only those names not appearing under a heading of their own in the main text or the introduction. *The text reference is in italic.*

Authors: Roger W. Laurilla, William L. Putnam
and Glen W. Boles. ROGER LAURILLA PHOTO

Artist and photographer **Glen Boles** has climbed extensively throughout North America and Europe, but his first love is the Canadian Rockies, where he has summited over 450 peaks, often by difficult new routes. Many of his climbs were first ascents. Glen, who lives in Cochrane, Alberta, is the author of *Glen Boles: My Mountain Album. Art & Photography of the Canadian Rockies & Columbia Mountains* (Rocky Mountain Books, 2006).

Raised in Revelstoke, British Columbia, **Roger Laurilla** was exposed to the mountains at an early age. His images have been published in such magazines as *Canadian Geographic, British Columbia Magazine, Ski Canada, Powder Magazine* and *Backcountry.*

Honoured by mountaineering societies at home in the United States and abroad, **William Putnam** is a highly decorated veteran of the 10th Mountain Division (Second World War). He has been frequenting the world's mountains and writing about mountaineering history for most of his life.